choice

True Stories of Birth, Contraception, Infertility,
Adoption, Single Parenthood, & Abortion

Edited by Karen E. Bender & Nina de Gramont

choice

True Stories of Birth, Contraception, Infertility,
Adoption, Single Parenthood, & Abortion

Edited by Karen E. Bender & Nina de Gramont

MACADAM CAGE

MacAdam/Cage
155 Sansome Street, Suite 550
San Francisco, CA 94104
www.MacAdamCage.com

Library of Congress Cataloging-in-Publication Data

Choice : true stories of birth, contraception, infertility, adoption, single
parenthood, and abortion / edited by Karen E. Bender and Nina de Gramont.
p. cm.
ISBN 978-1-59692-063-7
1. Women—Literary collections. 2. American literature—Women authors.
3. American literature—21st century. I. Bender, Karen E. II. Gramont, Nina de.
PS509.W6C487 2007
810.8'354—dc22
2007019568

Paperback edition: October, 2007
ISBN 978-1-59692-062-0

Book and jacket design by Dorothy Carico Smith
Printed in the United States of America

10 9 8 7 6 5 4 3 2 1

Some of these essays first appeared, often in a partial or slightly different form, in
the following publications: Sandy Hingston's "It Could Happen to You" in *Philadelphia Magazine*; Susan Ito's "If" in the anthology *It's a Boy!*; Janet Ellerby's "Bearing
Sorrow" in her book *Intimate Reading*; Deborah McDowell's "Termination" in her
memoir *Leaving Pipe Shop*; and Kate Maloy's "A Normal Woman" in *New Woman*.

This book is dedicated to the writers
who shared their stories with all of us

TABLE OF CONTENTS

INTRODUCTION

by Karen E. Bender and Nina de Gramont

A WOMAN HOLDS a pregnancy test, waiting for a line to appear. In three minutes or less she will have her answer. One pink line. Two pink lines. A blue or pink line. Pregnant. Not Pregnant.

Every day, all over America women stare at this stick and wait.

This woman could be an unmarried teenage girl, crouched in a locked bathroom while her unsuspecting mother makes breakfast downstairs. She could be a childless woman in her late thirties, her husband holding her hand and hoping this time the answer will be different. She could be married to an abusive husband from whom she must hide this test. She could be an exhausted mother of young children, not knowing how she will be able to afford another. She could know that she carries the gene for a frightening disease and be anticipating the answer with hope and dread. She could be the mother of the teenage girl, taking the test herself in a downstairs bathroom, excited about the possibility of starting again on the other side of her reproductive life.

The line appears.

Thirty-four years ago, these women would have had to live with whatever results the pregnancy test delivered. In the near future, some of their choices may be lost. But today—at this precise moment in history—there are many possible paths that they might follow. At this moment in the United States, they have a choice.

This anthology began on the last day of 2005, when we were at a New Year's Eve party. The kids had commandeered the living room, tooting noise-makers; we huddled against the wall, trying to hold an adult conversation.

When the conversation turned to politics, we began talking about South Dakota's proposed law to ban all abortions in the state. We couldn't believe such a draconian measure could be instituted in a democracy in our lifetime.

Growing up in the 1960s and 1970s with reproductive freedom a given, the idea that such a basic right could be revoked astonished and disturbed us. Though neither of us had had abortions, we'd thought about the issue a great deal and had both explored abortion in our fiction.

Karen said, "I've always thought about compiling an anthology about abortion."

We looked at each other. What would that mean?

We are writers; we have committed ourselves to the power of story as a way of reaching people. First we thought about a book of fictional accounts about abortion. But events in the real world are already dramatic; we wanted a book that would bear witness to the reproductive stories that make up real women's lives.

A few days later at a friend's birthday party, someone told us that in South Dakota it was already extremely difficult for a woman to procure an abortion. There is only one clinic in the state that offers the procedure: The Planned Parenthood in Sioux Falls, which performs abortions one day a week. Four doctors from Minnesota fly in on a rotating basis.[1]

How could such a prohibitive law arise from such a minimal practice?

We started talking about what our anthology could include. We told each other experiences of people we knew, traded stories from our own personal histories. As we talked, we realized that every woman we knew had some sort of story involving her reproductive life. What if our anthology focused on true stories—not only about abortion but about adoption, infertility treatments, the morning-after pill, birth control? Doesn't the word "choice" refer to all forms of reproductive options?

In this country people can be eager to speak but reluctant to listen. Political division may lead to simplistic, clichéd presentation of ideas. As writers and writing teachers, we are sensitive to cliché—we urge our students to get to the specific. With specific examples, we tell our students, your ideas will have authority. How could specific stories about choices transcend the clichés of politics?

In South Dakota, Leslee Unruh—one of the prime lobbyists for the abortion ban—had said, "I want abortion to end."[2]

This simplistic statement mirrors the easy proclamations we see and hear every day. We started talking about the bumper stickers we see in Wilmington, North Carolina, where we live:

Against abortion? Don't have one.

Choose life: your mother did.

Keep your laws off my body.

*Abortion doesn't make you un-pregnant. It makes
you the mother of a dead child.*

These statements are, ultimately, glib. None of these stickers tells us a story about a person who has made a particular decision. None of them really tells us what it is like to make a choice.

"That's what we could call our book," Nina said. "Choice."

In 1992 in an interview on NBC's *Dateline,* the first President Bush admitted that, despite his pro-life beliefs, he would "stand behind" a daughter or granddaughter who chose to have an abortion. He said, "I'd love her and help her, lift her up, wipe the tears away, and we'd get back in the game." President Bush's statement illustrates the stunning complexity behind this issue. It's one thing to oppose an idea in theory, but once the notion becomes personal and the faces familiar, even a staunch opponent of abortion can imagine not only tolerance, but can imagine supporting a woman's personal decision. When nuances are explored and empathy is applied, condemnation gives way to compassion.

In this country, we can be too eager to set compassion aside in favor of judgment. We are not attuned to complexity—but we need to be. As a nation striving to define itself as moral, we need, frankly, to become smarter. How can we rise above having our most potent discussions by bumper stickers, or pundits trading barbs on talk shows? How can we better understand each other as complex, as human?

The answer lies in telling our stories. After all, one of the women taking that pregnancy test could be your daughter. She could be your mother or your best friend. And her story might not end in that bathroom. She could discover that her fetus has a terrible genetic disorder. She could be unable to afford raising a child at this moment in her life, or simply be too young. She might not have a partner. She could learn that carrying the pregnancy to term might put her own life in danger. She might have been coerced into the encounter that led to the pregnancy. She might have been raped.

The word "choice" encompasses much more than abortion. It includes any of the numerous ways a woman might decide to have or not have a family. As Catherine Newman writes in her essay about conception, "Choice in all its many forms—adoption, abstinence, technology, choosing to be anti-choice, pleasure, abortion, birth control, kids, no kids, and even, I know, regret—is what makes human sexuality truly human and parenthood truly viable."

When an issue is as polarized as abortion, people on both sides see the world in black and white. In order to preserve these extremes, stories that reveal gray areas are kept secret. The woman who regrets placing her child for adoption suffers in silence, lest someone think she would have been better off aborting. The woman who undergoes a painful abortion keeps quiet, lest the complexities of her situation be construed as an argument against reproductive freedom. But when these stories are suppressed, so is our empathy. Instead of listening to each other's stories and drawing lessons from each other's lives, we are turning a deaf ear to human experience.

This collection explores the ramifications of many different forms of reproductive choice. In these essays the complexity behind these decisions—and the gray areas evident in all of them—come through. Even we, who went looking for these stories, were stunned by such stark and unvarnished honesty. Because the truth is, when a pregnancy is unplanned any subsequent choice is bound to be complicated. To deny this is to make the issue something less important than it is.

In her essay "Portrait of a Mother," Stephanie Andersen writes, "Almost ten years ago, when I was seventeen years old, I decided not to be a mother. Instead, I chose what the world told me was a better life. I chose college and a career for myself. I chose a stable, married mother and father for her, a two-story house in the country." At a glance, this makes Andersen sound like a poster child for the pro-life solution to unwanted pregnancy: giving a child up for adoption, often painted as a simple and easy alternative. But Andersen—who for seven months of her pregnancy planned to keep the baby—agonizes daily over the loss of her daughter. Listening to her child's voice on the phone for the first time, Andersen experiences an unbearable physical longing: "When I hear your voice, see your picture, I want the pain in my breasts and abdomen to go away. Forgive me. Let me kiss your face, your arms, your ears, your fingers."

Janet Mason Ellerby placed her daughter for adoption over twenty years earlier, when abortion was not yet a legal option. Her parents coerced her into hiding at a home for unwed mothers, and convinced her she had no choice but to relinquish her child. The wrenching separation left a permanent mark on Ellerby's psyche; in her mind she refers to the child as Sorrow.

Nor is there a simple answer in Kimi Faxon Hemingway's essay about abortion gone awry. Faxon Hemingway's mother had told Faxon Hemingway her own cautionary tale of a dangerous infection following an illegal abortion. Like so many of us who grew up in the 1960s and 1970s, Faxon Hemingway assumed that a legal abortion equaled a safe abortion —and was astonished to encounter nightmarish repercussions after taking the drug RU-486. Her experience underlines both the need for a focus on the safety of abortion, and the importance of conscientious medical care. Instead of arguing over the accessibility of a drug like RU-486, we should be putting our energy into making sure the drug is administered with meticulous attention.

Did Faxon Hemingway's harrowing experience turn her into a pro-life activist? It did not. Her essay is no more an argument against abortion than Andersen's and Ellerby's essays are against adoption. The essays simply embrace and explore the complexity and the contradictions of reproductive decisions. The idea that a woman might place a child for adoption and then proceed with her life content in the nobility of her decision, is simplistic; so is the idea that a woman may move on from abortion completely free of sadness or uncertainty.

These essays also reflect the vulnerability and poignant confusion of youth. We see mistakes born of simple confusion, of ignorance about how reproduction works; should this ignorance be deemed criminal if the resulting pregnancy is one a woman wants to end? In Ellerby's essay, she says of herself at sixteen: "My body was not my own. When it had escaped my parents' control, Alec had immediately taken it up, and when he had abandoned it, a baby had claimed it; I did not completely understand that my body was my own dominion." We see this confusion echoed in Sarah Messer's essay. "I had convinced myself that the clinic would say I wasn't pregnant," she writes of her 18-year-old self. She held "some strange belief that the condition only existed while I was in my apartment."

Another theme in these essays is the difficulty of finding a good male partner. We see men who vanish, who are abusive, or who simply do not love their partners. As Denise Gess writes of the man who distances himself when she becomes pregnant with his child, "I've watched the gestures of his departure as a way of steeling myself, of acknowledging that his departures are all I can count on." We see the disturbed young man in Carolyn Ferrell's essay "Summer, 1959," punch her in the ribs, beg her not to go to college; we see the boyfriend in Velina Vasu Houston's "Dragon Slayer," who, when he drinks too much, becomes a frightening *oni* (demon) from the fairy tales she read as a child. Pam Houston says, "I have never even been on a date with a man whom I would trust to raise a child."

We see the need for women to wait—to find the right person to love. And we see the women choosing to separate from problematic men in a way that is often different than the route their own mothers chose. A decision to have an abortion or to raise a child alone can be a decision about choosing an alternative future—one characterized by hope. Women may choose not to repeat the damaging marital experiences their own parents had. As Ferrell's mother notes in a narration in Ferrell's essay, "If you had to name my story, it would have to be called *No Choices*."

And we also see a woman's desire to create a family with the person she loves. Ashley Talley's mother falls in love, gets married, and is trying to have a baby in her forties; in the essay "Donation" she tells Ashley, "You'll understand when you meet someone you really love. You'll want to create life with them."

We see in these essays both the exquisite preciousness of independence and self-reliance, and the profound quality of maternal love. As Katherine Towler, who chose not to have children, says, "The truth—and it was a hard truth to acknowledge...was that I was happiest when I was alone, seated at my desk, writing. Everything else in life was simply what came before writing or after it."

And we see other women whose fierce desire to have children inspires them to go ahead with their pregnancies despite other peoples' advice to terminate. Katie Allison Granju, whose baby would have a 25 percent chance of being infected with primary cytomegalovirus, be at high risk for neurological impairment, physical problems, mental retardation, and infant fatality, is advised to have an abortion by her doctor and a minister. She schedules one and then cancels it. She decides, finally, to go ahead with her pregnancy and gives birth to a baby who has been remarkably healthy. After her child's birth, Granju feels "graced with this experience, which has allowed me to see that the blessing is sometimes as much in the struggle—from which I have learned so much—as in the outcome."

When Velina Hasu Houston considers becoming a single parent, her mother initially tells her, "You can have an operation and be done with the problem." But Houston tells her that she had a feeling that the baby was meant to be born. "The decision, however, was not political at all," she writes. "It was personal. Purely. And nobody's business."

Throughout these essays, again and again we see moments of profound dichotomy. Although the women in this collection write about extremely different experiences, there's an amazing thread of connection: a moment in each where striking contradictions meet and shimmer and meld in an unexpected way. In Susan Ito's "If," she writes about being adopted and her newfound relationship with her birthmother—whom she calls when she finds herself unexpectedly pregnant. "It's what I would have done, if it had been available to me," Ito's birth mother says, when Ito explains that she plans to abort. It's an extraordinary moment: a mother admitting to her child that she would have aborted her. And yet in this situation, it is somehow feasible as a statement of comfort. It doesn't mean on any level that the mother regrets having her or doesn't love her child. It only faces the truth with amazing honesty.

These essays dramatize what the Supreme Court justices call the "raw edges of human existence," as Francine Prose notes in her dissection of the beautiful, elegant language of *Roe v. Wade*. In her essay, Prose says, "You can read the rest for pleasure and for the chance to observe the workings of a mind (or group of minds) expressed in measured language that is blessedly simple and logical as it endeavors to take on a subject that, as Blackmun suggests in the paragraph above, is the very opposite of logical and simple."

And what happens once we absorb these stories, these "raw edges?" What do we do once we read them? As we read these essays, their exquisite honesty and individuality simply affirms what we knew when we began this anthology: *Choice is such a personal and complex issue, it cannot be dictated by the government.*

A woman's reproductive decisions need to be made by herself and with her medical provider. Her options need to be safe, available, and legal. The perception of what constitutes life—and when is the right time or situation for a life—is so personal, it needs to come from the woman herself. The truth is, a woman may become depressed after an abortion, may grieve her entire life after placing a child for adoption. These experiences must not be veiled or hidden for fear of giving the opposition political fuel. These experiences must be shared and discussed.

Government should not be involved in a woman's—and her partner's—decision to create a life. Rather, women should be honest about their experiences, without shame or apology. Only honesty will lead to the sort of epiphany Sandy Hingston experiences when she tells her pro-life teenage daughter that she herself had an abortion as a young woman. At her daughter's unexpected understanding, Hingston writes: "What I feel at that moment is electrical, biblical, as though I have gone up into the mountain in fear and trembling and emerged blessed."

There are so many circumstances that might lead to an abortion, an adoption, a pregnancy. We owe women who might find themselves in any of these circumstances nothing less than the truth of our own experiences. As Kate Maloy writes, "Nothing is ever sure, and sometimes, with no warning, life will bring us more than we feel we can handle…The important thing is to be as true to ourselves as possible under the circumstances." This theme is echoed in the essay "No Stone Unturned," by an anonymous mother who has devoted her life to her son's hemophilia. Explaining her decision to end a subsequent pregnancy when prenatal testing indicated a recurrence of the blood disorder, she writes, "I could not find the resolve or hope within myself...to feel optimistic about having a second child with hemophilia." Later, when she finds herself walking by a group of pro-life protesters, her resolve deepens: "I had made my own decisions about life's complexities, not for political or religious reasons, but for *my* body and *my* family."

There is no simple answer. There is only the necessity for options.

One thing became clear to us as we read these essays. In order to be truly moral, our country needs to put its values—and energy—in the right place.

According to the National Women's Law Center, four states—Georgia, Mississippi, Arkansas, and South Dakota—have explicit policies that allow pharmacists to refuse to dispense drugs. In Georgia and Mississippi this can include any drugs. In Arkansas pharmacists and physicians can refuse to provide contraceptives; in South Dakota pharmacists can refuse to provide any drug "believed to cause abortion or death." Only five states— California, Illinois, Maine, Massachusetts, and Nevada—explicitly require pharmacists to fill valid prescriptions, despite the fact that, according to the National Women's Law Center, "80% of Americans believe that pharmacists should not be able to refuse to sell birth control based on their religious beliefs. This was true across party lines and religious affiliations."

Although the South Dakota abortion ban was defeated in 2006, eleven other states—Alabama, Georgia, Indiana, Kentucky, Louisiana, Mississippi, Missouri, Ohio, Rhode Island, South Carolina, and Tennessee —considered similar bans in legislative sessions.[3]

The ban proposed in Ohio, which is still pending, would not only prohibit abortion in all circumstances, but would make it a crime to accompany a woman to another state for an abortion. Right to Life bills in Rhode Island and South Carolina would have established life at fertilization. While these bills did not explicitly ban abortion, establishing life at fertilization would make abortion illegal throughout all stages of pregnancy, without exception, and could potentially outlaw most contraceptives, fertility treatments, and stem cell research.[4]

As we went to press with this anthology, several state legislatures were considering abortion bans in their 2007 sessions—Georgia, Mississippi, Missouri, North Dakota, Oklahoma and Texas.[5]

In addition to watching our legislatures, we must investigate and question some of the prominent medical professionals in this country entrusted to creating health policy. For example, the deputy assistant secretary for population affairs at the Department of Health and Human Services is a man named Eric Keroack, who runs the Title X program, a $280 million federal program that is intended to help low-income people have access to contraceptive supplies and information.[6]

Dr. Keroack's background includes directing an organization that opposes contraception, claiming that it is "demeaning to women." How will putting such a person in a position of such significant social responsibility help women?

And finally, we need to carefully watch the actions of the current justices of the Supreme Court. Justice O'Connor, who recently resigned, was the fifth vote that prevented significant restrictions on abortion. In April 2007, the newly configured Supreme Court upheld *Gonzales v. Carhart*, for the first time restricting a medically approved procedure with no exception to protect a woman's health. According to the NWLC, the Court ignored the judgement of medical experts, and weakened the "undue burden" standard to determine whether an abortion restriction was unconstitutional. In her dissent, Justice Ginsburg noted the threat to *Roe v. Wade*. Justices Scalia and Thomas have both said that *Roe v. Wade* should be overturned, and Justice Alito and Chief Justice Roberts have not supported a woman's right to choose in the past. The pivotal vote to uphold *Roe* may be Justice Kennedy, who has both supported a woman's right to choose and also upheld restrictions. However, he voted to uphold the federal ban in the *Gonzales v. Carhart* decision.[7]

And what if *Roe v. Wade* were overturned? A 2004 report by the Center for Reproductive Rights found that thirty states could make abortion illegal within a year of the ruling.[8]

The study found that 21 states were at high risk for making abortion illegal—Alabama, Arkansas, Colorado, Delaware, Kentucky, Louisiana, Michigan, Mississippi, Missouri, Nebraska, North Carolina, North Dakota, Ohio, Oklahoma, Rhode Island, South Carolina, South Dakota, Texas, Utah, Virginia, and Wisconsin. These states could pass new bans or bring back old laws, as their state constitutions did not protect the right to choose. In nine more states—Arizona, Georgia, Idaho, Illinois, Indiana, Iowa, New Hampshire, Kansas, and Pennsylvania—protection of a woman's right to choose would be uncertain.

Would criminalizing women who have abortions actually affect the number of abortions performed in our country? Historically, making abortion illegal hasn't changed the abortion rates: it has only changed the stories.[9]

In this country, individual states began to pass laws banning abortion in the mid-1800s; the prohibition of abortion came under the same Comstock laws of the 1880s that also criminalized obscenity and the use of birth control.[10]

During the years when abortion was illegal in the United States—between the late nineteenth century and 1973—millions of women underwent the procedure, and many of them did not live to tell the tale. Rickie Solinger's book, *Pregnancy and Power,* cites a study that clearly established the safe practice of abortion-providing doctors in the 1930s. The study found that 76 percent of self-induced abortions resulted in complications. In fact, this was such a common problem that a textbook for coroners written during this time contained a list of substances and methods that women turned to for abortion when they could not get safe and professional medical care. This list included: Aloe. Alum. Ammonia. Catheters. Darning needles. Ergot. Jumping up and down stairs. Lead. Lysol. Methyl salicytate. Phenol (carbolic acid). Quinine. Salts of arsenic. Slippery elm sticks. Turpentine. Umbrella ribs. White phosphorous (scraped from the tips of kitchen matches.)[11]

The textbook also listed the results of these self-induced abortions. They included: acute supportive peritonitus, chills, coma, convulsions, delirium, perforated intestine, septic endometritis, stupor, suffocation, and death.[12]

Criminalizing abortion does not keep a woman from getting pregnant; it does not help her if she has an unintended pregnancy. Making abortion illegal is simply a policy of intolerance. How can we develop a deeper understanding of complexity and create a policy of compassion?

Instead of using governmental power to criminalize abortion and the women who seek it, why not make sex education widely available in school? This education can include information about abstinence and the right to say no, but also information that allows young women and men to clearly understand the reproductive process and thus make informed decisions. Statistically, states that allow comprehensive sex education in schools have significantly lower rates of teen pregnancy. And the opposite holds true as well. For example, school districts in southern states are almost five times more likely than schools in the northeast to provide abstinence-only education. Not coincidentally, southern states have significantly higher rates of teen pregnancies.[13]

Instead of banning late-term abortions, why not create a test for genetic abnormalities that will detect problems earlier in pregnancies, so that women can learn about the health of their fetus earlier and make the choice that is right for them?

Instead of trying to limit access to contraception or the morning-after pill, why not make it part of every employer's health care plan? And make it free and available for low-income women? We should make it illegal for a pharmacist to refuse to fill any valid prescription, regardless of personal beliefs. With education and access, we can significantly decrease the numbers of unplanned pregnancies and their corollary—abortion.

Instead of cutting federal funding for abortions, thus making it more difficult for low-income women to obtain them, why not make sure this option is available to all women, so the issue of access is not an additional burden a woman has to face?

Instead of making women juggle the arduous task of working while also caring for a newborn, why can't we offer our mothers the right to paid maternity leave—like every other industrialized nation (except Australia)? Currently, the United States is one of only five countries (the others are

Lesotho, Liberia, Swaziland, and Papua New Guinea) which do not guarantee any paid maternity leave for mothers.[14]

Why can't we emulate a country like Sweden, which offers parents up to sixteen months of paid family leave?[15]

Why not have more federally funded childcare?

How can we, as a nation, create ourselves in a way that shows how we truly celebrate the living?

We called for these essays believing that a woman's right to choose must be preserved; we wanted to illustrate the spectrum of possibilities in a woman's reproductive life. But perhaps the most important and surprising thing we learned was the consequence of not having choices; if you take away a woman's reproductive rights, you take away her human rights.

When a woman has no choice, she may be shuffled off to a home for unwed mothers, giving away a child she dearly wants, as in Janet Mason Ellerby's essay, "Bearing Sorrow."

When a woman has no choice, a family court judge may terminate a mother's parental rights to her own children, as in Jacquelyn Mitchard's essay, "The Ballad of Bobbie Jo."

When a woman has no choice, her fate may fall into the hands of a morally bankrupt doctor, and her body into the hands of incompetent and illegal practitioners, as in Deborah McDowell's essay, "Termination."

When a woman has no choice, she may mark her baby with a small brand—a burn or a cut—before abandoning her at an orphanage door in rural China. "It's a sign of love," Ann Hood writes in her essay, "Mother's Day in the Year of the Rooster."

When a woman has no choice, her desperate poverty may force her to relinquish her daughter to a woman of a wealthier country, as in Elizabeth Larsen's essay, "A Complicated Privilege."

When a woman has no choice, she may be in the position of Harriette Wimms, a lesbian dealing with infertility and desperately trying to conceive a child. She battles with insurance companies, for a long time unable to conceive because her insurance will not cover fertility procedures for lesbians—only married couples.

Or a woman with no choice may die of medical complications, as Susan Ito would have if she'd attempted to carry her dangerous pregnancy to term.

When a woman has no choice, she has no freedom. The path of her life is not her own.

We sit, typing this foreword in a house in a neighborhood like thousands of others across this country. What if we could glance through the curtains to see our neighbors? What if we could not just see their actions, but hear their thoughts and know their histories? What would we find that we have in common? The women in this anthology have lifted their curtains so that, for a moment, we can see into each other's lives and understand each other's choices.

What kind of stories do we want our children and grandchildren to be telling about this country in fifty, a hundred years? Do we want them to describe a country that criminalizes women for making the reproductive choices right for them, or do we want them to be able to describe a nation that has preserved all choices for all women?

There are 60 million women between 15 and 44 in the United States.[16]

Forty-nine percent of the pregnancies that occur each year in the United States are unplanned.[17]

About one point seven million households contain adopted children.[18]

More than one-third of American women will have had an abortion by age 45.[19]

If one of these women came up to you, holding her pregnancy stick, wondering what decision to make, what would you tell her?

Wouldn't you want to give her a choice?

Notes

1   *S.D. Makes Abortion Rare Through Laws and Stigma*, by Evelyn Nieves, Washingtonpost.com, December 27, 2005

2   *S.D. Makes Abortion Rare Through Laws and Stigma*

3   *Abortion Ban: Coming to a State Near You?* National Women's Law Center Website

4   National Women's Law Center Abortion Ban Page

5   NWLC Abortion Ban Page

6   "And Women Are At This Guy's Mercy," by Stacy Schiff, *WilmingtonStar News*, January 24, 2007

7   www.nwlc.org/pdf/ChangingSCt0307.pdf

8   www.reproductiverights.org/pdf/bo_whatifroefell.pdf

9   *How the Pro-Choice Movement Saved America*, by Cristina Page, pg. 58

10 National Abortion Federation website, www.prochoice.org/about_abortion/history_abortion.html

11 *Pregnancy and Power: A Short History of Reproductive Politics in America,* by Rickie Solinger, New York University Press, NY 2005, pg. 121

12 Solinger, p. 121

13 Page, pp.78-79

14 "U.S. Policies on Maternity Leave 'Among the Worst,'" by Tamara Schweitzer, Inc.com, February 16, 2007

15 "U.S. Stands Apart From Other Nations on Maternity Leave," Associated Press, July 26, 2005

16 http://www.americanpregnancy.org/main/statistics.html

17 "Unplanned Pregnancies Rise Among Poor Women," by Linda Feldmann, csmonitor.com:
    http://www.csmonitor.com/2006/0505/p02s01-ussc.html

18 "The Child Within," US Census Bureau,
    http://factfinder.census.gov/jsp/saff/SAFFInfo.jsp?_pageId=tp10_relationships

19 "An Overview of Abortion in the United States," The Guttmacher Institute, http://www.guttmacher.org/media/presskits/2005/06/28/abortionoverview.html

THE BALLAD OF BOBBIE JO
by Jacquelyn Mitchard

IF I SAY, "CHOICE," you think, "abortion."

But there are myriad permutations on a woman's privilege to make private decisions about her reproductive capabilities. Bobbie Jo Arness, a mother of two and a civil engineer from the small (and for reasons of privacy, fictional) town of Marianna, Tennessee, chose to have a baby—and the story of what that choice cost her made legal precedent and national headlines.

She chose to be a surrogate mother.

I know about it, because she did it for us.

She carried our son, Atticus—conceived through in vitro fertilization at a clinic in our home state—to a healthy, full-term birth. She endured stinging criticism from friends and strangers, a cesarean birth, and a brutal legal judgment to proudly fulfill all her obligations to us—although fulfilling all her obligations to us cost her everything she thought was real, and brought down criticism on all our heads. Still, she would be the first to tell you that giving Atticus life was a choice that brought her "as much grace and pride" as anything she had ever done—as much as giving life to her own two children, Daphne and Michael, whom she now sees only every other weekend and on Wednesday evenings for church.

But I am getting ahead of a story that really is a modern-day parable, as graphic as a gospel tale in its proof that the political is personal indeed.

Bobbie Jo wasn't the first surrogate mother who worked with us. At the time we met her, we had a son through surrogacy who was 18 months old.

Why had we chosen surrogacy at all?

We had several children through birth and adoption, and wanted one more. But adopting our daughter, Mia, five years earlier had lead to a painful legal battle when her birthfather sued for custody, so that path didn't feel safe to walk. I was past 40 by then, and had never been in the gifted program for carrying babies to term. So we set out to use our biological products to create an embryo that would grow in someone else's body.

It took several attempts. But finally, along came big, bonny Will. Our family was complete.

There was only one snag, and it kept tugging at us.

We had three frozen embryos left over—embryos we'd decided to donate or destroy. But whenever I'd casually ask my husband to call the clinic and deal with the embryos, he'd never quite get around to it. And neither did I. It wasn't that we considered those embryos "snow babies," the cloying phrase abortion foes use for embryos that are left unused. But we also couldn't shake the truth that *these* embryos had been created with love and intention, not by mistake. And it was this fact that kept us from feeling not quite right, somehow, in disposing of them.

We didn't want another child, but we didn't *not* want another child, either. And so we made a tentative choice to roll the dice once, and be at peace with whatever happened.

At the same time in another state, Bobbie Jo and her husband were struggling with a deeply personal decision as well.

Though she didn't want to raise another child ("Mikey has broken me," she often joked of her wild man toddler) she wanted to give another couple a chance at having a child, using her strong and willing body as a mechanism. At first, her husband balked: he thought the whole process might be embarrassing. Later, he agreed that hers was a gesture of consummate grace. As Bobbie Jo later told me, "My best guess is that it's something I felt called to do, and I usually end up doing what I think is right. I'm pretty determined that way. You might say stubborn."

It turned out to be an understatement.

Bobbie Jo not only talked the talk, she walked the walk, even when the walk took her over hot coals.

I like that in a person. I liked Bobbie Jo before I ever saw her face.

We were introduced by a friend of a friend; we had nothing at all in common except that we'd both majored in biology.

A deeply religious Southern Baptist ("Jackie," she explained, "This isn't the Bible Belt. This is the buckle!") she also was one of the only people I've ever met who gave born-again Christians a good name. Forthright about her beliefs, she was never preachy or sentimental. And she never said a phony word. Once, before the procedure, when Chris and I were going back and forth on whether we should really proceed, she wrote to us, "You need to want this with your whole heart. If you don't, no matter how sweet an idea it is, it's the wrong idea."

Wait, she said, on the Lord. The answer would come.

And it did.

Once we decided to go ahead, Bobbie Jo endured many days of painful injections to give her body the best chance of accepting the embryo. She and her husband, Cal, went to counseling, so that a psychologist could be sure that they could handle the stresses surrogacy can put on a marriage. The psychologist asked Cal if he could deal with questions and emotions raised by his wife carrying another family's child, and Bobbie Jo if she could handle the possible negative reactions from some people she met and the inevitable pain of relinquishing a child she'd given birth to. They both passed with honors. Finally, Bobbie Jo, Cal, and the fabled Mikey—who, at not quite two, had an unerring arm when it came to placing a french fry directly into the upswept hairstyle of the lady at the next table—came to our city for the implantation of the embryos. That would only take place if those embryos "survived" the thaw—there was only about a 15 percent chance that they would.

Bobby Jo was beautiful and comical with her mad french fry bomber. Her husband was gentle, quiet, protective; a heavy-equipment operator who treated Mikey and Bobbie Jo with amused tolerance. We saw pictures of their 7-year-old Daphne dressed as a pirate queen in her Halloween costume. Bobbie proudly explained that she was already reading at a third-grade level and taking tumbling to become a competitive cheerleader.

It was I, alone, who went into the small room with Bobbie Jo. Though we barely knew each other, we had to suppress nervous schoolgirl giggles. The doctor and the embryologist entered by separate doors, with our unknown destiny in a pipette: all three had "survived" and were of good quality. As Bobby lay with her hips raised and covered by a drape, the embryos were placed into her uterus through a small plastic tube.

"That's it?" she asked, incredulous. "I'm theoretically pregnant?"

We held hands tightly, and on impulse I put my head on Bobbie Jo's shoulder. It felt right. When we parted, it was with a small sense of loss and regret. If this didn't work, we would never see each other again; fate would never have brought women from two such different worlds together—would never have shown us how two such women occupy so much common ground. Bobbie Jo would never, on her own, have considered aborting in the unlikely event that all three embryos implanted. I would never have chosen to have triplets or expose Bobbie Jo to the dangers of such a pregnancy.

When, two weeks later, Bobbie Jo phoned to say that there were two gestational sacs and a pink plus sign on the stick, I was standing outside a copy shop. I was so floored I dropped my copies and my wallet. Again, there had been a mere 15 to 20 percent chance of this working. As I watched my copies fly in four different directions in the parking lot, my emotions followed them.

"Are you happy or worried?" I asked my husband that night in the dark.

"I'll know more when it's real," he told me.

But not long afterward, Bobbie Jo called to say that an early ultrasound showed one sac dissolving and no heartbeat in the other. Our own hearts deflated. Of course we wanted this baby, this angel of the outside chance. The doctor was apprehensive; so were other parents I knew who'd gone through this process. Bobbie Jo told me calmly, "Wait on the Lord, Jackie. That's all we can do."

She was absolutely certain that the three-minute procedure at the clinic would change all our lives forever. And she was absolutely right.

A week later, there was a clear flutter, then a little critter with arms and legs, then someone who was declaratively a boy, and then the last weeks began to run down through the glass of time.

That was when the roof fell in.

One day, I called Bobbie Jo, as I did a couple of times each week. She wasn't at work; she answered at home only after I'd tried four times, with increasing apprehension. *Pick up,* I willed her. *Pick up. Pick up.* Finally, she did, and said she'd been asleep, as her allergies were "kicking up."

Shocked, before I could think of a more diplomatic way to phrase it, I said, "But...you're lying. Something's wrong." An ancient presentiment of alarm made me stiffen—as if I were hearing a siren far off, getting nearer.

To my shame, I was relieved when she told me that the baby was fine, but that Cal had decided to divorce her. His coworkers were making fun of him as the pregnancy began to show. Small-town gossips, including members of Cal's family, had convinced him surrogacy was tantamount to adultery. "This is the man I thought loved me for twelve years," Bobbie Jo said, and no more than that.

It was only when I put down the phone that I began to cry. When I turned to him, my teenage son was blunt: "You weren't even sure you wanted this baby, Mom. And it's wrecking her life."

Still, I didn't believe that the Cal I'd met, the affable giant, would actually do this thing. It was a summer storm, and would pass, a natural over-reaction as the moment of birth neared.

I was wrong.

Within weeks, Cal served Bobbie Jo with documents of divorce, requesting full custody of the children. Although it was a closed pro-ceeding, she told me later that the circuit court judge admitted that he was not familiar with surrogacy "but that it didn't sound like a very psycholog-ically healthy thing for the other children." In any case, nearly nine months along, the judge said, Bobbie Jo was in no shape to be a single mom. He gave Cal the house and the keys to the door. He gave Cal cus-tody of the children. He gave Bobbie Jo her half of the mortgage payment, a child-support schedule, and the dog.

When she phoned, we couldn't find words to encompass our distress and helpless empathy. We couldn't even pay her more than we'd agreed to pay her (little more than travel expenses and lost wages) because Cal's lawyer was already baying about selling babies, callous Yankees who stuck contracts under poor, bewildered, innocent Cal's nose and made him lean on the hood of a truck to sign them—even hinting, according to Bobbie Jo, that my husband and I were going to "sell the baby to some same-gender couple up north."

We were outraged, at the ignorant implication and the calculated nas-tiness just beneath its oily skin. Only Bobbie Jo did not condemn, nor did she condescend or judge. She believed God's will would be done, and that, in our case, she was His agent on earth. We should concentrate on our baby's welfare.

"This is not the important thing," she told us, though coworkers had lined up for and against her, former friends had taken to crossing the street to avoid talking to her, her in-laws sneered at her at public gatherings, and even her government-protected village job strangely dried up after the controversy began. "You're going to have a baby. You need to concentrate on him."

But subsequent hearings brought only more bad news: Cal would not, as he had agreed, sign the pre-birth order that would allow our names on our child's birth certificate. Technically, no matter what the circumstances, a woman's husband is legally the presumptive father of any child she bears. There was an electrical tingle of fear in our days. Cal had not said he would claim our baby, but if the judge had ruled Bobbie Jo unfit even to share custody of her own children based *only* on the fact that she had agreed to be a surrogate mother, what else might the judge allow? Would he forbid Bobbie Jo from giving us our baby? There was no law in the matter to consult. It had not ever happened before.

Still, despite all this—and the fact that she could barely force herself to eat and only did for the baby's sake—Bobbie Jo kept reminding us that when she set her mind to something, she generally did it. If I had respected Bobbie Jo before for her honest simplicity, her absence of guilt, of games, of a hidden agenda, my esteem for her now approached awe. Most surrogates asked five times what she had asked us; she could have used her situation to manipulate us into giving her five times that—if we'd had it to give. Other people, and not evil people, might have done so out of sheer human need. But Bobbie Jo would not sully her own word once she'd given it. "That's Cal's department," she said, the closest she ever came to truly bashing the man.

And so, knowing that the baby we were already calling "Boo" because he was due somewhere around Halloween, was on his way, Bobbie Jo and her aunt left Marianna—left in anguish because weeks would pass before she would have even her pitiful overnight with her children—got on a plane and came to live with us until the baby was born. It was a risk, but Bobbie Jo's doctor had evaluated her and believed that the birth was not imminent. The fact that she was broad-shouldered and nearly six feet tall helped hide how far along she was. Bobbie Jo would not even risk our baby being born in Tennessee. Cal could have his way in Kelly County, she told us, but not "in the real world."

When she walked in our door, even though I barely came up to her shoulder I wanted to hold her on my lap and comfort her like a child. We comforted each other; between us, I felt Boo roll and shift.

We waited; gradually, the news of Boo's imminent birth leaked out. We stopped answering the telephone, for fear of reporters. Relatives of Bobbie Jo's called her with hints and bits of news. Though Cal had sworn (quite probably on a stack of Bibles) that this surrogacy was the only reason he would *ever* have considered leaving his marriage, it was difficult for them (and for us) to believe that a physical circumstance that would end in a month or two was the only cause Cal truly had to want to be free—and to refuse marriage therapy or any intervention.

Bobbie Jo believed Cal had someone else.

And finally she told us the full truth about what Cal and his lawyer had sworn in court. Lying on the floor beside Bobby Jo, who sat with her feet propped in the big chair, I let tears leak out of the corners of my eyes—unable to believe such things could happen in our time, in my country.

"Cal told them he had no idea how the baby was conceived because he wasn't in the room," Bobby Jo said. Clearly, his lawyer insinuated, it was possible that my husband had caused Bobbie Jo to commit an immoral act. He went on to explain that she was obsessed with her pregnancy and was ignoring Mikey and Daphne—a stone lie. I'd heard Mikey and Daphne playing in the background in a dozen phone conversations. "Daphne won her class spelling bee," Bobbie Jo's email from August 21 read. "They're going to evaluate her for the gifted program. But Mikey got a fever that just wouldn't go down last weekend. I was up half the night in the urgent care center. All I could do was read to him and rock him, the poor baby."

Were these the words of an unconcerned, uninvolved mom?

Yes, according to Cal. "He told the judge," Bobbie Jo said, "that his parents filled the role I should have filled."

Even Bobbie Jo's country lawyer, who had no experience with anything of this nature, was certain that no judge would rule against a blameless woman, who had done nothing except that to which her husband had agreed—and in all chastity, in a room with only a doctor, a nurse, and me.

But the judge saw Cal's point.

More than that, he refused to recuse himself from the case. He wouldn't talk to the press; but word was he was proud he'd taken a stand for good, old-fashioned values.

"But how could Cal say he didn't understand how this process worked? It was described to him a dozen times," I argued with Bobbie Jo.

"Because it's good to be a man in Kelly County," she said.

As the days passed, the buzz over Bobbie Jo grew.

Dozens of her friends and family cheered for her—ready to spit on their hands and cite the Constitution if anyone said a word against her. But others started a Web chat group, and wrote in no uncertain terms about "rich people" (we aren't, though because I write novels there's some measure of recognition to my name) taking advantage of a poor Tennessee girl.

Hardly. Bobbie Jo rode the Internet like a Hawaiian surfer. It was she, not our lawyer or hers, who pointed out that *Cal* would have to give consent to have our baby's DNA tested if he wanted to determine his paternity—unless a judge in our state granted our pre-birth petition declaring us the baby's parents before Cal could make a move. The woman the Web chatters tried to portray as a barefoot hillbilly knew that if Boo were born in our state, we had a far better chance of prevailing—no matter what, even if it took years for us to legally claim him as our son.

But everything dissolved in her tender concern over the baby.

She knew she hadn't been eating enough; the baby would be smaller than she'd wanted. She knew that if he didn't come soon, she'd need a planned cesarean to get back to her own family and her own battle. We walked the streets, talking as intimately as I've ever spoken with another human being—of men and law, fairness and stupidity, love and disillusionment. For miles we walked, trying to prompt a labor that just wouldn't come. During one walk, Bobbie Jo wondered aloud how the man who swore to love her could use such cruel lies against her. Had she done so much that was wrong?

"Bobbie," I told her. "There are those who'd say that Mary was a surrogate mother, too. And her man stuck by her."

Finally, all those walks having come to naught, we scheduled a C-section, for November 1, All Saint's Day, a day that has always been lucky in my family. We woke at dawn and drove to the community hospital. I went into the operating room with Bobbie Jo; for that moment, the focus of all the light in the universe narrowed to a single point. Would our baby be healthy? Would our baby survive? In a hundred thousand rooms in a hundred thousand places, a hundred thousand women, at that very second, asked themselves the same ancient question.

Then he was there.

He was fair, and had huge hands and reddish-blond hair and the perfect shape of babies who don't have to go through the rigors of labor.

We named him after an old friend I met when I was in about seventh grade, and whom each of his older brothers had met, through a wonderful book, in their time. A man of justice. A man who did the right thing, even when the world was wrong.

Atticus.

The moment when Bobbie Jo surrendered Atticus into my arms was bittersweet for both of us. Here he was—at once the hoped-for result of so much celebration and the cause of so much suffering. How could we help but adore him? And how could we live with what we wouldn't say, but felt—that her gift to us had come at too great a price?

A few days later, I was nearly overwhelmed when we had to say goodbye.

"Don't worry," she said. "Atticus was clearly meant to be. And who knows? He's a blessing for you, and he just might be a blessing for me, too. I might have gone on living in a marriage that was nothing but a lie, for the rest of my life."

And yet, it had been her life. And she would fight on, until all her resources were gone, to see it made right. "I know you are there for me," she said. "I'll wait on the Lord."

When she got home, Bobbie Jo's father, who had not been a fan of what Bobbie Jo had done but who now supported her full-heartedly, handed her a checkbook and told her to use what she needed to pay her legal bills. Many asked us why *we* didn't pay them. In truth, we wanted to, even clandestinely. But to do so would have savored of coercion, the last thing Bobbie Jo needed. Her honorable intentions and her evident lack of greed intact, Bobbie Jo went back to court—clearly no longer pregnant and able to share in the care of her children.

And again—yes—the judge ruled against her, saying that the children seemed fine where they were and he just wasn't sure that the surrogacy wouldn't somehow harm them, especially given all the gossip and press coverage. Even when teachers spoke up, saying that missing Bobbie Jo was clearly putting Daphne under stress, the judge saw no reason for a psychological evaluation.

The judge denied the standard of law in his state—joint custody. Bobbie Jo had promised Daphne and Mike that they would spend Christmas with her. Now, they looked at their mother as having broken her word. There were even rumblings that Cal's parents, devout members of a fundamentalist sect, thought perhaps our son might be better off with a "more Christian" couple.

But meanwhile, a judge in our home town had granted our lawyer's pleading and ordered Atticus's birth certificate issued with our names as his parents.

I hated Cal by this point.

But Bobbie Jo did not. She saw him as misguided and misled, not evil. He was the father of her children.

Months later, in Nashville for a speaking engagement, I visited Bobbie Jo, bringing Atticus with me. New motherhood had taken a toll on old me. I fell asleep in a rocking chair. When I awoke, I found the two of them curled on the bed, watching Olympic figure skating on TV. The tears spilled over. Here she was, this gallant woman, still caring for my little boy, as she had so tenderly for nine months. How could I ever repay or repair?

I couldn't, of course, and as we again parted, Bobbie Jo assured me that I didn't have to.

She had brought Atticus down from the stars to our arms. It was enough.

Now Atticus is nearly a year old.

Rarely does a month go by that I don't hear from Bobbie Jo, never a day I don't think of her. On our end, our family opened like a sea and closed around its new member without a ripple. On hers, the slow drip of irrational torture went on.

There were more hearings. Finally, a psychological evaluation was scheduled for the children. But it was set for months down the road. Daphne and Mikey were becoming used to their mother as a visitor. Bobbie Jo was trying with all her considerable might to get in shape, make new friends, go back to nursing school.

But nothing she did could change the fact that a town that once knew her name only because she was funny and smart and sweet-natured now would always know her name for another reason.

We'll always know her name.

And so will Atticus.

I don't suppose she will ever vanish from my life, as birthmothers and surrogates sometimes do, an awkward chapter closed, a payment made but a debt incurred. I think I will always be grateful to know Bobbie Jo and to call her my friend. I think that telling Atticus the story of his birth will be a pleasure, and I hope he will feel a righteous anger on behalf of the woman who gave him life and had her life's precious branches ripped from her for her trouble. There are those who still say that Bobbie Jo got what she deserved for getting mixed up with Yankees and weird science. There are those who see her as a hero. And yet, although clearly the law has failed her, she still does not give in to hatred and spite. She is a far better person than I will ever be, even though justice is not impartial in this case, but cold and blind.

Last year, for Atty's baptism, Bobbie Jo sent our son a casing for his baptismal certificate and a onesie t-shirt that read, "Miracle." It's not a misnomer. This babe wasn't really planned nor meant to be, and all the heaven and hell that evolved from his conception might have been something the world would have been better off without.

Perhaps.

Perhaps not.

The trials of Bobbie Jo will one day be a subject for a legal journal article, as this business of assisted reproduction, in which science has outpaced the law, becomes codified to make human sense—for the women who perform this precious work and for those who seek them.

Until then, and since I have no other choice, and though I'm not sure it will help, for Bobbie Jo's sweet sake, I wait upon the Lord.

IT COULD HAPPEN TO YOU

by Sandy Hingston

"Ephram has got Madison pregnant."

I've just hauled the laundry basket into the living room to do some sorting when my daughter Marcy gives me the news. She's watching *Everwood*, one of the teen TV dramas she tunes in to on a regular basis.

"Which one's Madison?" I ask. All these smooth-skinned, hard-bellied actresses look alike to me.

"The babysitter."

"What's she going to do?"

"Ephram's dad offered to pay all her expenses if she got out of Everwood and didn't tell Ephram about the baby."

"Did she take him up on it?"

"Don't know yet."

"Just once," I say, "I wish one of these girls who get pregnant on TV would wind up having an abortion. But no. It's always got to be, 'We're all behind you, honey. We'll help you out just so long as you do the right thing.' Why is the right thing always the same thing?"

Marcy is rolling her eyes. She's heard this speech before. "Why do *you* always assume it won't work out if she *doesn't* have an abortion?" she counters.

"Because they're—what? Sixteen? Eighteen? That's too young to have a baby. It's too young to even have any idea what having a baby is *like*."

"But if they're really in love—"

"Oh, please. Remember when you went out with Ernest?" I snap. "Remember how embarrassed you are by that now? You don't know what love *is* when you're in high school. It's stupid, just stupid, to trust your feelings about anybody at that age."

My vehemence ticks my daughter off. "So it's better to just kill the baby," she sneers.

"It's not a *baby*. It's a fetus."

She looks at me, levelly. "I can't believe you. You're the most moral person I know, and you're talking about murdering a baby."

I take a deep breath. The TV blares in the background. Marcy's eyes haven't left my face. This isn't the first time we've had this discussion. It always ends the same way: with her waiting and me breathing.

"You'll understand when you're older," I say.

* * *

The kids my husband and I have raised are good Democrats. They've heard enough around the dinner table to be able to argue against tax cuts for the wealthy, the war in Iraq, privatizing Social Security, drilling for oil in the Arctic National Wildlife Refuge. Abortion stymies Marcy, though. When a teacher assigned her to argue the "pro" side in a debate last year, she complained tearfully: "There's nothing pro to say!" She's gaga for babies; she smiles whenever she sees them, coos over them, aches to hold them. For most of human history, she'd be, at fifteen, already a mother one or two times over. Her baby-love is instinctual. Evolution works against me in this.

Still, I've done my best to explain to her why the issue of abortion is so important. "It's all about choice," I've said. "I'd never, *ever* force *anyone* to have an abortion. But President Bush and his gang are dying to force you *not* to have one. That's the difference right there." I've pointed out how the rich white men who run this country wish to hell we were still stuck back in 1950, and don't want women to be educated or intelligent or empowered in any way. Look at the ones they idolize, I've said: Dewy-eyed Nancy Reagan. Prim Laura Bush. Then look at who they vilify: Hillary Clinton. Teresa Heinz Kerry. Women with careers, not just jobs. Women willing to stand toe-to-toe with men. Women who are figures in the world absent their husbands' sheen.

I've argued that outlawing abortion would be forcing women to don a biological burqa, dooming them to give birth to unloved, unwanted babies, the offspring of rape and incest and, yes, just lousy planning, even if it costs them their health or their lives.

I haven't made much headway.

Maybe that's because my arguments always falter against bedrock. "What is the difference, then, between a fetus and a baby?" Marcy demands.

I look at her, levelly. "I'm not sure there is a difference. But that doesn't mean women shouldn't have the right to decide that for themselves."

* * *

"Jared has got Rebecca pregnant," says Marcy.

It's not TV this time; it's real life: kids she knows, kids her age. I catch my breath. "What are they going to do?"

She shrugs. "They're happy about it. Well, sort of. She's already had a baby shower. Their families are supporting them."

What a waste, I think, picturing smart, hard-working Rebecca, and handsome Jared. (Those aren't their real names.)

"I know what *you* think they should do," Marcy grouses. "I know what you *always* think they should do."

"It's the end to so many dreams," I try to explain.

"Or the beginning! They could stay together. They could wind up being happy together."

How brutal should I be? "Are they going to get married?" I ask.

Marcy's puzzled. "I don't think so. Why would they?" *marriage issue*

It's my turn to be ticked off. "Because they have a kid, maybe? So their baby has a father *and* a mother? The girl's parents used to *make* him marry her, you know. That's what's wrong with society nowadays. Nobody is ashamed of anything anymore. There isn't any shame."

"What do you want?" my daughter asks, her voice clear, like a bell. "For Jared and Rebecca's parents to be ashamed of them instead of happy for them? How would that help now? What good would it do?"

"It could help keep other lunkheads from getting it on—or maybe convince them to put on a condom!"

She glances at me sidelong. "Shame never did anybody any good," she says emphatically.

I breathe.

She waits.

I can remember a time when I knew right and wrong as surely as Marcy does. Smoking was wrong. Drinking was wrong. And sex was very, very wrong. These things were forbidden because if you partook, your parents might find out about it, and if they did, they'd…what? It didn't matter what they'd do. What mattered was that they'd *know*. The prospect of discovery was deterrent enough; we would have died of shame.

But I grew up in interesting times, and even as that iron curtain of parental disapproval hung, stiff and unmoving, a breeze was beginning to buffet it. The wind ruffled our granny gowns and long hair and bell-bottoms, and there was an answer blowing in it, an answer to war and loneliness and fear and pain, and the answer was…love. If we could all just make enough love, we would change the world.

It's a beautiful notion, making love not war, and the women of my generation took to it readily, naturally, because now sex wasn't just something that felt good. It was political, the act of love—an act of rebellion, a means of defying authority, a way of saying *No! We won't be bound by your mores, your judgments*. In that thin, sweet slice of time between the dawning of the Age of Aquarius and the advent of AIDS, we rutted like rams, boffed like bunnies, tupped like tigers, caught up in the wind that had swelled to a tornado, that blew us helter-skelter from one partner to the next.

Free love ruled. But free love cost us.

I have done my best to explain to Marcy why the issue of abortion is so important. I've never told her, though, why it's so important to me.

* * *

"The Rebecca-Jared thing has gotten…complicated," Marcy announces, looking troubled as she wanders into the kitchen. It's only a few months now until the delivery date.

"How so?" I ask, stirring chicken curry at the stove.

"Well…there's this other girl who's pregnant. I don't think you know her. And supposedly there are, like, four different guys who could be the father. She doesn't know which it is. So they have to take paternity tests."

"And?"

"Jared's one of the guys."

In her voice, I hear the first crack in the happily-ever-after scenario she has generously, good-heartedly, constructed for Rebecca and Jared. The baby-shower goodies, the apartment they'll share, the families standing behind them—the love-will-conquer-all wallpaper suddenly doesn't seem to fit, to cover all the flaws. Her distress obviates any inclination on my part to crow. What I find myself thinking about instead is a moment thirty years ago when I saw that same crack in the wall. I was locked in my parents' bedroom, dialing the phone, following the directions I'd been given at the Planned Parenthood clinic: "You can call for the results in three days."

I already knew. I had just gotten home for the summer after my sophomore year of college, and I could sense that my body had turned on me, that the boffing bunny was kaput. I gave my name to the calm, polite woman who answered the phone, and she delivered the news: "You're pregnant." In the three days of waiting, I'd imagined myself at that moment crying, going into hysterics, maybe even hanging myself. When it came, I was dry-eyed.

"You have a number of choices," the polite woman said.

"How much is an abortion?" I asked.

Two hundred dollars, she told me. I didn't have $200. I didn't have $20. It didn't matter. I'd find it, somehow. "I'd like to schedule an abortion," I said.

I borrowed the money from a friend. A year later, I'd be the lender, for a different friend. Still another friend drove me into the city on the morning of my appointment. We were a network—bright, caught-in-the-act college girls looking out for each other, a grim conspiracy of silence, sworn in our sisterhood to keep this secret from our parents: we were not who they had hoped we'd be.

My friend found a parking spot near the clinic. There weren't any pro-life pickets; no one was shoving photos of fetuses in my face. But she still held my hand. Inside, there were forms to fill out—disclaimers, warnings. I was nineteen. I'd never been to an ob-gyn. I'd never lain back on the table and put my feet into stirrups. I did now.

"You may feel some pressure," the nurse said as the doctor came toward me. What I felt wasn't pressure; it was pain. The speculum was cold and hard; the vacuum seemed to be sucking my insides out. *Was* sucking my insides out. I was six weeks pregnant. The fetus was the size of a garbanzo bean.

There was a mimeographed sheet of instructions: Tylenol for the pain, warm compresses. I read it while I lay in the recovery room, sipping orange juice. Call immediately if you experience intensive bleeding, sharp pains, dizziness, fainting. Nothing about pangs of conscience.

There didn't have to be. We girls—women—friends—didn't need that. We did what we did, most of us—and there are millions and millions of us, 45 million since *Roe v. Wade*; I long to tell Marcy that, relatives of hers, friends of mine, teachers she has, coaches, actresses, athletes, doctors, lawyers, Indian chiefs—without much hesitation, and without much guilt. I think so, anyway. We haven't gone back and compared notes, my friends and I; those appointments at the clinic just get glossed over, aren't brought up at reunions or in visits with old roommates. No other choice. Whatever we might have been destroying, we knew we were salvaging our lives.

keeping the dream I was salvaging Marcy's life, too. No—not her life. Just the *possibility* of it, no more than that. I was preserving a wisp, the frail hope that somewhere down the road there'd be a man I'd fall in love with, and we'd marry (white dress, white cake), and buy a little house, and in due time—in due time—have a baby, a perfect little baby to call our own. My parents' dream for me. Happily ever after.

That's the way it worked out, as it happens.

But how do I tell my daughter I owe all this to the baby—the fetus, dammit—I had vacuumed away?

No wonder we get to that point in the abortion discussion where she waits and I breathe.

* * *

My widowed father recently moved from the house where I grew up into an adult living community. The process entailed a lot of letting go, on everyone's part. Pop and my siblings and I had to decide what of the past we wanted to keep and what to jettison. Golf clubs, punch bowls, yearbooks—his moving into the future required us to reassess the past. How much should one carry through life from place to place? How much do you press on the next generation? What we keep for ourselves defines us. So does what we give away.

One weekend night, Marcy and I go for our first visit to the new place. It's nicer, roomier, than we expect. Marcy loves it because everything—carpet, appliances, paint—is spanking new. The dining room table, with its familiar lace tablecloth, is in an utterly unfamiliar setting. I cook dinner with timeworn pots and heirloom utensils taken from strange cabinets and drawers. Pop tells stories we've heard before. We laugh at them again. I realize with relief that nothing much has changed. I had been afraid that love might somehow get left behind in the old place—that it might not follow Pop here. And I think about how scared I was, thirty years ago, that *[place & time]* love would get left behind if he knew what I'd done.

"Everybody makes mistakes," I always tell my daughter. "Nobody's perfect." Still, typical first child, she does her damnedest to be. I try to imagine how I would feel if she came to me and told me she was pregnant. I know how she thinks I would feel: the same way I'm afraid *she'll* feel if she finds out what I did when I was nineteen. Repulsed. Disgusted. I can't bear the idea that her love for me might not hold up if I make that confession—that the ties between us might be irreparably frayed.

Then I imagine how I would feel if she *didn't* come to me.

As she and I drive away from Pop's, where we've been discussing the Bush-Kerry debates, I mention how heartened I am by Kerry's strong pro-choice stance, and how vital it is that he win the election if we hope to preserve women's rights. Marcy looks at me from the passenger seat.

She waits.

I breathe.

I think: *George Bush will win because I always stop here. Because, by my silence, I've let the "abstinence-works" and "condoms-don't-prevent-AIDS" and "good-girls-don't" lies live on. Enough. Enough.*

admission

"When I was a sophomore in college, I had an abortion," I say, shakily. There's no response from the seat beside me, nothing at all, so I rush on into the silence, trying to head off my fear: "I was stupid. My boyfriend and I weren't using birth control. I didn't think it could happen to me. But it did."

There is a pause, in which I imagine her fumbling to take all this in: *Mom. Sex. Boyfriend. College.* So much to work through before she even gets to the point I'm trying to make. Finally, she speaks up, breathless: "Wow. I didn't think people really *did* that—got pregnant and got abortions. I mean, you hear about it. The statistics. But I never thought that anyone I *knew*..."

"I know. That's why I'm telling you this. Are you...shocked?"

"Well—*yeah.* I didn't think that you...you know. Had sex."

"Let me emphasize. I was nineteen. I hadn't been having sex for long."

She says something touching and amazing: "I don't want for you to think that I think you're dirty or anything, because I don't."

What I say (blushing in the dark, in the car) is: "Good." Then I keep going: "I got a pregnancy test at Planned Parenthood after I missed my period. They told me to call for the results in three days. But I already knew. And I knew I couldn't have the baby. I didn't *want* the baby. So a friend took me into the city, and I got an abortion."

"What about adoption?" she asks.

"I..." She, my child, should appreciate this. "I didn't feel I would be able to give the baby up. I would have wondered for the rest of my life where it was, what it was doing. Whether it was okay." Something becomes crystalline in my mind: "I've never once wondered that about the fetus. So maybe that's the difference between it and a baby."

She's quiet for a while. Then she asks: "Did you ever feel guilty?"

"Not ever. Not for a moment." Then I reconsider. "Well. After your father and I were married and I had a miscarriage, I thought that maybe God was punishing me."

She says, "But you would have felt that anyway."

I say, "What?"

And she says: "Even if you hadn't had the abortion, you would have felt the miscarriage was a punishment from God."

I think: *This child is wise.*

Then she says, "What did you think Pop would do if you told him you were pregnant?"

What I say is: "That's the thing. It didn't matter what he'd do. What mattered was that he'd *know*. I couldn't bear that shame."

She says: "Well. I guess I won't be afraid to tell *you*."

What I feel at that moment is electrical, biblical, as though I have gone up into the mountain in fear and trembling and emerged blessed.

IF

by Susan Ito

WE HAD BEEN MARRIED just less than a year that spring of 1989. My husband had a medical conference in Washington. He left our home in California early in the week. I planned to meet him there later, for a long weekend. When the airport van arrived at our house, I loaded my suitcase into the back, strapped myself in, and fell asleep before we reached the bottom of our street. The driver shook me awake at the airport; I had been drooling on my jacket collar. I had never experienced such overwhelming somnolence before. I stumbled through the corridors of the airport, feeling drugged, my head buzzing with a strange, sparkling heaviness. Passengers rushed past me with their wheeled luggage, their tickets flapping in their hands, and all I wanted to do was curl into a corner and sleep. It was all I could do to stagger onto the plane and doze, waking only to devour the plastic tray of rubbery food and sleep again.

"I think I'm sick," I told John as I got off the plane. "I feel woozy."

But it had been the first month of sex without birth control, the little cervical cap far, far away in the bathroom cabinet, the spermicide buried in the underwear drawer. We had thought it would take months, maybe even a year. Not so soon as this.

I sat on the edge of the bed and flipped through the yellow pages, searching for a clinic that would be open on a Saturday. While John was in a darkened auditorium, studying the dark red planet of a diseased liver shining huge and luminous on the wall, I climbed into a taxi, trembling, and gave the driver the address of the Georgetown Women's Center.

They took a tube of blood from my arm and then told me to call back in three hours. I wandered the streets of a city I didn't know, the jeweled boutiques, bookstores, a café with colorful bowls of salad crowded together under a glass counter. I sat there, eating stuffed grape leaves, staring at my watch, the tiny needle of the second hand jerking through space.

I thought about my blood, the tablespoons of blood that lay in the glass tube in the clinic. Blood that was waiting to speak, its language translated by chemicals and microscopes. Blood of the birthmother I'd tracked down and met when I was twenty, who had been glad to know me, but wanted me to stay a lifelong secret. Blood of my invisible birthfather, whose name she wouldn't reveal to me. Blood of so many unknown relatives. This blood was going to inform me of the presence of another, of one whose face I would finally see, a child to name and hold.

The woman on the phone said yes. "Congratulations," she said. News that she delivered dozens of times a day, altering lives with one syllable. Yes. No. I stared at the plastic receiver, the telephone. The phone was bolted to a wall outside of a B. Dalton bookstore. I bought a book on pregnancy, and ran my finger along the due-date chart, counting months. Early January. New year, new life.

I remember almost nothing about that pregnancy except the way it ended. I remember a walk along the grassy trails of Sea Ranch, the wild wind, my bursting energy. I was wearing John's blue jeans to accommodate my five-month pregnant belly.

In August, we took a trip to the Outer Banks in North Carolina with his brother's family. I swelled in the humidity like a sponge, my breasts enormous, my face squishy with fluid. "Look at me," I said, frowning in the mirror. "You look wonderful," he said. It wasn't what I was talking about. I hadn't been complaining about feeling fat or unattractive, although I was fat, in a strange, swollen way.

John, a doctor, went from that family vacation to El Salvador, heading a medical delegation to the war zone of Guazapa, under a volcano. My father-in-law disapproved, told me outright that he felt John was abandoning me. But I was proud of the work we were involved in. While he was in Central America, I drove to Davis to help load a container of wheelchairs, crutches, and medicine bound for Nicaragua. It was then that I noticed I couldn't lace my sneakers. My feet were the size of small footballs.

I picked him up at the airport, saying, "Don't you think I look fat?"

"You're pregnant, sweetheart," he said. "That's how you're supposed to look."

Sunday morning. September 17, 1989. I had gained thirteen pounds in a week. I pulled out the pregnancy book. In red print, it said, *Call the doctor if you gain more than three pounds in one week. If your face or hands or feet are swollen.* If. If. If. I checked them all off. While John was in the shower, I called my obstetrician and friend, Lisa. I whispered under the sound of running water, "I think something is wrong."

Lisa's voice was so smooth, so calm. "Swelling is very common," she said, "but it would be a good idea to get a blood pressure check. Can John do it?"

We stopped by his office, two blocks from the restaurant we had decided on for dinner. We were going to see a movie, then browse a bookstore; our usual date. I hopped onto the exam table, held out my arm. I couldn't wait to get to La Méditerranée. My mouth had been dreaming of spanakopita all day.

I heard the Velcro tearing open on the cuff, felt its smooth blue band wrapping around me. I swung my feet and smiled up at John, the stethoscope around his neck, loved this small gesture of taking care of me. I felt the cuff tightening, the pounding of my heart echoing up and down my fingers, through my elbow.

I will never forget the expression on his face, the change in color from pink to ash, as if he had died standing at my side. "Lie down," he said quietly. "Lie down on your left side. Now."

The numbers were all wrong, two hundred plus, over and over again, his eyes darkening as he watched the mercury climb on the wall. He shook his head. "What's Lisa's phone number?"

His voice was grim as he spoke to her on the phone—numbers, questions, a terrible urgency. He told me to go into the tiny bathroom and pee into a cup. "We've got to dipstick your urine, see if there's any protein."

I sat on the toilet and listened to him crash through the cupboards, knocking over samples of ulcer pills, brochures about stomach cancer, looking for a container of thin paper tabs. I gave him the paper cup, the gold liquid cloudy and dense. The dipstick changed color quickly, from white to powdery blue to sky to deep indigo. My protein level was off the chart. "No," he whispered. "No, no, goddammit, no."

I asked what, over and over, not believing that things could be as bad as what his face was telling me. "Your kidneys aren't working," he said. He pulled me out the door, across the street to the hospital. He pounded the buttons of the elevator, pulled me flying to the nurses' station, spat numbers at them. I thought, don't be a bully, nurses hate doctors who are bullies; but they scattered like quail, one of them on the phone, another pushing me, stumbling, into a room. There were three of them, pulling at my clothes, my shoes; the blood pressure cuff again; the shades drawn; they moved so swiftly, with such seriousness.

I had a new doctor now. Lisa, obstetrician of the normal, was instantly off my case. I was assigned a special neonatologist named Weiss. He was perfectly bald, with thick glasses, wooden clogs, a soft voice.

A squirt of blue gel on my belly for the fetal monitor, the galloping sound of hoof beats, the baby riding a wild pony inside me. What a relief to hear that sound—although I didn't need the monitor, I could feel the baby punching at my liver.

There was a name for what I had. Pre-eclampsia. Ahh. Well, pre-eclampsia was certainly better than eclampsia, and as long as it was pre-, then they could stop it, couldn't they? And what was eclampsia? An explosion of blood pressure, a flood of protein poisoning the blood, kidney failure, the vessels in spasm, a stroke, seizures, blindness, death. But I didn't have any of those things. I had pre-eclampsia. It felt safe.

They slipped a needle into my wrist and attached it to a bag of magnesium sulfate that hung over my head. This is to prevent seizures, they said. You may feel a little hot. As the first drops of the drug slipped into my bloodstream, I felt a flash of electricity inside my mouth. My tongue was baking. My scalp prickled, burning, and I threw up onto the sheets. I felt as if I were being microwaved.

I was wheeled down to radiology. Pictures of the baby onscreen, waving, treading water. A real child, not a pony or a fish. The X-ray tech, a woman with curly brown hair and a red Coca-Cola T-shirt, asked, "Do you want to know the sex?" I sat up. "There you go." She pointed. A flash between the legs, like a finger. A boy. I nearly leapt off the gurney. "John! Did you see? A boy! It's Samuel!" Sahm-well, the Spanish pronunciation, named after our host family father when we lived in Nicaragua studying Spanish, the most dignified man we knew.

He didn't want to look, couldn't celebrate having a son. He knew so much more than I did.

Weiss came to stand next to my bed. Recited numbers slowly.

"Baby needs at least two more weeks for viability. He's already too small, way too small. But you..." He looked at me sadly, shook his head. "You probably can't survive two weeks without having a stroke, seizures, worse." He meant I could die.

"What are the chances...that we could both make it?" Doctors are always talking percentages.

"Less than ten percent, maybe less than five percent." The space between his fingers shrunk into nothing.

This is how they said it: I was toxemic, poisoned by pregnancy. My only cure was to not be pregnant anymore. The baby needed two more weeks, just fourteen days.

I looked at John hopefully. "I can wait. It will be all right."

"Honey. Your blood pressure is through the roof. Your kidneys are shutting down. You are on the verge of having a stroke."

I actually smiled at him. I actually said that having a stroke at twenty-nine would not be a big deal. I was a physical therapist; I knew about rehab. I could rehabilitate myself. I could walk with a cane. Lots of people do it. I had a bizarre image of leaning on the baby's carriage, supporting myself the way elderly people use a walker.

We struggled through the night. "I'm not going to lose this baby," I said.

"I'm not going to lose you," he said. "And think of the baby. Chances are almost certain that a baby born this small will have problems. Severe problems."

I knew about children with problems; I had worked in a children's cerebral palsy clinic for years. Many of them had been born at the same gestational age as Samuel was now. I knew children who could not walk or speak or look into their mother's eyes.

After the longest night of my life, I relented.

I lay with my hands on my belly all night, feeling Samuelito's limbs turning this way and that. There was nothing inside me that could even think of saying goodbye.

At four in the morning, I called my parents. "We're in trouble," I said. My mother wept, frantic, alone. "I've got to find Daddy." He was on the road, traveling somewhere—where? North Carolina, Kentucky, Tennessee? On the road meant invisible, unreachable, gone. "I'll come out there tomorrow," she said. "There's no reason," I told her. She hung up sobbing.

At six, I called my birthmother. She was calm, optimistic, her voice smooth as water.

"I've known women who've had the same thing, and everything always turns out fine."

"It won't be fine, it's too early, way too early…" I wanted to tell her I wasn't like the others she'd known, that 95 percent of pre-eclampsia cases happen when the baby is nearly full term.

She wasn't listening. "I'm sure everything will be fine." Her voice was flat, gentle. She didn't offer to fly out to California. I wondered about the stroke—if it really happened, if that would bring her to my bedside. I began to get a small glimmering inside me, of understanding what it means to be a parent. And seeing for the first time that this was what she was not.

I had met her when I was twenty after a heart-racing, detective-story search. She was beautiful, glamorous, sophisticated: I felt I had hit the birthmother jackpot. Over the years it became clear that she was willing to be my friend and confidante, that she liked me. But there were two key conditions I had to adhere to if I wanted a relationship with her: one, I had to keep my own identity a secret in front of anyone she knew; and two, I had to not ask her who my birthfather was. At the time, it seemed worth it. I was young and infatuated by her charisma; I was willing to agree to anything. She also charmed my parents, who had fully supported my searching for her.

September 18, 1989. Another day of magnesium sulfate, the cuff that inflated every five minutes, the fetal monitor booming through the room. No change in status for either of us.

I signed papers of consent, my hand moving numbly across the paper, my mind screaming, I do not consent, I do not, I do not.

In the evening, Weiss's associate entered with a tray, a syringe, and a nurse with mournful eyes.

"It's just going to be a bee sting," he said.

And it was: a small tingle, quick pricking bubbles under my navel, and then a thing like a tiny drinking straw that went in and out with a barely audible pop. It was so fast. I thought, I love you, I love you, you must be hearing this, please hear me. And then a Band-Aid was unwrapped, with its plastic smell of childhood, and spread onto my belly.

"All done," he said. All done.

My child was inside swallowing the fizzy drink. It bubbled against his tiny tongue like a bud, deadly soda pop.

This is what it was. A drug, injected into my womb, a drug to stop his heart. To lay him down to sleep, so he wouldn't feel what would happen the next day, the terrible terrible thing that would happen. Evacuation is what it is called in medical journals.

Evacuees are what the Japanese Americans were called when they were ripped from their homes, tagged like animals, flung into the desert. Evacuated, exiled, thrown away.

I lay on my side pinching the pillowcase. I wondered if he would be startled by the drug's taste, if it was bitter or strange or just different from the salt water he was used to. I prayed that it wouldn't be noxious, not like the magnesium sulfate, that it wouldn't hurt. That it would be fast.

John sat next to the bed and held one hand as I pressed the other against my belly. I looked over his shoulder into the dark slice of night between the heavy curtains. Samuel, Samuelito, jumped against my hand once. He leaped through the space into the darkness and then was gone.

All gone.

This was my first experience of being a mother. I went home at the end of the week, gushing fluid, peeing and sweating quarts of the liquids my body hadn't been able to release. I wept oceans.

My parents called me several times a day. "Is there anything you need? What can we do for you?" I could imagine them wringing their hands, pacing, feeling helpless.

"Nothing," I said dully. I need my baby.

It was a week before I called my birthmother again. Her voice was bright.

"Oh!" she said, surprised. "When I didn't hear back from you again, I assumed everything must have turned out all right." Seven days, I thought, seven days and she never called.

"It didn't turn out all right," I said, my voice as dull and heavy as a stone. First grandchild swept away and she never picked up the phone.

"Well," she said (how could her voice be so calm?), "I'm very sorry. You're so young, though…"

Is that what she told herself at twenty-nine, when she had me and then let me go? Did she just set her vision to the future, the other children she would have? Was it really that easy?

There weren't many choices for my birthmother when she was pregnant with me back then. It's possible that she could have taken a knitting needle or rat poison and tried to terminate the pregnancy herself; I'm thankful—for both her sake and mine—that she didn't do that. She might have run away to an anonymous town where nobody knew her, and passed herself off as a widow with a child. But that would have meant tearing herself away from her family, her community, everything she knew. So she did what felt like the only viable option at the time: she bought a girdle. She ate like a bird. She did what she could to assure that I would be as small as possible; then she traveled to a faraway city and gave birth to me two months prematurely.

And then she gave me up for adoption.

Her choices had begun narrowing long before that day, however. They started shrinking when, in 1941 our country went to war with Japan, whose people looked like her family. Her family had no choice when their Los Angeles business was shut down and they were told to pack their lives into a single trunk, and they were forced to show their allegiance by moving into a barbed-wire compound in the high dusty desert of Colorado. She was ten years old then.

They had little option when the war ended and they were offered sponsorship, a job and a home and a place in a tiny town in the Midwest. Everyone in this town originated, one generation or two or three, from the same small country in Europe. Her family would become a charitable, benevolent experiment: loved but untouchable. When she reached adulthood, it was expected that she would choose a solitary life, the life of a schoolteacher or a nurse. The life of a wife did not seem an option because who in that community could openly marry such an outsider?

She chose love, a secret love. She chose a married man with a family. And that was how I came to be.

When I was twenty-five, and in a fragile, new relationship, I felt myself experiencing strange sensations: swollen, hypersensitive breasts, and the impulse to weep every five minutes. It took a while for me to understand what might be happening.

I picked up the telephone book, scanned the millions of numbers, flipping the thin yellow pages, and dialed. Crisis Pregnancy Center. I certainly felt like I was experiencing a crisis. I spoke with a woman who told me to come that day. I pressed the white buttons on the phone and called my boyfriend. My mouth was dry as I told him where I was going. He had only the year before gone through a pregnancy with another girlfriend; had seen her through the entire thing, held her hand through labor and birth, and together they had signed relinquishment papers for their daughter's adoption. He didn't say much when I told him what I feared; he was in shock.

He drove me to a place in the outer Richmond district by the beach, a small white door in the basement of a church. A woman in a plain brown dress opened it, scouring us both with her eyes. "Did you call this morning?" I nodded and handed over a brown paper bag that held a mayonnaise jar, sloshing with warm urine. She told us to wait in what looked like a daycare room, with blue and yellow padded mats on the floor and a plastic playhouse littered with stuffed animals. We sat on short chairs, our knees tilted up to the ceiling. Thirty minutes later, the woman called us into a windowless room, sat us down on a worn loveseat and said that I was pregnant.

The world became very quiet. I believed that I could hear the little ball of cells, popping and dividing underneath my skin. I imagined a tiny seahorse, rocking in a crimson pear. The woman began talking about baby clothes and financial assistance for unwed mothers, and then paused and squinted at me. "You aren't considering abortion, are you?"

I couldn't lift my eyes. "I don't know."

"Well. Let me tell you about what really goes on in that procedure." Her lips curled away from her teeth. "What happens is this: your baby is sucked out of your body by a machine that is fifteen times more powerful than your household vacuum cleaner! Can you imagine?"

I told her that I couldn't imagine. Then I stood up to leave, telling her I would think about it. My boyfriend's face was gray as stone. He reached out to take my hand.

The woman moved to the door, blocking us a bit. Taking slow long looks at each of us, she warned, "You might want to consider the fact that the majority of relationships deteriorate after an abortion." We thanked her and walked to the ocean.

Pregnant. It couldn't be possible. I clutched at the front of my jeans, stumbling in the sand. "I'm scared," I said. Tears ran down into the collar of my shirt. And then, "No wonder I'm crying all the time."

He squinted out at the ocean, his eyes bright. I knew what he was thinking. Not again. Not again.

It seemed that there were three possible options: abortion, adoption, or keeping the baby ourselves. Adoption was out of the question: there was no way I was going to relinquish my first blood relative, and there was no way he was going to endure that particular hell again. Keeping the baby, at that point in our lives, seemed as abstract and unrealistic as becoming astronauts or movie stars. Our relationship was too new, we were way too unequipped. My parents were extraordinarily conservative and old-fashioned, and I couldn't imagine even admitting to them that I had had sex. Some people might, at the age of twenty-five, decide to up and raise a baby with a person they barely knew. But it seemed absolutely incomprehensible to me.

Abortion felt like the only avenue.

I was fascinated though—horrified and fascinated—to realize that my body was capable of doing such a thing. Growing a human being. I patted the skin over my belly, trying to feel something, although it was ludicrous; surely it was no larger than a paper clip. I knew that its days were numbered, and I resolved not to miss any part of it, to feel everything I could until it was gone.

I called her. There was no question of calling my parents. I called my birthmother because I knew she would understand. And of course she did. She had been an alarmed, unmarried pregnant girl, twenty-five years ago.

Her voice was bright when she recognized my voice. "Su-san! How are you?"

I felt something crumple inside me. The words came out brokenly. "Not so good."

I could hear her breath catch over the phone. She inhaled, then let it out. "What is it? What's the matter?"

"I'm pregnant."

"Ohh." The vowel sound she made was filled with empathy, pain, and recognition. It was exactly the sound I needed to hear. Thank you, I said silently.

"What will you do?" Her voice was solemn and soft.

"I've got an appointment. On Monday." I didn't say the word out loud.

"Ah. Well, I think that's probably for the best, isn't it?" She knew that my relationship hadn't turned out to be The One, that I wasn't anticipating a long future together. I'd confided in her just as thoroughly as I had with my best girlfriends.

I sighed. "I'm sure it is. But it's still…hard."

"Of course it is. It must be very hard." I could feel the tenderness coming through the receiver and I closed my eyes. It was as if her palm was on my forehead, stroking it.

"You're lucky that you have this option."

"Yes."

"It's what I would have done, if it had been available to me…" And then she stopped short, realizing what she had just said.

I blinked. I tried to keep my voice steady. "Of course. I know." I was balancing on a tightrope. I wanted this support, this ability to confide in her. I needed her to be my understanding, forgiving mother. And yet she had just told me that she would have killed me if she had had the chance. The rigid voice of the woman in the church basement came back to me. I saw the deadly vacuum cleaner. I thought of coat hangers and bottles of X-labeled poisons. I blinked through tears, harder, and pushed it all away.

She tried to smooth over her own words. "Susan, is there anything you need? Can I do anything for you?"

Come to me, I wanted to say. Come be with me and hold my hand. But I couldn't choke the words out. To hear her say no would have been unbearable.

"No," I said. "I'm sure it will all be fine."

Maybe she was just echoing my words four years later, telling me what she thought I wanted to hear.

I have two other children now, daughters. After losing Samuel, I was frightened and alarmed at my body's betrayal. My husband and I began pursuing adoption instead; it seemed safer than running the gauntlet of another pregnancy. But our two daughters insisted on showing up in our family, despite our feeble efforts at contraception; I am infinitely grateful that they did. And yet I do not forget that son, small cowboy, the way he galloped through me. Nor do I forget the microscopic, unnamed seahorse of a child who came before that. There is still a part of me that believes that I failed the test of motherhood, the law that says your child comes before you, even if it means death. I put myself first when it came to Samuel, just as my birthmother had with me. And sometimes I cannot bear what that feels like. I look at my girls, the life that fills this family, and I think, none of this would be here if I had chosen differently.

If I had stayed with that old boyfriend and never had that first abortion. If I had refused to give up on Samuel's chances. Maybe I wouldn't be here today. Maybe I would have a severely disabled son. If my birthmother had taken a coat hanger to me instead of hiding me under a girdle and then delivering me in a faraway state. If she had stolen away with me and pretended to be a widow in a new town. If that married man, my birthfather, had left his wife and children. If, if, if.

There are lifetimes of ifs to consider. But in the end, my birthmother and I made the choices we did. One time I chose one way, and another time it felt less like a choice than a gun at my head.

I am inching toward fifty now. I no longer condemn her or myself for what we decided for ourselves, years ago. Did we choose wrongly? Were we selfish? There is no way to truly answer those questions. My life has been steeped in the tea of reproductive choice since the moment of my own conception. I wish us peace for all that we have chosen.

BEARING SORROW:
A Birthmother's Reflections on Choice
by Janet Mason Ellerby

June 1964

ALEC GREETED ME eagerly at the stately front door of his parents' manicured home in our affluent bedroom community of San Marino, California. It was almost one year to the day since we had met on a church retreat at Big Bear Lake. I had been charmed by him and his boyish efforts to catch a fish, and he, in turn, had seemed quite taken with me. One week after the retreat, he called and awkwardly but sweetly asked me out. We went to see *Bye Bye Birdie* at the Academy Theater in Pasadena. Two years older than I, he was skinny, pimply, and growing toward handsome but not there yet. Little by little, I moved from shy ingenue to girlfriend. He gave me a yellow St. Christopher medal to wear on a long silver chain around my neck—the marker in our circle for going steady.

My sophomore year was almost entirely taken up by my devotion to Alec. I found myself agreeing to each step in our sexual passage. I castigated myself for each capitulation, but he was so insistently single-minded. Most of what we did, when we could, was make out. I had wanted to be a dutiful daughter, a popular girl, a smart girl, but I wanted Alec to love me more than I wanted all that.

And so that night, shortly after his high school graduation and my sixteenth birthday, I drove myself to his house, having only that week gotten my license. His parents and sister were away, so we got right down to the serious task at hand. He undressed me but he remained dressed, our usual modus operandi. He would explore my body. I would passively acquiesce, a typical sexual arrangement of the times. I remember his freshly ironed button-down shirt and his baby blue, v-neck sweater. His sparse facial hair tickled my upper lip and the astringent smell of his acne medicine, a white smear still visible on his chin, could not be ignored.

I would like to say we made love that night, but I was too intimidated and ashamed to find love in that dark encounter. I had dreamily, romantically anticipated a Catherine and Heathcliff blending of souls, but it turned into a joyless hour, one I stumbled through submissively. Still, it was not date rape or nonconsensual sex. I was willing.

We were lying on the family couch, gray in the TV half-light but unfortunately avocado green. The textures of the evening come back with amazing clarity. I can still feel that ugly couch, nubby, almost warty—weirdly appropriate in its toad-like hue. This time Alec did manage to enter me by prodding, pressing, and pushing, slowly but persistently. I was too shy to touch him, to guide him, too scared to respond in any way; instead I just held still like an obedient child. Rather than passionate, I was fixated on the idea that we must be doing something wrong. This was just too painful; and then suddenly he pulled out.

Trembling, I turned my back and pulled up my underpants and jeans. I never did see his penis; I was too inhibited to look, more ashamed than curious. When he turned on the unforgiving lamp, the avocado cushion showed a dark red stain, our sad version of the telltale bloody sheet. Alec ran for towels and we scrubbed at the offending spot. Our zealous concern for the couch helped us deny what had just happened.

Time to go home. He walked me to the door, murmuring that he loved me. Then he said something puzzling: "We can never do it *like that* again," and then he added, "Go home and take a hot bath, as hot as you can stand it."

What did he mean by "*like that?*"

I drove home shakily, already lonely and full of trepidation, but it wasn't until I got into that excruciatingly hot bath and watched the thin stringy blood seeping out of my sore vagina that I realized what might have happened. Had he come inside me? Is that what he meant by "*like that?*" The blood on the couch, in my underpants, and now this! I put on a clean pair of white underpants and fiercely scrubbed the ones I had been wearing, hoping that it was menstrual blood. In the morning there was one more spot, and then it stopped—no more blood, none.

I had just turned sixteen. Although it was 1964, we still lived in the fifties; I was sheltered. Brought up in a culture where sex was never articulated, neither Alec nor I knew know how to talk about it. Layers of inhibition, self-consciousness, and shame made it impossible for me to ask him, "Did you come?"

I did not, in any practical way, prevent my pregnancy. I had never had a conversation with my mother, with a teacher, not even with my older sisters about birth control. I whispered about it with my girlfriends, but they knew next to nothing. I did know that conception occurs when a sperm penetrates an egg, but I did not know when this would happen during a menstrual cycle, which means I didn't even have a basic understanding of the rhythm method. What I did have was the classic, erroneous folklore that mysteriously circulates in adolescent subcultures then and now. My best friend Jackie must have gotten a bit of advice mangled because she told us that you couldn't get pregnant right in the middle of the month, and we all knew a girl couldn't get pregnant the first time. My only sex education had occurred four years prior, in the sixth grade: the girls went to see a film about menstruation and hygiene and the boys a film about—well, I don't know, but certainly not birth control. By the time we got to high school, those brief and vague films with their embarrassing diagrams were no defense against reality. And so, there I was: fertile, passionate, and unprotected.

So that was it, the first time. No transcendent melding of body and spirit, no conflagration of souls, no unbreakable seal that would now bind us to one another forever. We had fumbled through an awkward, embarrassing overture to sex, not atypical in its gracelessness, not unusual in its uncertainty. But the consequences for me would be profound and enduring.

September 1964

My mother and I were on the doorstep of her obstetrician's office when it opened that morning. Late the night before, she had found me crying, and asked, for the first time in a long time, "What's wrong?" When I wouldn't answer, she finally asked the obvious question: "Are you pregnant?" I answered her the only way I could: "I don't know."

I was not lying. I was still not sure if what Alec and I had done back in June counted as sex. He had said, "We can't do it like that"; but that was our only time doing it "like that." It had been so painful and embarrassing.

Surely this could not be the way a baby was conceived. My stomach was still flat and taut. I never felt like throwing up. I had no cravings. Surely pregnancy had to feel like something.

Dr. Cook ushered us into his office and the explicit questions were asked: "Was his penis inside you?" "Did he ejaculate?" "Did you bleed?"

My answers were inconclusively vague. Frustrated, Dr. Cook said the only way to find out what had really happened was to examine me. Flushed with rage, infuriated by me and my obfuscation, my mother rose to follow us into the examination room, but he asked her to wait. We went alone.

This was my first pelvic exam. I knew that doctors helped women have babies, but I didn't know about the table, the stirrups, the position, and the instrument. I followed each of his nurse's instructions, taking off my clothes, putting on the huge paper gown, placing my heels in the stirrups, scooting down on the table, and arranging my legs in a way that felt obscene. As Dr. Cook inserted the cold speculum, he tried to cheer me by commenting on my suntan. With the gloved fingers of one hand inside me, he pressed hard on my stomach with the other hand. I squeezed my eyes shut, but tears still spilled out, sliding down my temples into my hair. Slowly he removed his fingers, rose from the stool, took off the gloves, washed his hands at the sink, and walked to the head of the table where I still lay. And then those words: simple, blunt, devastating: "You're pregnant."

Was I brave? Did I receive the news stoically? Not really. My tearful reply reflected my steadfast denial:

"No! I can't be! It was only the one time."

But he was adamant: "You're pregnant. Get dressed."

From that moment on, I would make no more choices. I would do only as I was told. I mechanically redressed. The nurse led me back to the office where Dr. Cook and my mother waited.

My mother asked, "Is there anything you can do?"

"No—nothing," he answered. "It's much too late for that. If she had come to me right away, I could have given her something. But not now. There's nothing I can do."

It was 1964. *Roe v. Wade* was still nine years in the future and I was three months pregnant.

Where was I that morning? In complete psychological retreat. If anyone had thought to ask me, "What do you want?" I would not have known how to answer. I watched the adults around me as they began to make important decisions for me, and I put up no resistance. I was shocked by what was happening to my body, that I had no control over it, that it was doing something monumental without my knowledge or consent.

My body was not my own; perhaps it had never been. When it had escaped my parents' control, Alec had immediately taken it up, and when he had abandoned it, a baby had claimed it. It may sound as if I am unwilling to take responsibility for my actions, but in fact, I did not completely understand that my body was my own dominion, that I could say what did and did not happen to it. In significant ways, women were not led to believe that they owned their bodies—the state, their husbands, or their fathers did. I willingly handed my body and my future back to my parents. Their money and authority took over, and I surrendered all bids at self-control. I would not be allowed to make another decision for a long, long time.

What about an abortion? My parents certainly had the means to pay for the travel and the procedure, but the hermetic life of our well-heeled suburb prevented them from knowing how one might proceed with such a plan. When I tell people who grew up in working-class neighborhoods this story, they are always amazed that no one considered that option. But there were no back alleys in San Marino, nothing illegal whatsoever, and my parents' principled moral rigor would have prevented them from considering anything unlawful in the first place. If an abortion had been obtainable, would I have been able to make my own informed, thoughtful choice? Regrettably, no. I was in my parents' hands entirely with no more free will than a newborn. The baby I carried was theirs too, to do with as they saw fit. I would have agreed to anything.

The next morning, my clothes were packed and I was put on a plane for Cleveland. My aunt had agreed to care for me throughout the pregnancy. When my parents and I said goodbye at the terminal gate at LAX, my mother's anger helped her avoid any signs of grief or reservation, but my father seemed defeated, unsure. I had never seen this tall, confident, controlled man in any kind of emotional distress, but there he was, noticeably stooped, weeping. Despite his great disappointment, he was suffering from the decision to send me away—a necessary banishment, he must have reasoned, but exile just the same.

I turned, leaving them there, watching me, and started up the ramp and into the plane. The die was cast; there was no turning back. I found my seat and stared blankly, utterly empty, out the window as the plane accelerated, the first step in a perilous journey that no one could have anticipated. The plane gained altitude, the smoggy maze of the LA grid spread out beneath me, and I knew that nothing would ever be the same.

January 1965

I lived with my aunt, uncle, and cousins in their affluent Cleveland suburb for the fall, attending school and hiding my pregnancy behind a tight girdle and bulky sweaters. On the day after New Year's, my aunt drove me to the Florence Crittenton Home for Unwed Mothers in Akron. I was well into my seventh month and even my wool jumper, the last article of clothing roomy enough to disguise my vanished waistline, would no longer do the job.

The home looked like something out of the nineteenth-century novels I was so fond of: a massive, three-story Victorian mansion. Surrounded by snow-covered grounds, the place loomed dark and ominous behind menacing wrought-iron bars. We drove up a short driveway to the solid front door and parked. My aunt pounded the knocker and the door swung open. In the foyer a tiny, gray-haired woman—the housemother—greeted us.

I realize this sounds like the hackneyed beginning of a horror movie—and I was indeed horrified during that initial introduction—but the home itself turned out to be quite benign. I fell in love with that ponderous, vast old house, with its heavy, dark wood paneling and ornate fixtures that impressed me greatly after the relatively unadorned stucco homes of Southern California. Rather than acknowledge to myself the point of being there, I pretended I was entering a Victorian boarding school. That I was there to have a baby still did not register.

There were many such homes for unwed mothers at that time, at least for privileged girls like me. There were no African American or Hispanic girls, not while I was there. About thirty girls lived there at a time. Their parents, like mine, had sent them there to protect everyone from the shame of their pregnancies and to facilitate the adoption process. It was a rule that every girl who came to live at Florence Crittenton would, without question, "give up" her baby for adoption.

Although I did cry when my aunt left me that day, I adjusted to the routine at Florence Crittenton. On that first evening, I thankfully peeled off the girdle and stuffed it in the back of a drawer. Then I locked myself into the old-fashioned bathroom and ran steaming water into the fabulously huge, claw-footed bathtub—another prop for a captive princess in an enchanted castle. After bathing, I looked at myself in the long, speckled mirror on the back of the bathroom door and sighed, deeply dismayed by the reality before me. Complicated blue veins crisscrossed my swollen breasts; a dark brown line extended down from my distended belly button into my pubic hair; my round stomach seemed impossibly to be growing hairs. Disbelief was difficult to suspend given this reflection, so I quickly pulled on my underpants, fastened my bra, donned one of my new smocks and a pair of elasticized slacks, combed my hair, and headed down to dinner. I was determined to be good, no matter what, and my uncomplaining forbearance worked to make this newest phase of my pregnancy easier on everyone.

For the girls at Florence Crittenton this was a secret time, a shameful present that would become a forgotten past. We thought if we obeyed the rules (i.e., do not disclose your real name; keep up with your schoolwork; gain no more than twenty pounds; do not tell the baby's father your actual whereabouts; rub your belly with cocoa butter to avoid unsightly stretch marks), we would emerge untarnished and free. We believed in the rituals and wisdom of the adult world. If we followed these elaborate procedures, surely our salvation was around the corner.

My aunt took care of the arrangements for the adoption and my medical care. Although all the girls at Florence Crittenton were required to attend a one-hour class to prepare for childbirth, I still could hardly believe I was pregnant with a baby. My aunt encouraged me to think of my "condition" as a temporary setback—like a badly broken leg or a serious appendicitis attack. When I did think of giving birth, I pictured myself asleep since my doctor planned to sedate me as heavily as was safe.

I never actually talked about the baby itself. My aunt must have believed that by avoiding that reality, I would continue to discount the baby's actual presence in the world. It was common practice at the time that unwed mothers never see the baby or even know its gender. That was the plan for me. I would have no recollection of the birth or the baby. It would be removed and then whisked out of the room and out of my life. My trespasses would be forgiven, the secret would be ensconced, and I would return to life as a junior in high school. It was a nice way to anticipate the event, but as often happens, these plans would go terribly wrong.

March 1965

On a wintry evening two weeks before my due date, I began noticing my stomach tightening—no pain but definite contractions. Mrs. Reilley, our nurse, was busy dispensing medications to girls who needed them. When I told her what I was feeling, she dismissed the mild contractions as false labor. In fact, no one was due to have a baby in the upcoming week, so she had arranged to visit her daughter in Youngstown. She assured me I'd be fine and hastened out the door.

False or not, it was my turn to sit in the special rocking chair for girls in labor, and in the tradition of the Home, other girls sat cheerfully around me, timing the irregular intervals between contractions. It was exciting until we all had to turn in.

Alone in my bed, I kept checking my watch. At 1:00 a.m., the pains were ten minutes apart; at 2:00 a.m., eight minutes; at 3:00 a.m. I decided to stop counting, willing my body to halt a process that was escalating all too rapidly. The illuminated hands on my watch were approaching 4:00 a.m., when, in the middle of an intense contraction, my water broke, seeping into the mattress, warm, plentiful, and alarming.

Given this new development I had to notify Mrs. Williams, which meant waking her. I reluctantly knocked on her door, apologizing for getting her up. She was clearly tired and annoyed by the disturbance, chastising me for choosing this night of all nights to go into labor. This part of her job must have been one of the most unpleasant. She sent me back to my room to dress and pack an overnight bag. Since Mrs. Reilley was far away by now, Mrs. Williams had to call another nurse to come from across town to get me. As if to deepen the melodrama, it had been snowing heavily for several hours; the nurse called back to say that rather than try to drive herself, she had called a cab. I was to wait for her in the downstairs hall. Mrs. Williams went back to bed.

I waited for her alone for over an hour, wondering how I would live through this nightmare unaccompanied. The pains were shocking; I could not help but cry out every time one gripped me, so I kept stuffing my mittens in my mouth to muffle my insuppressible yelping. The house was cold, dark, and profoundly still. Above me on the second and third floors, everyone slept. My stifled cries and whimpering awakened no one.

Finally, a little after 5:00 a.m., a woman I had never seen before walked in the big front door and hustled me out to the cab waiting in the snow. She seemed inexplicably angry, exasperated by my tears and moans. When the cab driver showed concern, she irately dismissed him, snapping that there was plenty of time. My labor pains were by now coming one on top of the other, yet I was unable to convince her that they were valid, that I was desperate. Completely distraught, I frantically begged the cab driver to help me—which infuriated her; she shouted, "Shut up!" and slapped me hard across the face. I was dumbfounded by her malice and utterly helpless. When we finally arrived at the hospital, she shrilly cursed me when I told her I couldn't walk and hauled me out of the cab. More afraid of her than of the pain, I hobbled up a ramp, across the entryway, through the doors, and into a brightly lit hall.

The kind cab driver did help me; he had run ahead and found an orderly who now moved swiftly to guide me into a wheelchair. Leaving the sputtering nurse behind, we quickly moved down a long white hallway, into an elevator, up a few floors, down another hallway, and finally into a room where a gentle hospital nurse was waiting to help me undress.

Just as I have never forgotten the off-duty nurse's inexplicable fury, I have also not forgotten those others that helped me: the cab driver, the orderly, the hospital nurse, and the intern who would deliver my baby. With compassion, they saw me for what I was, a lost child in baffling pain.

6:00 a.m. March 20, 1965

I give birth to my daughter, whom I have already secretly named Sorrow, in a frigid delivery room. Because of the saddle block the intern has quickly administered, I do not feel her being born, but I immediately hear her crying. Even before she completely emerges from my body, she's crying. She is not placed on my stomach, like most newborns, but when I ask, I am allowed to look at her for about a minute. I am allowed to touch her rosy, glistening cheek and her wet, dark hair. I see that the umbilical cord has been cut; the small, yellow-gray stump extending from her navel is all that is left of our intimate connection. Her tiny perfect hands are furiously grasping at the shockingly cold air around her, so different from the peaceful, watery warmth of my body that had rhythmically cradled her.

She won't stop crying, but I know I can soothe her if they will just give her to me. I am crying too, much like her, with big, gulping, cadenced wails. I realize that this is my one and only chance to claim her. I beg the nurse:

"Please, please, just let me have her. Please give her to me. Please."

The resolute nurse shakes her head. "No, I'm sorry. I can't."

I am left with an image I will always carry, a terrible burden yet a treasured memory: My baby is crying hard, her fists and legs frantically beating the air—her high, shrill command to me to comfort and suckle her. My arms are outstretched; they extend before me, supplicating, ready to receive her forever. And then she's gone. I push up, panic-stricken, trying hysterically to free myself, to get off the table, but I cannot move my deadened legs, still tied to the stirrups.

Because there had been no time for my regular doctor to get to the hospital and because I was fully conscious for my daughter's birth, some of my aunt's instructions were not carried out. How grateful I am to the people in the delivery room for giving me that minute with Sorrow. My wailing baby girl remains crystalline in my memory. I cherish her endurance.

Sorrow's birth was an irreparable tear in the fabric of my adolescence, a rent that became the most consequential event of my life. Her birth ignited an implosion of a self that I had only tenuously pieced together at sixteen. The centrifugal force that held me together—a bright, sunny girl—was obliterated that night as I turned into a helpless, unfamiliar, straining body consumed by unimaginable pain. I had no idea what was going to happen to me or who would finally find me in that lonely hall at Florence Crittenton. That I was found and delivered to the hospital did not make it easier to cope with the knife in my heart—surrendering the baby I loved instantly and completely. She was, I believe, the only thing in the world that might have repaired me, recentered me after the pain and terror of that night, but she was taken away. And so my selfhood imploded into fragments of hysteria.

Later, I would spin an intricate personal narrative, weaving my memories, constructing a passable identity: on the surface, I appeared serious, studious, and quiet, but underneath, I was inexplicably prone to bouts of melancholy brooding. I ended up with a tangled and conflicted orchestration of selfhood that consistently failed me. Somehow I could never faithfully incorporate either the actual events of Sorrow's birth or my inextinguishable grief at her loss. My inexorable past would always insinuate itself into my present, and I would break apart, falling into sloughs of depression so deep I feared I would never climb out.

When I woke later that day, a metamorphosis had occurred: the girl I had been was gone. Indeed, two births could have been registered that morning. Sorrow began her life, and I had to begin my life anew. But this time, I had to start over, hobbled by a complex psychological wound, shell-shocked from a shattering night.

Despite my aunt and my parents' dicta not to feel and not to recall, the night I lost Sorrow remains. I encounter the memory over and over again: the icy delivery room; the precise sounds of Sorrow's cries and my own wailing; my dead legs in the stirrups; the image of my tiny baby, so vulnerably naked except for the whitish, chalky substance that covers her; my own outstretched arms. Despite my earnest, most concentrated efforts, I am inundated by the flood of feeling this memory releases, leaving me, even now as I write this, in disarray—discomposed, stranded, utterly alone.

April 1965

I returned to Florence Crittenton for the required ten-day, post-delivery stay, this time to a dull, gray room for the newly delivered. Unlike the rest of the house, this room looked and felt like a cell; my meals were brought up to me on a tray. The other girls avoided me, just as I had avoided the downcast girls who preceded me. I lost the will to wash or eat, and sleep was almost entirely elusive. My aunt did not visit since, as she put it, the worst was over, and she had long ago told me that my parents had to be protected from the details of my pregnancy. They did not call. Alone in that room, laden with a barrage of grief I could not restrain, I deteriorated in ways too deep to express.

After ten days in the gray room, I was asked to bathe, dress, and come downstairs. Ushered into Mrs. Williams's darkly formal office, I was introduced to a social worker and a representative from the adoption agency. Again complete loneliness and utter helplessness overwhelmed me. No one informed me that I did not have to do this, to sign away my baby. In fact, I did not understand that until I signed those papers, she was *my* daughter—that no one else could have her unless I consented. I was handed a pen and showed where to sign. I mutely and obediently did as I was told and was excused.

For years after, I excoriated myself for my ignorance, but I have since learned that this was a common deception. Girls were deliberately not informed of their parental rights—not informed that keeping their baby was an option, even if they were not yet adults, even if their parents did not consent. I realize now that I was coerced by well-meaning people into doing something that was for me deeply unnatural, aberrant. But then, at sixteen, with no sense of self-reliance, no means of self-support, and no informed legal council, there was no other conceivable choice. I had never been encouraged to be decisive or to think for myself, and my previous tries at independence had gotten me into grave trouble.

Recently I was corrected when I told someone I "gave up" my daughter for adoption. Today, I am supposed to say that I made an "adoption plan." And in fact, there was such a "plan." The representative from the adoption agency told me that the baby (never "my" baby) would now be the daughter of a professional couple. The baby's parents (not her "adoptive parents") were stable people in their thirties. Their occupations would ensure that she would be raised in a home free from financial worries— just like my upbringing. But the "plan" provided no comfort. It was meant to sound soothing and rational, but it masked acute pain and cruel separation. The "plan" allowed Sorrow to be taken away from me, and completely cloaked any possibility of a reunion.

Even today, when I think that I could have demanded my daughter, that my rights were primary, that others would have had to comply, my anger still bubbles up, livid and raw. That I could have said, "Let me feed her," and nursed her with the milk I was still plentifully producing; that I could have bathed her, clothed her, and comforted her with my healthy body that ached for her touch as hers must have ached for mine. But all I could do was shamefully wipe away the milk, tears, and blood. If she was anyone's, I was made to believe, she was my parents', and they did not want her. What I wanted was so irrelevant that I did not even hazard asking it of myself. I was shattered even though I was told over and over that I should feel relieved, fortunate, that the worst was over. That was cold comfort. It would never be over.

For girls like me, choice was not a concept, hardly even a word in our vocabulary. If we had been poor girls or girls of color, most likely we would have been required to marry as soon as our parents found out about our pregnancies, or perhaps our mothers or grandmothers would have taken on the responsibility of raising another child. But illegitimate children and shotgun marriages with a full-term baby coming only six months after the wedding were anathema to our parents. Adoption was the only possible solution for girls like us and there was definitely a market for our healthy, white babies, just as there is today.

In 1965, there were businesses like Florence Crittenton in every large city in America to hide us, and hundreds of adoption agencies to take care of the sought-after product of our fruitful nine months. No one thought about social programs that might have created homes for us to return to with our newborns, places where we could have learned how to be competent mothers. Cultural codes were so punitive that such a solution to unplanned pregnancies was unthinkable. We had to agree to a stunningly simplistic, unexamined agenda: to be secreted away, give birth without a fuss, willingly relinquish our babies, and return, grateful and contrite to the lives that had been planned for us. We agreed to adoption, we agreed to our own unsuitableness, we agreed to a shameful interpretation of our actions, we agreed to take on the secret of our lost babies because we had no means to question the values that informed those decisions. Still influenced by the cultural rigidities of the fifties, we had no means to become the loving, responsible, proud, and capable young mothers we might have been.

Looking back now at those last incomprehensible days at Florence Crittenton, I can understand the new, forlorn girl I was, pacing around that bleak room. Now I can take the word "trauma" and apply it to that night of solitary physical pain and my unanticipated agony in that cold delivery room. I know now I was feeling the torment any new mother feels who loses her baby. When a woman loses her child after carrying it for nine months, when her baby dies, we feel tremendous sympathy for her. It seems the worst possible misfortune. We wonder how she will cope with her grief; we hope she will become pregnant again soon so that her pain can somehow begin to heal. Yet I was expected to feel happy, relieved, unburdened after losing Sorrow. No wonder I was baffled. In the struggle between nature and culture, I lost.

Perhaps there are those who believe the decisions made for me made my life easier, that I had more choices—or different choices—because my daughter was given away. Returning to California at sixteen with a newborn to care for would have dramatically changed the direction of my life—at least for a few years. Instead of the supposedly burdensome responsibilities of motherhood, I was allowed to return to what would presumably be a carefree adolescence and untroubled university education. This rosy scenario was not to be. My remaining adolescence was careworn, my university education discordant, my world travels lonesome. I was a mystery to myself, confused by waves of sorrow and a recurring sense of difference, separation, and loss. I was haunted by my tiny daughter and prone to fits of inconsolable anguish over her loss. Rather than safeguarding me, secrecy worked to sabotage me. Rather than free me from disapprobation, secrecy shackled me with guilt. As my parents expected, I adopted a pleasant exterior, a facade, a performance that kept me perpetually off-kilter, uncentered, and sad.

My daughter's adoption into a loving home is a kind of testimony to the well-meant intentions of the adults around me. For my parents, it was the best possible outcome for an onerous obstacle; for her adoptive parents, it was a longed-for wish finally granted; for my daughter, it was a more dependable future, perhaps. I am the one who could not, cannot, will not find surcease for bearing Sorrow, for relinquishing my daughter, for having no choice at all.

THIRTY-FOUR YEARS OLD TODAY

by Pam Houston

TODAY IS THE 34TH anniversary of *Roe v. Wade*, and I am forty-five years old. What that means is that I got my first period the same year that the history of women's reproductive rights changed (hopefully) forever. To the best of my recollection it was the same month. Possibly it was the same day. This means that there has not been a single day of my life when it was physically possible for me to get pregnant that it would have been legally impossible for me to decide what to do about it.

Until I wrote this essay I had no idea that I had arrived at the smug expectation that my body was my own domain by such a narrow margin. My elders will no doubt remind me how lucky this proves I am, but hard as I try, I can't imagine a world in which a woman does not get to choose whether or not she will have a baby. In the same way that when I was little, I couldn't imagine a country in which the Protestants were killing the Catholics; in the same way that in my country, I can't imagine why any woman would ever vote for George W. Bush, in the same way that I don't understand why, if we have the right to bomb countries who make weapons of mass destruction, why the conversation never turns to the fact that we have weapons of mass destruction ourselves.

I can follow the logic behind all of the counter-arguments, but for me to truly believe that somebody like Kansas senator Sam Brownback could tell me that I am required by law to carry a child for nine months, to give birth to that child and raise it for eighteen years, I would have to see it with my own eyes.

In high school I had a friend named Nicole who, to this day, can talk to her father about nothing besides sports. When she was thirteen years old she went to a baseball game with her parents, who were on the verge of divorcing, and her boyfriend, who was a little older than she was and who her parents liked more than the boyfriend before.

The Phillies were up in the bottom of the seventh inning when Nicole realized that the low-grade nausea she had been feeling all afternoon was blossoming into something more and she ran to the bathroom. After she got sick, it hit her like a ton of bricks: how unsteady she had been feeling, how hard she had been sleeping, how her period—which she had only had a year and a half to get used to—was two-and-a-half weeks late.

She could hear the crowd roar in response to Mike Schmidt hitting what would turn out to be a game-winning triple, and she sat down on the toilet seat vowing never to leave the ladies' room again.

Eventually her mother found her crying in the stall and asked her if she had had a miscarriage. Nicole shook her head, not because she was still pregnant (though she *was* still pregnant), but because she had not yet heard the word "miscarriage," and had no idea what one was.

In my own life, I have had two abortions, which feels like at least one too many. The first one came after getting pregnant around (through) a diaphragm, *with spermicidal jelly*. The second one, after a slightly less odds-against accidental pregnancy, came after my boyfriend of two years went back to the East Coast to fight some more with his ex-wife. The combination of abandonment and hormones plunged me into a depression so deep that my therapist said, "I can get you through this pregnancy alive if you want me to, but you might think really hard about whether or not you want me to."

These two stories make me sound, I suppose, pretty much like a loser, and yet there are many, many areas of my life at which I excel. At picking men, however, I am a loser. Some days it makes me laugh and some days it makes me cry, but every day it is true. I have never even been on a date with a man whom I would trust to raise a child. I pick smart men, handsome men, funny men, talented men, artistic men, athletic men. And no matter how different from one another they might look on the surface, inside they are complete responsibility-phobes, arrested in their emotional development somewhere between eight and sixteen years old.

I have tried as hard as I know how to change this troubling pattern. I have had many thousands of dollars worth of incredibly valuable therapy that has helped me immeasurably in all other areas of my life, but in this one area no progress has been made. Because of my failure to change this, my single remaining self-destructive behavior, I am grateful to have lived in the post-*Roe v. Wade* era. Not as much for the two abortions I did have as for the knowledge that I would have the same choice again, if another diaphragm failed, if I forgot to take a pill, if I had been raped and mugged (instead of just mugged) that October night along the panhandle of Golden Gate Park.

Choice. There is a problem right off the bat: something about the very word suggests polarization. Is there something in the actual diphthong that suggests that *one* will be bad and *another* will be good, *one* will be right and *another* will be wrong, and that these categories will remain static and mutually exclusive as the days and months and years that follow the choice tick by? Do the pro-lifers truly believe that women who have abortions do so carelessly, callously, without a second thought as to what they are choosing in favor of, and what they are choosing against? One day I would like to meet the woman they imagine, the one who strides in and out of those off-green rooms in thigh-high boots and a miniskirt, grabbing a couple of Nilla Wafers and a cup of juice on the way out and saluting the abortion counselors, *see you in a couple of months, gals!* I'd like to meet the girl for whom a mother's or a minister's or a congressman's condemnation begins to compare to all the fear and shame and guilt she has already heaped upon herself.

In college I had a suitemate named Claire, whose extremely loyal hometown boyfriend got her pregnant in the fall of our freshman year. It was 1979 and we were in the dead center of Ohio, and when Claire went home to Cleveland for Christmas she told her mother about her plight. I don't remember whether there was any discussion about keeping the baby, I don't know if anybody offered Claire *that* choice. What I do remember is that when they pulled out of the driveway on their way to the abortion clinic, Claire's mother made Claire lie down on the floor of the back seat of their expensive taupe sedan, all the way down their street, all the way through their subdivision, all the way onto the highway, so a passing neighbor wouldn't grow curious about where Claire and her mother were going so early in the morning, and later force Claire's mother into some kind of lie.

I was a child born to two people who had no business being parents. They met late in life; neither one had ever been married. My mother was an actress. My father had been the most eligible bachelor in Trenton, New Jersey. They both drank way too much.

Hardly a day of my life went by when my mother didn't tell me that she gave up everything she loved to have me, and for years and years I believed her. Then one day, quite recently, my therapist had me make a list of everything my mother loved: tennis, sewing, acting, travel, vodka; and in doing so he made his point. There was nothing on that list that my mother *had* actually given up—that she ever gave up—she had done three out of five of the things she loved most on the very day she died.

My father let his scowl and his rage and the back of his hand do the talking for him, but we decided to make a list of things that he loved too: tennis, (lots of) women, travel, vodka; and sure enough, he hadn't given up any of his favorite things either. The only thing my therapist and I could come up with that *would* go on the list was *life before each other*, and considering how miserable they made each other for the thirty years that followed, I can vouch for the significance of that.

And still, I wonder, if my mother had lived in a culture of choice, would she have decided to have me? She was a 13-year-old runaway who transformed herself into a Broadway showgirl. She had had illegal abortions in the back alleys of Manhattan—I don't know how many but I know there was more than one. But at forty-two, after snagging the most eligible bachelor in Trenton, New Jersey, those back alleys of fear and freedom must have seemed very far away.

I have a hard time feeling sentimental about the next step in this line of thinking—the "then I wouldn't be here" part of the argument. If I weren't *here* I would be somewhere else, and if I weren't anywhere else, I wouldn't even know it. My parents would have gotten to keep whatever it was that they loved and lost, and I would not have been blamed for the anger and recrimination between them.

I have heard it suggested that if everyone who had no business being parents did not have children, we would have a hard time keeping the world in people. But as I look around I see plenty of people. It seems like it would be a good long time before we ran out.

There is a woman I know named Sherrie, who had an abortion when she was eighteen. She was filled with regret almost instantly, a regret that grew through the years until finally, at twenty-five, she adopted two girl children, siblings from an extremely troubled family, to try "to pay it back." Twenty years later, one daughter in rehab, the other gone off to join the Marines, she calls the double adoption the biggest mistake of her life. "As soon as the youngest turns eighteen," she says, "I'm moving someplace warm, and I don't really care if the husband comes or not. For once in my life there is going to be some Sherrie time."

Two months later, when the older girl gets kicked out of the Marines for drugs and comes home from the base in South Carolina pregnant *and* strung out, Sherrie, now fifty-one, does the only thing she can think of, which is adopt her daughter's twin baby girls.

The first time I got pregnant was exactly nine months before my first book came out, exactly nine months before I was to go on a national tour. I told my editor first, and she encouraged me to think very carefully about my choices, to think very hard about a decision that would, no matter which way I went, have a tremendous effect on the rest of my life. Next I told my mother, who spoke more plainly than my editor had done. "You have a very special talent, Pam," she said. "One that makes you unique and valuable. If you decide to skip the book tour and have that baby you become instantaneously ordinary, just like everyone else."

As of today, 62 percent of the population believes that *Roe v. Wade* should not be overturned. Twenty-nine percent of the population (including at least two presidential candidates) believe that it should. Two questions occur to me immediately: first, what is the demographic of the 9 percent who have no opinion whatsoever? And second, with such clear-cut numbers, why do we keep talking about this year after year after year?

Maybe we are still talking about abortion because—unlike say, decisions about going to war in the name of democracy, or detonating weapons of mass destruction, or even about whether or not to put convicted criminals to death—abortion is the place where moral authority, policy, and the general public collide.

"People are pro-life because it gives them a way to proclaim their potential innocence in the eyes of God," my friend Lucy says. "I'm pro-choice because I've never had any illusions about my own innocence. God has been able to see through me right from the start."

I have a friend named Seeta who takes the most unapologetically anti-child stance of anyone I have ever met. If we are out to dinner and a child comes careening anywhere near the legs of her chair, she will hiss like a cat at them until they slink away. I'll admit that this is one of the things I love most about her.

"I will never be sorry," Seeta says, on our ride home from one of these dinners, "that I don't have children. I'm just sorry that I live in a time when *not* wanting to have children is still not at all okay."

There is a man I know named Frank whose Bolivian girlfriend turned up pregnant. He was at that time spending part of every year in Bolivia, and he offered to help her raise the child, part time when he was "in country" and not visiting his other girlfriend—the married one in Budapest—or living with his ex-wife in D.C. The Bolivian girl gratefully accepted the offer; evidence Frank said, of how poorly Bolivian men treat their women, how little support the women expect from men who father a child. Unfortunately or fortunately for all involved, the Bolivian girl miscarried late in her third month.

A few years later, when I had my own little pregnancy scare with that same man (just a late period as it turned out) he said (by way of reassurance) that if I turned up pregnant in the future he would offer me the same deal as he offered the Bolivian, which I immediately began calling "North American serial rights." It was the last time we had sex with any enthusiasm, and very nearly the last time we had sex.

I wonder, is it serendipity or coincidence or just plain old logic, that women got the right to have abortions at almost the same time that men got the right to remain in adolescence for twenty or thirty or sometimes even forty years?

Since I have just turned forty-five, and since I am not in a committed relationship (still working on it...), it seems that the final decision about me and children has at least unofficially been made. I don't spend a great deal of time thinking about what it would have been like if I had taken one of those pregnancies to term and raised the baby. I don't really believe that there is any way to measure my life of book tours and universities and world travel against a life of children and home and domestic pleasures. I have no doubt that they both have their high moments and their low ones, they both have their regrets and their *grass is always greener* feelings. What I do think about sometimes is what it would be like to have the options taken away from me, what it would be like to witness human rights moving in the wrong direction and so clearly at my expense.

The other day I was in a convenience store in Vacaville, California, where a skinny guy with thin greasy hair, a dirty white button-down shirt, and a Poindexter nose, was handing out pamphlets. When I saw the bloody fetus on the cover I changed my trajectory around the convenience store to give him an even wider berth, but he took a step toward me. "Aren't you concerned," he said, "about the slaughtering of babies going on right across the street from this gas station?" I looked out the window at the sign that bore the familiar Planned Parenthood logo, put my tampons and my Gatorade down on the shelf full of oil filters and air fresheners in front of me, squared my shoulders, and headed for my car. What I wanted to ask him is, *Where are all the hunky good-looking pro-lifers?* What I wanted to ask him is, *Why are the only men willing to hand out these pamphlets the men who will never get laid?"*

Almost every close female friend of mine has had an abortion. There is not one of us who does not still think about it, does not still mourn the loss of the child—or, if we don't think of it as a child, perhaps we mourn the loss of possibility. Nearly all of us still believe that we made the right decision. What we would like Senator Brownback and his supporters to understand is that we did what we thought was best for ourselves and the future; sometimes selfishly, sometimes selflessly, and always in the face of grief and regret and undeniable longing. What we would like Senator Brownback and his supporters to understand is that *far* more important than whether we call it a baby or an embryo; *more* important than stem cell research or the lack of it; and more important, *even*, than whether or not we bring a child into the world and by doing so change our lives and the world forever, is the fact that we do it freely, is the fact that we have a choice.

PERSONAL BELONGINGS

by Kimi Faxon Hemingway

1.

ON THE DRIVE to Chapel Hill that morning, I could only see small things: my ragged fingernails, lint on the dashboard, tiny, nascent buds on Bradford pear trees. Later, the picture would emerge, big, bulbous, and clear, but not yet. I was still inside it all, unable to see out. When the world goes black and your eyes are slow to adjust to the dark, you focus on what's in front of you. Your hand, for example. Maybe the stars. Any point of navigation at all.

It was the day before Easter and I was on my way to a city two hours from home, a city with an abortion clinic. I was thirty years old. It seemed suddenly that all former rules for living were out the window.

The sky stained the empty road pink. I curled into the front seat of Heather's small Honda, wrapped in a down comforter. The would-be father was crunched in the back, mostly quiet. We were all quiet. Heather's eyes fixed to the road as I breathed onto the cool, damp windows until the mist from my breath dissolved.

2.

The clinic was already packed by the time we arrived since it was one of two days of the week when abortions were administered. Heather and I shared a seat in the waiting room. The would-be father spread out on a patch of worn carpet and read our horoscopes from the city paper.

"You have been very fertile lately," he read, announcing my horoscope without the least bit of irony. Heather exhaled loudly, stood up and walked around between the clusters of people that I could not look at. I opened my eyes, pulled my legs into my stomach, and glared at him.

"What?" the would-be father said, hands up, half smiling. "It's funny."

This is all I'm going to say about him:

It was more than drunken sex with a man I didn't love, although, technically, that's exactly what it was. But it was complicated. We were complicated. It was dangerous and wrong in a way that looked right in certain light. Sometimes bad things are glittery and attractive and hard to ignore—it was the steadiness of his hands, that he could build a house with those hands and write a poem and touch me roughly, assertively, that kept me there longer than I should have stayed. We'd found each other at a friend's party one night and ended up at my apartment. Drunk, he neglected to pull out when I asked him. This, for a while at least, made him easy to blame.

A young woman with brown hair cut to her jaw read my name aloud from a clipboard. I stood up, legs like Gumby, cinched the drawstring of my pajama bottoms tighter, and then concentrated on walking through the crowded room toward the woman who stood in front of a door marked Private.

The woman, whose name was Rachel, led me to a desk in a small windowless room and asked how I was feeling. She was kind and had gentle eyes. It was this and the fact that she seemed like she might be my age that made my throat close up. I squeaked out some unrecognizable words.

"It's okay," she said calmly, pushing some paperwork my way. "Have you thought about what kind of abortion you'd like to have?"

I had not thought about it.

I knew immediately though what my choice would be the morning I peed onto that pink stick and waited for the boxes to fill in, knew that once they did, I'd finally have to act on what had always come so easily to my lips: every woman should have the right to choose an abortion.

"Well, because you are so early in your pregnancy, you might think about RU-486 as an option." I had only heard vaguely of RU-486. I thought it was similar to the morning-after pill, which friends of mine had taken in college.

Rachel explained that it was an ideal drug to take in the early stages of pregnancy, that the success rate was higher than a traditional, surgical abortion given the fact that I was only four weeks pregnant. She said that many women had had positive experiences with the drug, in part because they felt it was a more private option.

The fact that this drug was now available as a possible choice within the right to choose an abortion was a very big deal, Rachel told me. A lot of people had fought long and hard to make it safe and available.

I learned more about RU-486 later. That it really was a big deal that women like me had access to the drug. Even though RU-486 had been successful in Europe by 1988, the Reagan and Bush administrations had tried vigilantly to suppress the drug's entry into this country because of political pressure, a hypothetical increase in abortion, and the fear that women would use it as a form of birth control. But after ten years of negotiations between Roussel Uclaf (the French manufacturer and distributor of the drug) and the FDA, RU-486 finally became available to women in the United States in 2000. On a political level, it was something I could get behind: it was progress.

It turned out I could also get behind it on a personal level. These were the words Rachel used to describe the experience of taking RU-486: organic, natural, almost like miscarriage. I liked the sound of those words. I especially liked the sound of this advice: "make a ceremony out of the experience." She likened the pain of taking the drug to very strong menstrual cramps. I could handle that, I told her; I'd had menstrual cramps since I got my first period. That was old hat. I would bleed for four hours maybe, she informed me, and then I'd be up and around in a couple of days.

"Or, you could come back in two weeks and have a surgical abortion when we know that the success rate increases." She paused and looked at me, "Of course, this is your choice. You need to decide which option suits you the best."

On the one hand I was hard as nails, knew my choice. On the other hand, I wanted someone else to decide, to take over, guide me. I thought of my mother. And how desperately I wished I were strong enough to call her. How much I wanted her here right now.

The pills seemed manageable, I reasoned, seemed better than driving back to this clinic after two more weeks of waiting for something to grow substantial enough to be eliminated. Seemed somehow easier than slipping my feet into stirrups and having to listen to that terrible sucking sound my friends had told me about, the moment when the vacuum enters you and does its job.

I thought of the women in the waiting room, imagined recovering with them in a communal room, heating pads on our stomachs, buckets by our beds. Need to be in my home for this one, I thought.

I felt better imagining the women Rachel mentioned, the ones who'd liked the drug. They were women I could conceive of as friends, women who had ceremonies, and did yoga and baked bread. It felt almost, to use her word, a "natural" way to end a pregnancy. As if I were now connected to countless others who'd had abortions. It's the thing women say to each other after rites of passage like weddings and childbirth: welcome to the tribe.

"I'll take the pills," I said.

After I sat in that small office and swallowed two tablets of Mifepristone, Heather drove us all home. I tried to sleep in the backseat while the would-be father talked on his cell phone, laughing jollily with old friends as if he were on vacation. I prepared myself to take Misoprostol, the second set of drugs, the following day.

3.

One afternoon when I was a teenager, my mother and I stood in the bright light of our kitchen and chopped onions, talking about how weeks earlier I had held a handmade sign outside the courthouse in New Hampshire's capital with my teacher and a dozen other students, protesting for choice.

This is when my mother told me, almost matter-of-factly, that in the sixties she'd had an illegal abortion. I sat down, amazed. This was not something that happens to your own mother, I remember thinking. Her ability to tell the story with such detachment stunned me, as if she had easily extracted the lesson in order to pass on what was necessary. "It's so important that abortion always be legal," she said, looking at me.

A young woman who worked for the abortion doctor came for my mother at a friend's apartment in New York. The woman blindfolded my mother, then drove circles around the city to disorient her before arriving at the doctor's home office in Jersey City.

Weeks after the doctor injected a needle the length of my mother's forearm into her cervix, she was still gushing blood; the placenta and fetal tissue still remained and she had developed a horrific infection. She hemorrhaged for weeks, until one day, after losing so much blood, she fainted on a set of stairs in the Boston apartment building where she lived. She finally found a doctor who was willing to help her. He told her it was unlikely that she would ever become pregnant again.

The doctor was wrong, however, and on January 20, 1973, I was born. Two days later, on January 22, the world changed: *Roe v. Wade* had finally made abortion legal.

My mother's story and the lesson were inseparable in my mind. It seemed so uncomplicated: take the procedure out of the back alleys and put it in a clean, modern, medical facility. The assumption, the mistake, was in thinking that legal meant safe.

4.

I did what Rachel told me to do: I made a ceremony out of the event. I woke early, lit a candle, and tried to forgive myself for what was about to happen. It wasn't that I wanted a baby. I didn't, at least not yet. It was just that I was beginning to feel old, beginning to feel like my time was running out. It was also that my body was fighting to be pregnant. It wanted it, even if I didn't. The body change is instantaneous: moods shift, breasts swell, the uterus—already beginning to expand—pushes on the bladder.

I made a nest on the couch and piled pillows up, stacked toilet paper and maxi pads in the bathroom, played soft music. When the would-be father and Heather arrived for the showdown, I slipped the pills out of the small brown envelope, went to the toilet, and pushed them toward my cervix as far as they could go. Then I waited.

"This isn't so bad," I said as the first mild cramps hit about one hour after I'd taken the Misoprostol, half laughing with Heather at some silly love scene in a romantic comedy she had brought over in order to distract me.

One hour later, though, the story was different. I was running to the bathroom in ten-minute intervals, soaking up thick pads, then screaming on the toilet while tissue, mucus, blood, shit, spilled out of me. Heather came into the bathroom and rubbed my back, and then she started crying. The crying scared me. I wanted her to be stronger. *I* wanted to be stronger. I thought of my neighbors and worried they'd hear me.

Heather helped me back to the couch. I felt wrung out, but it had only just begun. It was the last time that day that I made it to the toilet. The five feet between the couch and the bathroom seemed insurmountable, and when the convulsions, fever, and chills hit, my body thumped to the floor. I stayed there excreting fluids I did not know my body had onto the wood floor. The would-be father scooped me up and put me back on the couch. Heather cried more.

One more thing about the would-be father:

As I writhed in pain on the floor, on the couch, on the toilet, he called his mother. I tried to ignore the fact that at that moment he was giving his mother, *his mother*, a play-by-play of how the drug was affecting me. The phone call was meant, perhaps, to comfort him, I guess, or me. Either way, it infuriated me. *There's nothing private about this*, I said in my head, arguing with the clinicians.

He tried to hand me the phone so his mother could speak to me, give me some words of wisdom, or support, or condemnation, I wasn't sure. This was a mother who thirty years earlier had considered having an abortion, but ultimately decided against it. The evidence of the choices she finally made? The man speaking on the phone in my apartment. How grateful she was that she had made the choice she did. How grateful he was, almost existential. He would not be here today if she had chosen differently, he reminded me the night before my appointment. Still a choice, I'd said back.

5.

One week later I was still wearing a nightgown and diapers, still calling the clinic in hysterics. "Why am I so weak?" I wanted to know. "You didn't tell me I'd be so weak. And why am I still bleeding buckets?" I asked, and always the same answer: "It is common to bleed heavily afterward. In a few days, you should see some relief."

My body was fighting against itself. Relief seemed a far-off word, an abstract idea. My hormones raged; I expelled liver-like blood clots the size of my palm most days, including the day I returned to the clinic for a follow-up visit. The physician's assistant who administered the pelvic exam and ultrasound chuckled while I lay on my back, a speculum holding me wide open. "You sure are a bleeder, aren't you?"

I asked her what would happen to the blood and tissue floating inside me.

"It will just get absorbed back into your body," she said and then, moments into the exam, she talked about fitting me for an IUD during the visit.

I began to cry, buttoning my pants. "This is just so hard."

"Why is it hard?" she asked.

Even the very company that championed RU-486 has warned women about the drug. In the French newspaper, *Le Monde,* Edouard Sakiz, the former chairman of Roussel Uclaf, was quoted as having said that women "have to be very confident to choose this method. It may be physically more natural, but psychologically it hits you much harder. You preside over the killing of the baby, completely unblinkingly. For women who are confused or vulnerable, and of course, so many are in this position, it is really quite terrible."

The idea that the drug would make a very difficult and personal choice private, is appealing. Except that it doesn't offer privacy. You still have to go the clinic, you still have to leave the clinic with your paper envelope of pills and cryptic instructions, and then you have to administer the drug to yourself when you get home, and there in your home is all the evidence, the haunting reminder of the choice you have made. At that point privacy takes on new meaning. As in *alone*, as in *private hell*.

6.

It was three weeks after that Easter Sunday, and I continued to hemorrhage. My body tried vigilantly to fight off bladder infection after bladder infection, my mind quietly, efficiently, detaching from my physical grief. I was divided into tiny compartments: this is what my body wants, feels, needs; this is what my mind wants, thinks, feels. I began to call my body, "the body" and the abortion, "the nightmare."

During these weeks, I was aware that my neighbor, Rocco, was watching me around the house, shuffling to the laundry room in slippers where I scrubbed blood from my clothing; carrying my garbage to the trashcans out back; passing by his windows like a ghost; crying with the would-be father on the back stairwell. I didn't mind that he was watching; in fact, part of me wanted him to know. There was a kind of disclaimer involved: *this is why I'm like this.* A confession could clarify things. A confession could explain. But there was also the feeling that if I told my story, I could get rid of it.

Rocco was a respected chef in town. One of the great perks of living in the house was that I was often the lucky recipient of his cooking, his guinea pig. The hallway perpetually smelled of yeast, garlic, and leeks. But even for all of his savvy in the kitchen, his sincerity about the French tradition of food preparation, his mature generosity, he was still twenty years old and driven by hormones. A couple of times, he propositioned me and my friends to spend a night with him, that doing so "ain't gonna hurt our friendship," so when he came to my door one afternoon, weeks after the abortion, and saw me green and hunched over and guessed that I was pregnant I was surprised by his perceptiveness. After I told him of the abortion, of my sickness since, everything in him contorted, like his face was a wet cloth being wrung.

"Good Lord, Kimi, you killed your baby?"

"Jeez, Rocco, please don't say that."

"Does your momma know?"

I looked at him, nodded, and gently closed the door. "Have to lie down now, Rocco," I said, through the crack.

I had finally told my mother about my abortion. I had not known how to say it to her, how to even begin. She wanted me to learn to forgive myself. But first she wanted me to be healthy again. It must have been excruciating for her to see her failed abortion story repeated over thirty years later in her own daughter.

Moments later, Rocco came back to my door with an offering, chicken broth. He said, "Tell me what to do; the only way I know how to take care of you is to feed you." But I could not eat, could not ask for what I needed, didn't know what I needed, except to erase all this.

My mother wasn't happy that Rocco knew about the abortion, that people knew.

"But Mom," I said, "don't you think it's a good idea that someone in my building knows? You know, just in case." According to my mother, I had been reading too much abortion literature. I accidentally came across a picture of a woman who died from an illegal abortion in a big book about women's health. The woman was lying in a yoga posture, child's pose, the soles of her feet smudged with dirt, the lower half of her body bloodied. Her naked skin appeared thick and stiff as plastic, her face invisible to the camera.

Looking at the picture, I thought of my mother, of all the other women I know who have had abortions, of myself, and I asked the *what if* questions. But there was an even stronger connection I felt to this woman, some self-recognition, and some sense that I was confronting my fear by looking at her, some sense that she'd been punished for what she'd done, some sense that I had been, too. I knew my mother was right when she said, *leave the books alone, don't ruminate so much*. But this is my nature, I am haunted, cannot lift myself out of the mire. She made a clucking sound with her tongue, loud and aggravated, "God, Kimi."

Once, as if to reveal the kind of person I am, as if to say, this is how sensitive my daughter is, my mother told a friend that I could never cut down a tree, even if it meant planting a new one in its place, that I could not even throw out a sickly house plant. "She just can't do it," my mother had said. "She doesn't like to hurt anything."

This kind of person, one who cannot throw away a sick plant, seems an unlikely candidate for abortion, I know—let alone the kind of abortion in which you "preside over the killing"—but for me this comes as close as possible to revealing the complexity of the choice. Most women I know who are pro-choice have a serious moral consciousness, so, if they're like me, the very thing that makes them pro-choice makes them particularly vulnerable to the consequences of the decision. Even the terms we use, pro-choice, and pro-life, seem misnomers—of course I believe in life. All life. But the life I chose first was my own. At first this seemed audacious, seemed like a kind of dare, one I'd certainly never been confronted with before. The kind where you become utterly conscious of your future and your own power in choosing it. I knew I had to save myself from a future I didn't want, one I was too afraid to imagine. That seemed the only choice at the time. Even if it meant ending another life.

7.

It had now been nearly three months of the same—bleeding through my clothes, wearing diapers, anemia—when I finally decided to see a new doctor a friend had recommended. He gave me vitamin supplements and antibiotics for my uterine and bladder infections. This wasn't the first time he'd seen this kind of fallout from RU-486.

"Chicken skin," he told me. "What's in your uterus—leftover tissue— it looks like chicken skin," he said looking away from the ultrasound machine and at me sympathetically, fatherly. "That's what's left over after the drugs. That and probably a bit of fetal bone. It could be causing the infection." Only as a last resort, he told me, would he perform a D&C given the high risk of infertility and scarring, and my lack of health insurance. He asked if there was some place I could go where people could take care of me, give me some support.

I decided to visit my parents at their home on an island off the coast of Massachusetts. Most days, I worked hard at pretending to be cheery, at concealing the dozens of maxi-pads I used, bent on not making my parents—my mom especially—worry. It didn't work. She was smarter than I gave her credit for. Such is the blindness of desperation. Part of me felt like I had gotten myself into this mess, and I was the one who was going to get myself out.

After the weeklong visit, my parents hugged me urgently and waved through a secure glass wall at the airport. I vowed to them to follow my doctor's advice and to have the surgery if the less invasive methods were ineffective.

In Boston, I rushed through two terminals to meet my next flight, but by the time I reached the security gate, I could feel movement in my uterus. I knew the feeling; I'd been experiencing it for months now. It usually began with a rumbling in my lower abdomen, then cramping, followed by the passage of clots through my cervix and then the dampening of my inner thighs. This day though it was an uncontrollable gushing, immediately visible on my pants.

I had reached my terminal by the time the bleeding raged so much that I could no longer walk. I hunkered down in a faraway corner and called my parents for advice. My father was stern. I asked if there was someone he knew in Boston, a doctor friend who I could call.

"Not on a Sunday," he said, "Just go buy more pads and try to manage the pain." All I could find in the airport gift shop were thin maxi-pads, and even if I had found something stronger it wouldn't have made a difference. I tied a scarf my brother bought for me in Mexico around my waist to conceal the blood on my pants. But it was futile, the scarf was soaked too.

I paced the airport between visits to two different bathrooms where I sat on the toilet and tried to wait it out, to no avail. I called home again. "I don't think I can manage it," I said to my dad on the phone. Going to an emergency room would be expensive and a long wait, he reasoned. "All you have to do is make it back to North Carolina," he said.

"All I have to do," I repeated to myself.

Then, moments after speaking with my father, I fell in front of a long ticket line.

I woke to a US Airways representative waving a flight brochure in my face. The Airport Health Clinic was closed on Sundays, but there was an EMT on duty, the US Airways woman told me. She helped me back to the bathroom where she said the EMT would meet me. The bathroom that, after my previous visits, looked like someone had been murdered there; blood was everywhere. My blood. That I could not manage.

The EMT pushed the stall door open and looked at me, a 30-year-old woman crouched on the floor beside the toilet, too embarrassed to meet his eyes. He set a heavy black bag down beside me, and I could see through occasional sidelong glances that he was muscular and that his expression was kind. The EMT told me that it could just be my period. That sometimes after abortions the first period is extremely heavy. I said, "That's possible, I guess," even though I knew it was not possible. I had been bleeding for months. There had been no respite. No period of menstruation, just varying degrees of bleeding. That I clearly could not manage.

At the hospital, I waited in my room, perched atop a very deep, plastic bedpan and let blood drain out of me. An older Jamaican woman, a nurse's assistant, called me Baby and wiped me down with a warm cloth. The other nurses were unfriendly. This was the emergency room on a Sunday night.

After the young resident assigned to my case tried to give me a pelvic exam—admittedly his first ever—with a speculum that was too big, I was sent to a separate wing of the hospital for an ultrasound.

The sonographer manipulated the wand around and around to get a better reading, and when I lost control once again of my bowels and made a mess of her sterilized bed, she muttered, "Oh, God" and placed plastic beneath me. She left the room to find someone who could give a second opinion while I lay on the table with a plastic wand in my vagina. The room was dark except for my uterus hanging off the lit ultrasound screen.

I cried for my choice, for my inability to control what was happening, for the humiliation I felt, the despair, for the mystery of my body. I was alone and without insurance in an emergency room in a city where my family had once lived; I had no idea what was wrong with me, or how to fix it. That's the thing about abortion, what starts out as a compelling and profound act of control over your life soon becomes an act of surrender. Suddenly a choice that had once seemed black and white boiled down to a simple desire: I wanted to make it out of this hospital whole.

When the sonographer and her colleague returned to the room they looked at the screen, then went into a back office where I could hear whispering. Moments later, they emerged, and told me what they were looking at. They were looking at a bad infection. They were looking at the placenta and an implantation site. They were looking at a partially developed fetus in my womb. My exceedingly high hormone levels, apparently, matched the information delivered on the sonogram screen. Information that suggested I was still pregnant. It had been three months since I had taken RU-486.

When there's failure in the choices we make, there is insurmountable regret. Later, the lesson resonates. But at the time, I had not been able to forgive myself. I felt that my choice had been wrong. I had chosen wrong. It wasn't that I felt particular regret for what could have been—a child. Though, to be fair, there were days when I did, but it was more specific than that. It was this feeling that I could not take care of myself, that I could not perform on a physical level. There are other women for whom RU-486 has not worked, like me, but there are more women for whom the drug has worked. I was part of a group that failed. It felt colossal. It felt like inadequacy. I couldn't even have a proper abortion.

The next morning, the hospital released me, and back I went to North Carolina where I would have the necessary surgery. I boarded the plane, my hair crumpled and matted to the back of my head, dried blood splattered to my back. The hospital had donated the outfit I wore—gym shorts and a Harvard T-shirt. My own clothes, soiled and crusted with blood, were folded inside a clear plastic bag that read, *Massachusetts General Hospital, Personal Belongings.*

8.

I can't say why the drug failed me exactly; no one can. As one of the doctors at Mass General examining my case said, "The thing is, we don't know what a uterus should look like three months after RU-486." A week after my doctor performed the D&C, I went to see him for a follow-up appointment. He was stunned, he'd told me, by what he'd found when he'd done the surgery, by what was still left in my uterus all those months later. "This is not an innocuous drug," he'd said, shaking his head.

It could be that the drug itself is less problematic than the way it is handled and prescribed in the United States. The protocol for RU-486 is very different in Europe than it is in this country. In France, for example, the drug is administered in hospitals where women are closely monitored in case of emergency. These women undergo a series of exams, blood tests, and evaluations before the drug is prescribed in order to ensure that it is an appropriate and effective method for each woman who considers taking it. But in the United States, clinics are often understaffed and may not perform the preliminary blood work or pelvic examinations necessary to better predict success for each individual woman. As my doctor told me, this is a drug still in its discovery phase.

Over half a million women in the United States have taken RU-486 since it was approved in 2000. Between 5 and 8 percent of these abortions fail, and ultimately require vacuum aspirations. All seven of the reported deaths related to this drug have resulted from systemic infections caused by the bacteria *Clostridium sordelli*. In five of these cases, the second drug, Misoprostol, was administered vaginally. The FDA, however, never approved vaginal administration of the drug. They recommended that it be taken orally, and claimed that this is "the only safe administration of RU-486."

Planned Parenthood does not agree. According to a spokesperson for Planned Parenthood, vaginal insertion of Misoprostol can "offer fewer side effects and also enables women to have medical abortions up to 63 days, as opposed to the 49 days the oral is approved for." But even so, despite this claim, six years after the drug first became available to American women, Panned Parenthood agreed to the FDA's demands to adjust their administration of the drug.

In my case, it's possible that the vaginal insertion of Misoprostol caused the failure. But it's also possible that the dosage of Mifepristone and Misoprostol I had been prescribed may not have been enough to end and expel the pregnancy, the milligrams reduced by the clinic as a way to temper the terrible toxicity of the drugs. The FDA recommends that women take 600 milligrams of Mifepristone and 400 micrograms of Misoprostol. I took 200 milligrams of Mifepristone and vaginally inserted 800 micrograms of Misoprostol. The drugs may not have been entirely effective if, as reading I have done suggests, I was pregnant with twins, which run in my family. The reason it took months to see that I was carrying more than tissue is that, as one doctor told me, "reading an ultrasound is like reading the Koran; it's all in your interpretation."

When I stood in that kitchen all those years ago and listened to my mother's abortion story, I had missed the point. Abortion is political, intellectual, and medical, as I had thought then, but for the women who experience it, who agonize over it, it is more than that: it is emotionally scary and physically dangerous, even when it's legal, modern, and the obvious choice.

9.

The morning I learned I was pregnant—hours after watching the pink squares on that plastic wand fill in—I went to class. It was a graduate seminar on pedagogy and it was boring and dry and I went only as a way to distract myself. This day, however, the professor surprised the class by bringing in William Stafford's poem, "Traveling Through the Dark."

In the poem, the speaker drives a river road at night only to stop when he comes across a recently killed doe. The speaker gets out of his car in order to roll the deer—now a "heap"—into a canyon so as not to cause accidents for other drivers. But he notices that the deer is pregnant.

The speaker hesitates after this discovery and then says, "I thought hard for us all—my only swerving—then pushed her over the edge into the river." The reader also hesitates at this image, at the moment of discovery, and the hush of "hear[ing] the wilderness listen."

After reading the poem aloud, the professor told the class—all teaching assistants preparing to teach composition classes of our own—

that some students might interpret this as an abortion poem.

"Where is the evidence to suggest this?" Methodically, he shifted the items on his desk.

The class collectively squirmed.

"It's the last stanza that suggests the speaker, and all of us, are up against something really big, the part where Stafford says, 'I thought hard for us all,'" one student said.

I thought to myself, what if Stafford means for the speaker to be a woman? I wondered how this changes our reading. The woman speaker contemplates saving the waiting, still-warm fawn. Is she more likely to save the deer? Less likely? Does she understand in a way the male speaker might not, what is at stake?

The odds of this discussion on the day I contemplated ending a pregnancy were eerie, enough to make me believe in patterns and signs, even fate.

The room was silent, except for the uncomfortable shifting of notebooks, legs crossing and uncrossing, throats clearing.

"This is a poem about making decisions in the dark," the professor said, looking up from his papers. "It's about how we are never allowed to make perfect decisions." Everyone nodded, the room quieted. Heather positioned her body in front of me, as a mother might, in an attempt to shield me from the professor's view. In case I was crying. Which I was.

10.

For months after the abortion, I had this recurring dream:

I am on a bed, a mattress, covered with white sheets. The windows are wide open; wind blows through the room violently, sanguine leaves scatter and make a mosaic of the bed. The would-be father gets up to close the window, says, "Watch out for the bugs, a lot got in through the window." I sit up and look at the bed, its white sheets pulled tight, and see a small salamander or snake, grotesque and deformed. A black stripe runs down its back and tentacles grip the sheets. I reach for a hairbrush on a nearby shelf and start to smack the animal with the back of the brush; the word that comes into my head is *bash*. I hit it with the brush until life bleeds out of it and it shrinks and flips over. I look again and see that on its other side, the animal was furry, a miniature kangaroo, or a squirrel, but now, after I killed it, it is simply a husk, a stain.

Even though I knew that having a child with the would-be father was a choice I wasn't willing to make, I still felt deep remorse. Maybe because it went on for so long, or maybe because I was afraid that I'd lost my opportunity, that I had damaged my body so much that I'd never be able to conceive. Would the fact of having a child with the wrong person be worse than not having a child at all? I thought of this often. I doubted myself often.

Just as my mother's doctor told her it was unlikely that she would conceive again, so did mine. He'd said that the scar tissue in my uterus, the months of bleeding, and the D&C that followed would make it very difficult to become pregnant when the time came when I actually wanted to be, when the time came when I chose to get pregnant.

I once read that the body stores memory in its cells, memory of injury and trauma and even pregnancy. So if that's true, then this story, my abortion story, becomes more than an experience that my brain registers and remembers, but a narrative that my body knows on a cellular level even when I stop telling it.

My mother confessed that it was not until she became pregnant with me that she began to forgive herself and move on. And even though I now understand what she means, even though it has been four years since I took RU-486, and even though as I write this, I am nine months pregnant and married to a man I love, the story still feels partially unfinished. Now, on the eve of the birth of my first child, I find myself thinking of that dream, of things we inherit and pass on, and I can't help but wonder about the life of this baby and the things he will be born knowing in his bones. I can't help but imagine the choices he will have to make.

The following essay is a chapter from Deborah McDowell's memoir about her family in Bessemer, Alabama. Strong women figure prominently in *Leaving Pipe Shop*, especially McDowell's elegant and ambitious grandmother, whom she calls Mother. McDowell leaves for college in Tuskegee in 1969, a time when young women under suspicion of pregnancy are pointedly excluded from events like the Bessemer Debutante Ball. Oft-repeated phrases from elders such as "Don't disappoint me" are a powerful code. "Mother drummed this message into my ear every time I saw her," McDowell writes, "and I knew, beyond a shadow of a doubt, just what she meant: DON'T GET PREGNANT." This essay describes the difficulties and dangers of abortions in the era just prior to *Roe v. Wade*.

—*K.E.B and N.de G.*

TERMINATION

by Deborah McDowell

THE CAMPUS PHYSICIAN made the rounds to each of the women's dorms (he never went to the men's) at the beginning of every year to lecture us on the importance of birth control. Of course, the lecture, like everything else I'd already heard about sex, was delivered in code. "Now you can get pregnant," Mama had said awkwardly as she handed me a box of Kotex and a brand-new elastic sanitary belt the spring I turned fifteen. When I paused, searching her face for the information about pregnancy I assumed was sure to follow, she added, "If you miss your period, that's the sign that you're pregnant, so remember to keep your dress down and your pocketbook closed." I swallowed two aspirin while staring out the kitchen window, then withdrew to my bed with a booklet on reproduction that the nurse had handed out in school; actually, it was a thin pamphlet with pastel drawings of a woman's pelvis: pale pink ovaries and lavender fallopian tubes.

The campus doctor sprinkled his dorm lectures not with references to pocketbooks that needed closing, but to barn doors closed too late, his metaphor for coitus interruptus, or as we used to put it, "coming out." "This method of birth control," he said, "is just like closing the barn door after the horse is out." Warming to the snickers he had coaxed from all of us who packed the "receiving room" of Rockefeller Hall, he laughed too, closing with the crowning witticism I was to hear from him over the next three years: "And for all of you who rely on that most favored method of birth control, let me make it absolutely clear: Hope is zero percent foolproof." I had certainly proved him right on that count. Timidly suggesting that my new college boyfriend, Richard, use a condom, I relented when he complained that it wouldn't feel the same. He would come out in time. And time after time, I hoped he would. He never did, and I did not protest, fearful that he would return to the homecoming queen, who reminded me of all the high school majorettes who got the sweetheart rings.

I had spent the whole first semester of college struggling to make it to
8:30 biology classes, to make new friends, finally finding my niche with a
group of four other southern firstborn women who lived on the second
and third floors of Rockefeller Hall. We walked together every day to
Tompkins, the dining hall, stopping to tease Tom Joyner, the campus disc
jockey, who sat inside a glass booth and spun the latest forty-fives. We
jerked and wiggled our bodies as we inched through the serpentine line
to reach the steam-clouded stalls and pointed again to turkey fricassee or
cutlets of mystery meat. Legend had it that the cutlets were ground
pigeons plucked from the huge flock that swarmed around Tompkins
Hall. On Friday and Saturday nights, we skipped the dining hall and
ordered fried chicken instead, from Thomas Reed's Chicken Coop.

Often of an evening, with orders for the others, Ginny Hitchcock or
Joan Floyd and I would walk down Old Montgomery Road to the Coop,
jeans pulled over pajamas, and scarves covering the pink sponge rollers in
our hair. Back in the dorm, we played dirty Hearts atop Ginny Hitchcock's
steamer trunk until the wee, wee hours of the morning. By the end of first
semester, we had all gained several pounds from this late-night orgiastic
feasting on chicken and french fries and vowed to break the ritual at the
very start of the new year.

Resolution still intact, I scouted around for alternatives to fill the
former gaps of weekend nights. Winston had stopped writing from Texas
because I had failed to "prove my love for him." That is, I had not gone all
the way. Worse, I had led him to believe I would, as a Christmas present
to him. His last letter indicated, in no uncertain terms, that "unless and
until you are willing to prove your love for me, it's best for us to start
seeing other people." With no prospects in sight, I became a basketball
junkie, which is how I met Richard Hancock, the near-seven-foot center
from Detroit.

He fell in step with Gwen Rigby and me as we headed back to Rockefeller Hall from a game. Tuskegee had won, and Richard was the leading
scorer. So engrossed were we in our conversation that we did not hear his
footsteps, muffled by pine needles strewn all along the unlit path that
wound away from Logan Hall. "How did you enjoy the game?" he asked

in that cocky way of his, as he approached us from behind. I jumped and said, "I didn't hear you coming."

There he was, the man who figured almost nightly in my diary, standing in the flesh, the thick white towel ringing his neck, forming a halo in the darkness.

"I been walking behind you-all since Logan Hall, but you so busy yakking and jabbering, it's no wonder you couldn't hear me."

Gwen laughed and called him "Hard-hearted Hancock," the name he got for wearing such a mean and fearless scowl at basketball, a face made still more scary by his beady, bloodshot eyes. I did not say too much that night, not even when Gwen left us to play Ping-Pong in the student union, and Richard walked on with me to my dorm. Underneath the lamp above the door at Rockefeller, he said good night and hoisted the red duffel bag onto his shoulder, the gold-embroidered Tuskegee tiger clawing at the sides. "You played a good game," I said, and rushed inside to join the late-night card game and to boast that Richard Hancock had walked me home. "No shit."

When the team made it to the SIAC finals one month later, I bought a ticket to the tournament and showed up in a pair of green velour hot pants and knee-high boots and watched the team from third-row center, near the court. They lost the championship, and I seized upon the idea of writing a personal letter to every member of the team. On the deckle-edged blue velum paper that Mother had given me for Christmas, I praised the rebounding skills of this one, the passing skills of that one, and the dribbling of another. For Richard I reserved the most heaping praise for shooting, since he had scored a record thirty-two points. It turned out that he was the only one of the team who answered my letter, hand-delivering it to Rockerfeller Hall.

He was glad to see me again and couldn't quite believe I was the kind to write letters to a whole basketball team. I seemed so shy. "That's why I write," I said. That's how it began—with the letter, and quietly, before I realized it had happened. We started meeting on the side of the George Washington Carver Museum. He always waited for me on the top step and, together, we descended to the building set in a hollow several feet below street level. I was still stuck in the groove of heavy petting, then retreat, but, after just a few meetings, Richard echoed Winston's words: There were many girls who'd give him more, who had already. He had no time for teasers. I gave in the very night he ran back up the steps, leaving me with the parting shot of insult, "Call me when you get tired of acting like a goody-goody little churchgoing girl from 'Bama." "Don't go," I said, and there, at the Carver Museum, while steadying myself against a pebbled concrete ledge, I first had sex, hidden behind the wall of hemlock trees whose ominous branches reached out to touch our shoulders. His spasms ended, we walked together in silence until we reached the front of the dormitory. The lights in the foyer were brightly lit and people milled about the office. I lingered on the steps, wanting urgently to wipe away the glob of semen wet between my legs, yet not wanting to answer any questions about my "date."

"What was the date of your last period?" the doctor asked. Richard had borrowed a teammate's car and driven to Opelika, where, he explained, we would not run the risk of having anybody see us. I took the pocket calendar from my purse and showed the doctor the date. It was circled in red. For almost nine weeks I had counted and recounted the days of the calender, cramming the tiny blocks with points of red and blue and green. "Fill this up with urine and give it to the nurse. When you finish, have a seat in the waiting room." I joined Richard there, where he sat flipping through *Sports Illustrated*.

"The urine sample was positive. Let's see how far along you are." The white paper rustled as he patted the edge of the examining table and asked me to remove my underwear. The examination finished, he said, without even casting a glance my way, "You can get dressed now," and pulling off the rubber gloves, he opened the door and beckoned for Richard.

His starched white lab-coated back to me, the rotund doctor faced Richard and said, "She's almost four months gone." Not a word did he say to me, but after the space of a gasp, I spoke up:

"I'm not four months pregnant. I can't be."

"Young lady, I've been delivering babies for thirty years. Trust me."

In the car, Richard let me know that I was on my own. I had tried to trick him, he said, but it had blown up in my face. If I thought he was going to marry me to take care of another man's baby, I had another think coming. Only later did I learn that the portly doctor from Opelika had used the ruse of "certain" dates to help many an athlete evade his responsibilities to a pregnant student.

In this era before *Roe v. Wade*, girls in dormitories all around the campus kept underground lists of abortionists. After many false starts and missed connections, making up my mind and changing it again, I settled on one, a midwife in Phenix City, Alabama. I could have gone to a woman who lived in the projects right outside the Tuskegee city line, but I was afraid someone might recognize me.

The woman was very tentative on the phone and gave me strict instructions: I had to come alone. I was to take the 12:30 bus from Tuskegee that arrived in Columbus, Georgia, at 1:30. Her son, who would be wearing a green fishing hat and a brown corduroy jacket, would meet me at the station and then drive me to her house on the outskirts of Phenix City, a short jump across the river from Columbus.

It took me a few minutes to pick her son out of the knot of people standing outside the station. His hat was really slate gray, not green, and he looked much older than I had imagined. "Are you Readus?" He nodded yes.

The faded yellow Buick rattled over winding country back roads still tracked from recent rain. Although it was unusually chilly for the last week of March, the sky that day was bright. I was glad I saw no hint of rain, for I had images of this rickety car, with its wire hanger for an antenna, rutted in the mud or, worse, the road itself transformed into one long wading pool.

Readus drove without a word, slowly, deliberately, looking straight ahead. As he steered the car around craters in the road, I fought the rising fear of what lay ahead by concentrating on the streaking countryside—the blackened timber, the roadside stores, the shrunken tar-paper shacks plopped down in the middle of rolling fields, white sheets, and feed-sack dresses pinned on clotheslines swaying in the wind.

As soon as Readus stopped the car just on the side of the shotgun house, my misgivings seized me and the morning coffee refluxed in my throat. I choked it down, but it rose up again as soon as I stepped into the house, which smelled of cold cooking grease and camphor. Gesturing to a large velour recliner pushed against the papered wall, Readus offered me a seat, then headed toward the back. I surveyed the room, which was dimly lit and spare of furnishings—a cold stove, a green plaid couch with matching chair, a floor-model television, crumpled balls of tinfoil on the rabbit-eared antennas, a bowl of plastic fruit on a side table. And above the mantel, in a dusty frame, a triptych of John and Robert Kennedy and Martin Luther King Jr.

A few more minutes passed before she limped into the room in lace-up Hush Puppies and said, "Come on back here." I don't know why, but I reached for my umbrella. "Leave your parasol in here." I could not meet her eye to eye; she looked too much like women in my neighborhood back in Pipe Shop. Grandmothers they were, not the ones like Mother, but like Miss Hattie and Grandma Edie, the ones who wore thick brown cotton stockings, sat and rocked on porches, went to midweek prayer meeting, and dipped Garrett snuff from tins nestled in their apron pockets. Whenever I try to conjure up an image of the midwife, I can only see the washed-out housedress that she wore and the two gray braids like drooping tusks on either side of her head.

I followed her back to a tiny box of a room where a brown metal chiforobe was opened to reveal dingy sheets and towels. A dingy floral bedsheet suspended from an overhead bar formed a makeshift screen around the corner cot, propped on one side with a mail-order catalog. She asked for the three hundred dollars right up front and I counted out into her hands the crisp twenty-dollar bills borrowed from one of my teachers.

"I don't need you to take off all your clothes, just your panties and your underskirt." I did as I was told and stood barefooted, shivering on the cold and gritty linoleum, hugging the garments to my chest. Taking them from my hand, she shoved them underneath the wooden bedside table with a kerosene lamp on top. Then, latching the door, she pulled the plastic windowshade, and next the string that lit the naked lightbulb dangling from the ceiling.

From the bed, I watched her remove plastic tubing and other supplies from a dresser drawer. First I lay there on the musty sheet, listening to her hum an unfamiliar tune, then terror seized me once again. I raised up on my elbows, prepared to change my mind, I thought, then remembered Mother's "be goods" and lay back down again. In the middle of a bar, the humming ceased and she stood beside the bed to prepare me for what would happen "way over in the evening": labor pains and blood and then the baby. Like Readus, she was taciturn, saving her words for only what seemed absolutely necessary. I wanted her to grip my hand, just like husbands grip the hands of wives in childbirth scenes in movies, but she didn't. She squatted down on a three-legged stool and resumed the dirge-like tune.

"Scoot down," she said, then pushed my skirt around my hips and pried my legs wide open.

"Don't go closing your legs now. You shoulda closed 'em long 'fore now." I had heard this caustic language all my life, spewing from the mouth of every older woman that I knew.

An hour passed, maybe two. I don't remember. I stepped back into my panties, my stockings, my slip, and followed the humming midwife to the front door. She whispered, "Remember, don't go making mention of my name to nobody or I could get in a whole heap of trouble and, if that happen, y'all girls over at the college will be in a sho-nuff fix." I nodded my head and mumbled, "Yes ma'am."

Calling to Readus, who was napping on the couch, the woman said, "She ready." He pulled on his scuffed-up brogans and lifted his coat and hat from the recliner. The front door banged behind him and I soon heard the motor gunning. "I don't reckon you'll have no trouble, 'cause you ain't but two months gone, but if something go wrong, go on over there to John Andrew Hospital and they'll take care of you." I tiptoed down the steps to the waiting car parked just outside the doorway.

Days later, the infection set in—fever, chills, blood—and I knew I had to go to the hospital. Checking me right in, the doctor gave me the bare facts, fastening on me a candid look that said, "How could you?" but a touch that said, "I understand." He had to do a D&C, but because I was under twenty-one, he needed my parents' permission. Dying would be easier, I thought. He cut a deal with me, explaining that this was a simple procedure, and I could explain it to my parents as such. They could then send a telegram of authorization. But if they called to ask him any questions, he was legally bound to answer them.

I plodded to the phone booth at the end of the hospital corridor, closing the narrow folding door behind me as the light flickered on inside. Dropping the dime into the slot, I placed the collect call and struck up my familiar banter when Mama accepted the charges. I don't know now what I told her, but I do remember hearing fear, motherly concern, and intuition rising in her voice.

"I'm taking the bus down there in the morning," she insisted.

"But, Mama, that's not necessary." I began to sweat inside the telephone booth as she reiterated her plan to come by bus tomorrow. Daddy could pick her up on the weekend if Mother had improved.

"What's wrong with Mother?"

"She had a stroke."

"When?"

"Almost a week ago."

"What? I don't believe it. I just got a letter from her last week. Where was she?"

"She was at home."

"But I thought she was on a job in Mobile."

"Yeah, that's where she was, but she had come back home. Hadn't been back from down there much more than an hour when she had the stroke. Mr. Fred said they were just sitting at the kitchen table talking when she slumped over, right there. She was still in her uniform, hadn't even taken off her shoes and stockings."

"Why didn't anybody call me?"

"We didn't want to worry you before we knew anything. Plus, we knew you would be coming home anyway for Easter."

"But Easter's almost a month away."

I recovered my wits and persuaded her that she should stay at home with Mother. A telegram was all the doctor needed. This was a routine procedure that would probably rid me of the awful cramps that confined me monthly to the bed. That's where we left it. I hung up the phone and stumbled out of the booth.

I couldn't believe it. Just last week—the very week I'd scheduled the abortion—I'd received another of Mother's famous "be good," "stay-on-the-course" letters, along with a clipping from the *Birmingham World* about the Debutante's Ball. It was a newsy letter, longer I think than any she had ever written. She was on her way to Mobile and wrote that the Bessemer Board of Education had finally granted Reggie's petition to be transferred back to Brighton High from W.A. Bell, where he could get a decent education from teachers who were competent and caring. "These people are bound and determined to ruin black children's education," she had written, but, "Thank God, Reggie is a fighter." The letter sounded hurriedly written, and some words were, uncharacteristically, illegible. It took me a few seconds to puzzle out "determination," a word that cropped up in all her letters to me. "Never lose your determination," she had written, but the "de" of "determination" was blurred, and so it looked like "termination." But even without the prefix, I knew that it could be no other word.

She enclosed a book of stamps, a ten-dollar bill, and the clipping of the Debutante's Ball:

I've been meaning to send you this since the first of the year, but it's just been first one thing and then another. You look so nice in the picture, Mrs. Berger says you've grown up to be a lovely young lady. I haven't had a chance to get the pictures developed from the ceremony, but will send you some as soon as I do. I talked to Papa yesterday and he sends his love to you. He says look out for a lemon pound cake in the mail next week. Well, let me bring these few lines to a close. Just stay on the path and keep on making us proud. I'll see you Easter Sunday. With all my love, Mother.

The story filled two narrow columns:

18 DEBS MAKE FORMAL BOW TO SOCIETY

They created a perfect picture of winter beauty in floor-length dresses of winter white and the traditional single strand of pearls. Geraldine Lantaffeta, ornamented with iridescent sequins. Miss Clara Oliver and Sonya Gamble lighted the eighteen candles, which cast a soft glow on the decorative background of red poinsettias.

Mistress of ceremonies, Mrs. Mable Ravizee, presented the parents of the debs, who were themselves visions of grace and dignity as they took their places at the festive hall.

It was classic reporting for *The Birmingham World*. All the language and the frippery of high society for a ceremony in a gymnasium, the orange basketball hoop above Miss Ravizee's head.

Presiding at the refreshment table were Mesdames Sylvie Haynes and Mahlia Vaughn. The table was covered with white tulle over a red satin under-skirt, with a centerpiece of red and white chrysanthemums resting on a blanket of ferns and magnolia leaves. Completing the picture was a large cut-glass punch bowl brimming with cranberry juice. Approximately 150 guests enjoyed the occasion.

"Mesdames?" I scanned the rest, shaking my head and clucking as I read the last paragraph:

Mrs. Mable Ravizee, debutante committee chairman and mistress of cere-monies for the occasion, expressed hope that the presentation of the debs will serve as inspiration to other young girls to be morally and spiritually above reproach, so that they too may be presented to the Bessemer social world as young women representative of the best our city has to offer.

CONCEIVING IS NOT ALWAYS THE SAME AS HAVING AN IDEA

by Catherine Newman

IN THE SILENCE we could hear the kitchen faucet.

Drip.

Drip.

Drip.

Our friends had been telling us a story—a story that made the very air in the room crackle with feeling. We sat on their deep purple couch while upstairs our two children and theirs enacted various scenes from *Little House on the Prairie*, and they described the conception of their older daughter. These friends—two women filled up and spilling over with love—had borne a container of donated sperm out to the deserted end of a wild and beautiful beach. And not a minute later, the decade's most spectacular storm came barreling in over the Atlantic: a storm that illuminated the wind-swelled sea with great flashing crashes of lightning, a storm that evacuated the entire beach so that our friends wound up drenched and shaking back in their little car, correctly certain that they were now expecting a baby, their sought-after child, intentionally conceived in every sense of the word. The very same glorious daughter who, ten years later, popped her bonneted self into the room to grab a couple of clementines, and smiled at us—at me, with tears shining on my cheeks.

And I was still wiping at them with my sleeve, blowing my nose over the beauty of these people we are lucky enough to know, when they turned their open, curious faces to us, my husband and me, and said, "What about you guys?" and "Yeah, how were your kids conceived?"

Drip.

Drip.

In the movie version, you'd cut from the scene of their conception—complete with the swelling piano chords and the sepia-toned ocean waves—to circus music played at the wrong speed, a frantic montage of naked people humping damply against each other on the bed, on the carpet, their heads lolling around on their Jack-in-the-box necks, *yuh-duh duddle-uddle uh-duh-duh-duh*, with maybe a half-empty bottle of Wild Turkey in the foreground. To be funny, you might splice in scenes of other mating animals—rabbits, rhinos, Paris Hilton, Prince Edward Island mussels—everybody hump-hump-humping away with the circus music and a few *wicky-wicky* hip-hop samplings of creaky bedsprings. And in the silence of the film that was playing only in my own head, I must have grinned or grimaced in a particular way, because our friends suddenly shook their heads. They laughed and said, "Oh my god! Right!" They laughed and said, "Actually, no. Don't."

"Uh, let's see," I could have started, my lips hanging open like those of a frat boy, of a chimpanzee mother of two. First there was Ben's conception—and I use "conception" in the strictly *embryonic* sense here—when I had been more or less unconscious, brimful of narcotics after splitting my lip open during a roller hockey game. "Don't kish me," I'd slurred through my sewn-up mouth, "but the other stuff is okay." *The other stuff* being, you know, *the accidental creation of human life.*

And then there was Birdy's, when rain delayed our departure for a camping trip, and we'd lumped boredly around the house until one thing led to another: Michael, the love of my life, reaching around me to dry his hands on a dish towel; me up on the kitchen counter in an inseminating kind of a way. Nothing like *making another person* to kill a couple of minutes!

Our children are the very sun around which my small planet orbits. I've got nothing against straight people. And I'm all for sexual pleasure and reproduction both—I just happen to think that the muddling of the two together ranges from vaguely awkward to totally creepy. Especially when the suggestion—by, say, your minister, senator, or grandmother—is that getting off should be always and uniquely twinned with getting pregnant. Are you supposed to think about the baby you're trying to conceive *while* you're trying to conceive it? That seems kind of weird and incesty. Also kind of a, um, *turn-off*. (I have actually boo-hooed sentimentally into an intimate moment, "Honey, this is how we ended up with the kids!" and Michael has sighed and patted me on the head.) Wouldn't it be funny if other bodily indulgences had the same outcome as the sexual kind? *Oof— I ate a platter of sushi and a package of Ding Dongs, and now we're having another baby!* Or other kinds of friction? *Thanks to my rubbing of that butcher block with mineral oil, you're going to be a big brother!*

Sometimes the heterosexual female body seems to me like the kind of person who confuses sex with love.

At least mine is. I have gotten pregnant using birth control well, using it badly, and using it not at all. I have gotten pregnant with a bonfire raging in my heart, and I have also gotten pregnant with the matter-of-factness of boiling an egg. I have terminated, miscarried, and carried to term. And while my politics have been rationally, intentionally, and coherently pro-choice, my feelings—oh, my feelings have been a kite in the wind. At my most captive—with cells multiplying deep inside, hidden beneath flesh and muscle and occulted from intelligence—I felt powerful and excited. Even as I have also understood this excitement to be the hallmark of a certain kind of privilege: a restless mind clattering around inside a comfortable life. And even as this buzz has turned, on occasion, into a kind of droning grief.

"You need to ask me about it every day," I cried to Michael, whose body did not offer him a gory, cramping reminder of what to expect when we were no longer expecting. I was furious. I was depressed. Everybody around me suddenly seemed to be pregnant, absurdly huge, bursting open like ripe pomegranates spattering me with their juice. I took a lot of baths. At the drugstore, maxi-pads were the stone I was rolling and rolling up some kind of babyless hill. Dark shapes slid out of me into the toilet bowl like criminals, like poisonous sea creatures streaming bright, bloody tentacles behind them. My body had made so much so quickly! I knelt on the bathroom floor, held one in my hand; the ache of empty arms took me completely by surprise. There may be nothing more humbling than the wildness of human life: shaped but not fully constrained by our choices, as ravaging and spectacular as a freak summer storm.

The paradoxical beauty of choice is that it can't smooth the seams between reason and passion. It can't promise, for example, that you won't grieve for a pregnancy you don't want. Or that you get to keep a pregnancy you do. It doesn't mean you won't feel terribly alone when the nurse at a clinic takes your blood pressure with the coldness of her judgment glittering in her eyes or when, weeks after a miscarriage, the pathology report arrives in the mail like the ghost of your own melancholy. It doesn't even mean you won't feel terribly alone sitting and sitting in the glide rocker with a new baby leeched onto your poor postpartum person—even if your heart soars when her gaze flutters open to meet yours, when her face blossoms, smiling, like the sped-up film of a blooming rose. Even if that baby was conceived on the kitchen counter, amid half-empty bowls of macaroni and cheese, without the cloud of a child anywhere in that clear blue horizon of desire.

But it's not this contradiction that baffles me. It's the fact that the very people who believe that our pregnancies, despite their hydraulic origin, should dictate parenthood—many of them are the same very people who remain aghast over our friends, who mustered all of their love and consciousness to procreate. Don't get me wrong—I'm glad we didn't have to pass some kind of intentionality test to have our babies; I'm also glad that we could, when we needed to, choose to not, even if this gladness did not exactly feel, well, *glad*. Choice in all its many forms—adoption, abstinence, technology, choosing to be anti-choice, pleasure, abortion, birth control, kids, no kids, and even, I know, regret—is what makes human sexuality truly human and parenthood truly viable. Without it we are as witlessly tied to the mechanics of our bodies as salmon struggling upstream; as the camels groaning and grinding *in flagrante delicto* while my children stand openmouthed at the zoo; as a nest of snakes; as a cliff of lemurs.

Which is not to say that the children don't come tumbling into the room now like a litter of puppies. A litter of puppies wearing petticoats and suspenders and calling each other Pa and Ma and Baby Carrie. A year later my IUD will start dragging at the bottom of my poor old floppy uterus like an unhitched anchor and I will have it removed. We will get pregnant again and panic and then we will choose to keep the baby. We will rejoice and then miscarry. And these same friends will sit with me on their purple couch and share my grief—my private, incoherent, peculiarly heterosexual grief over an unchosen pregnancy, a chosen baby, an unchosen loss—and they will remember to ask me about it every day. But right now the children are laughing and pink cheeked and our friends are watching with merry, sparkling eyes. And I am watching them, struck anew and simply by the amazing grace of human being.

HARRISON:
Battling for the Chance to Make a Choice
by Harriette E. Wimms

I WAS SITTING ON the gravelly shore of the Patuxent River with a group of teenaged girls from the Catholic church my mother and I attended. The air smelled of salt and suntan lotion, and the sky above was picture-perfect blue as the gentle waves of the river lapped at the beach. It was the summer before our senior year of high school and our youth group minister, Annie, was asking us what we wanted to do with the rest of our lives. I had to make plans that would dictate "my future"—or so I had been told. Annie was twenty-two and seemed to me worldly and wise. She and I and several other members of the youth group had stolen away to the beach this day. We were nestled within the confines of a mostly white, upper-middle class neighborhood called Esperanza Farms, along a the portion of the shoreline that was only accessible to community residents. Since one of the girls in the group lived here, we were allowed access to the beach for the day.

Several of the girls talked about attending colleges I had never heard of: Vassar, Hood, Wellesley. "I'd like to study veterinary medicine," one girl mused while using a stick to write the name of her horse—and then her new boyfriend—in the sand. *their dreams*

Another girl said, "My parents want me to study business administration, but I don't know if I will."

My father and mother were both working-class folks—a retired aircraft electrician and a custodian, respectively, and we didn't talk much about colleges or future careers. My father had completed high school, taken night classes at Howard University to obtain an electrician's certificate, served as an army electrician in World War II, and worked as an aircraft electrician until 1971, when he retired to become my stay-at-home dad. My mother, who had grown up in a small Georgia town, attended school until the sixth grade—that was when her mother died and she dropped out to financially provide for her seven younger siblings.

As African Americans raised in the early 1900s, both of my parents experienced significant discrimination because of their racial and socio-economic backgrounds. These experiences, instead of making them bitter, instilled in them a desire for continued self-improvement—and the belief that education could powerfully improve personal and community cir-cumstances. They believed that a "good education" would help me live a life easier than theirs had been. Still, their advice about my future was fre-quently generic: "Get good grades. Never give up. If you're going to do it, do your best. Books now, boys later. Keep up the good work." Most importantly, they let me know that they loved me immeasurably and would embrace whomever I chose to become.

Back on the beach, a few other girls talked about the "handsome and well-off" husbands they hoped to lure and catch, about the weddings they had "always dreamed of" as they flipped through *Elle* magazine. One girl said, "Oh, I want a dress kinda like this one here with the lace and the low back and a long train and flowers in my hair that match little bouquets placed throughout the church…"

There was a lull in the conversation and a few girls looked in the direction of me and my friend Shawna: we had been conspicuously quiet. I took a deep breath; I had been thinking about the future, too, and I had come to a conclusion.

"Well, I don't think I'm ever getting married…"

An electric pause traveled among the girls as they stared at me. Some-where a cricket chirped. I swallowed hard and continued, "Mostly what I want is to have a baby. That's what I really want to be, a mother. Just me and my kid, you know? Then maybe also I could become a DJ or a radio station producer or something like that…" The end of the sentence trailed off as I began to lose my nerve. The silence that followed was just a few seconds too long, then a tittering of giggles erupted from the group.

"You are so funny! She's always saying crazy stuff like that."

I stared at them and then chuckled, too. My youth group minister wasn't laughing, though. Her face was flushed as she responded, "You can do so much more than have babies! Go to college. Get a job. Do some-thing so you can support yourself! You can have babies any time. You have your whole life to do that."

* * *

I made that pronouncement over twenty years ago; now I am watching my beautiful son sleep. For him, his life is a given. His existence is a certainty, as sure as the fact that the sun comes up in the morning, that on most sunny days we will go to the park after his nap, and that both of his mothers love him more than words could ever express. He is the center of our universe and knows only that his presence brings us boundless joy (and the occasional exasperated sigh that accompanies parenting a 2-year-old boy). He does not know—nor will he understand for many years to come—the legacy that surrounds my choices, as a woman, a lesbian, and a working-class person of color, to become his birthmother.

I am one of those women who always knew, in my bones, that I was meant to be a mother. During those high school days, while my private Catholic school classmates (I attended on scholarship) talked of plans to attend college after graduation, I dreamed of strollers and baby clothes. I had also decided that I never wanted to be married to a man and considered the possibility of being a single mother. My peers and mentors scoffed at my confessions, telling me that I should focus instead on my obligation to support myself before producing offspring (as if my desire to have a child as a single woman would undoubtedly end in my reliance on public assistance). It was also suggested that as an African American woman, I should strive to achieve educational pursuits and economic advantages first, that I should become "accomplished," and motherhood should be an afterthought. So I toddled off to a state university, received a degree in English, found a job in the marketing department of a publishing company, and pursued a number of unhealthy love relationships with men who "just weren't right for me."

This was before the AIDS epidemic truly hit our collective consciousness. In the early eighties, safe sex for me and many of my college friends simply meant ensuring you weren't going to become pregnant. Perhaps it was my maternal longings rising up from my subconscious—or maybe it was just stupidity—but I rarely used birth control. I know now, in retrospect, that I was a very lucky woman. Still, there were many times when I would feel a dull ache in my breasts and faint nausea in the pit of my stomach and look at the calendar and anxiously add up the days, wondering if I had made a choice by default. Sometimes weeks would pass and then finally my period would arrive and I would feel I had dodged and simultaneously been struck by a bullet: relieved and saddened that the choice to become a mother had not been made for me by my contraceptive choices.

In 1992, I married one of those "not good for me" men, and after a tumultuous and abusive year of matrimonial discord and unprotected sex, I still was not pregnant. The medical establishment and women's magazines told me that this failure to conceive was cause for concern. For a woman under thirty-five, a year of sex without pregnancy suggested there might be a problem and a doctor should be consulted. For a woman thirty-five or over, six months was the time frame for panic. I had, in fact, married my husband with the intent of having children—the marriage itself was an afterthought. And somehow, between our fights and his drinking, between the money problems and the lies, I had managed to chart my basal body temperature religiously for months and was having sex at all of the fertilely appropriate times. My gynecologist agreed that I might have some "reproductive challenges" and sent me to a specialist.

I was diagnosed with an endocrine disorder called polycystic ovarian syndrome (a disorder which meant I did not ovulate regularly), as well as a severe case of hypothyroidism and a hearty case of depression. An endocrinologist and a fertility specialist were eager to help me become pregnant. They talked cheerily about medications and procedures (from artificial insemination to in vitro fertilization) that could help me, and urged me to move forward as soon as I was able.

"There's much we can try—from oral medications to induce ovulation to more high-tech methods to help you achieve pregnancy. As your doctor, I can't make your life decisions for you. But given your health problems you may want to move forward on starting your family within the next several months. You've been married almost a year now, right? So it's about time to get started. And luckily, most employers in Maryland are now required to include fertility treatment coverage in their health insurance benefits packages." She rifled through my file and continued, "We do accept your insurance. So your treatments will be covered at 90 percent of the allowed benefit. We'll start with Clomid (a drug that promotes ovulation) and some fertility monitoring which should run you about $50 per cycle. If that sounds doable, we should be able to move forward as soon as you're ready. Perhaps your husband will be able to make it to the next visit?"

While my doctors were enthusiastic about me getting pregnant, my husband was not as enthused. He refused to attend appointments with me and was not very thrilled about the prospect of a fertility screening: he was more comfortable shrugging off our childlessness as my problem and leaving it at that. Still, my specialists were hopeful. The doctors, nurses, and insurance representatives all seemed to believe that our "right" to pro-create was a given, despite the ongoing havoc within our home.

* * *

My husband and I were on the outs for a number of reasons, the least of which being that I had fallen in love with a woman. As my marriage dis-integrated in 1993, the divorce was accompanied by a sense of relief and freedom. I had a job with good benefits and room for advancement, writing marketing copy and filing paperwork for a publishing company. I had a nice enough place to live: a rambling, drafty three-story Victorian I rented with three friends in a sketchy but culturally and racially diverse community in Baltimore City. I was finally living an authentic life: I joined book clubs, kissed women in bars, volunteered at the lesbian bookstore, co-edited a literary magazine, sat in cafés reading poetry, placed a rainbow sticker on the bumper of my car, attended coming-out support groups at the local gay community center—and I was still mightily determined to become pregnant.

In 1996 I met my future partner, Pat, who answered my personal ad in the *City Paper*. During our first conversation, while we flirted and talked about the music we enjoyed, I interrupted her to say, "You know, I like you and I want to get to know you better and everything. But in all honesty, I have to tell you up front that I'm planning to get pregnant next year, whether or not I am in a relationship. If you don't like kids, we should probably hang up now."

There was a moment of silence, and then—I could hear the smile in her voice—she said, "I'm still on the phone, aren't I? So, want to have dinner tomorrow night?"

We fell in love and, in typical lesbian fashion, we rented a moving van three months later. My parents fell in love with her, my nieces and nephews were awed by her video games and comic book collection. We planned a commitment ceremony for fall of 1997, and when we returned from our honeymoon, called the fertility doctor's office to make an appointment. Motherhood, as the doctors had told me five years prior, was only a few prescriptions and a syringe or two away. Unfortunately I hadn't realized that reproductive rules had changed drastically with my marital status.

Now that I was divorced, I was considered a single woman by fertility specialists and my insurance company, whether or not I was involved in a same-sex relationship. I learned of these changes when I went to an appointment with my reproductive endocrinologist. Once so enthusiastic, her demeanor was now somber as I entered her office.

"Well, now that you're divorced, things are a bit different," she said. "You need to call your insurance company first and find out if your treatments will be covered. Unfortunately, many of my single clients have a hard time getting these kinds of procedures covered."

"But I'm not single. Plus, I'm infertile."

"In the eyes of the law you are single," she said. Her jaw was set, almost defensive; she sat up straight in her chair. "This is just how the regulations are written. Insurance companies usually only cover fertility treatments for heterosexual married couples. But you can always pay out of pocket and see if they'll reimburse you."

I couldn't understand the words she was saying. They just did not compute. It couldn't possibly be true that insurance companies could discriminate on the basis of marital status, could it? Surely that had to be illegal. This, however, was just the beginning. I learned from talking to medical office support staff, the Maryland Office of the Attorney General, and the benefits coordinator at my job that this was, in fact, how my policy (and most policies) was written. The policies were blatantly discriminatory but legally so.

In 1997, in the state of Maryland, although most employers were required to include infertility treatments among the benefits covered by their employee health insurance packages, these benefits were requisite only if an employee was a member of a heterosexual married couple. Single women, lesbians, and even unmarried heterosexual couples were specifically excluded from these covered benefits.

Therefore, despite my diagnosis of medically caused infertility, fertility treatments were not covered because of my sexual orientation—I was married but my same-sex marriage was not recognized. Motherhood was no longer the medical necessity it had been when I was a heterosexual married woman. Procedures which would have cost me $50 or $100 while I was married to a man would now cost me several thousand dollars per month. I was afraid I would be denied the opportunity to become a mother because I could not afford the medical procedures I needed, procedures that had been offered so easily when I was married to a man.

I contacted my local ACLU office to find out if what was happening was legal. The representative I spoke to said I was not the first woman to relay this kind of story. He encouraged me to talk directly with the human resources department and the benefits coordinator of my employer. These individuals blamed the insurance coverage stipulations on the insurance company. Insurance company representatives replied that employers were responsible for developing their own benefits packages. (Many medical insurance policies are still written this way, although I have been told that employers may opt to change their benefits packages so that treatments are covered for unmarried employees.) The ACLU lawyer believed I had a case; however, if I chose to pursue it, I might draw significant media coverage. I declined their help, afraid that my job would be jeopardized by the negative press. *scared to fight*

I began writing letters: to the human resources department of my employer, to the appeals department of my insurance company, to the Maryland insurance commissioner and the Office of the Attorney General, encouraging them to change their policies. But in the end, I was told nothing could be done, regulations could not be changed for one person.

What's worse, many physicians seemed to believe that motherhood was no longer a right or even a reasonable consideration for me. My fertility specialist, over the phone, suggested that I find a different practitioner because my insurance would not cover her services. Several hospitals and fertility treatment centers refused outright to provide me with services not because of my ability to pay, but because I was a lesbian.

One day I walked into the office of a reproductive endocrinologist in the same professional building as my dentist. A picture of mother and child on the door had caught my attention; I thought, "Maybe this is a sign." The office was wallpapered in muted pink and blue swirls with faded silk flower arrangements on several end tables. The waiting room was empty. A receptionist pushed back a glass window, "Ye-ess. May I help you?"

"Yes," I said. "I have a quick question: does the doctor offer services to single women or lesbians?"

She said, hesitantly, "You'll have to talk with the doctor about that."

"Well, is the doctor available? I'm having a hard time finding a doctor who will work with me and I'd like to talk to him to ask..."

"No hon," she interrupted. "The doctor isn't available. He only sees people by appointment."

"What about a nurse or the office manager?" I replied in nearly a whisper.

"No ma'am. You'll have to ask the doctor about that."

I left the office after grabbing the doctor's card. That afternoon, the same receptionist transferred my call immediately to the physician. I asked him about his willingness to offer artificial insemination to lesbian couples.

"I can't help you," he said.

"I'm sorry?" I said.

"No, I cannot help you. I don't approve of that sort of thing." And he hung up the phone.

The next week I called the department of reproductive medicine at one of the most prestigious hospitals and universities in Maryland. When told that I could not access fertility services there, I asked to speak to the head of the department. The doctor returned my call late that afternoon. "How may I help you?" he asked.

I told him that I had been diagnosed with PCOS and had not become pregnant after nearly two years of unprotected sex with my former husband. And then I told him about my domestic partnership, and how none of the many doctors I had contacted would offer artificial insemination services to us.

"Miss Wimms," he said, "We simply can't offer those services to you because you are not married. This is, of course, not a value judgment. You must look at it from the hospital's standpoint. If we inseminate you and then let's say you die, the hospital would be liable."

"I don't understand," I said, perplexed.

"We could be sued for paternity."

I laughed out loud before realizing he was serious.

"Well," I said, recovering, "what if I sign some kind of contract that states you won't be sued if I die?"

"Our lawyers wouldn't allow us to do that. Good day."

Crying in my internist's office a few months later, I relayed these stories while we discussed which depression medication we should try next. The doctor pulled out a notepad and wrote down a name and number. "Call this woman. She's young and has just joined a practice in this neighborhood. She might help you."

Pat and I went to the appointment together. As we stepped into the doctor's office, I felt as though I were walking into battle. After shaking her hand we sat down in the overstuffed chairs in front of the desk. The doctor moved to the leather chair behind the desk and sat down, smiling.

"We are a lesbian couple," I said.

I looked up; she was still smiling.

"Great," she said. "How can I help you?"

Once Pat and I finally had located a doctor who was willing to help us get pregnant, she told us that Maryland law stipulated that an "unmarried" woman could only be medically inseminated with sperm that had been frozen, stored, and quarantined for six months at a cryobank. This would cost several hundred dollars. If we were using anonymous donor sperm, we could move forward. But if we wanted our child to have a relationship with his or her donor, we would have to have sperm processed. Pat and I had decided that we wanted our child to have the option of knowing his donor. We asked a dear friend to be our donor and he agreed. So we chose a sperm bank that had served lesbians for years and made preparations to have our donor visit the bank.

However, as the donor's sperm bank appointment date approached, the bank notified us that our donor would not be able to provide sperm specimens for us if he were gay. It was the policy of the bank to disallow anonymous donors who were gay, due to an "increased risk of HIV disease." This rule extended to known donors as well. Therefore, we had now lost our ability to use the donor of our choice.

oh no...

In the midst of our efforts, our gynecologist suddenly announced to us that she was pregnant and moving to Colorado. After three years of fighting the system, with the news of our doctor's pregnancy, my partner and I decided to give up. We were tired. A choice had been made for us, born out of our frustration and inability to access the technology to support our reproductive choices. We had networked with many women who were making the choice to become parents as single women or lesbian couples; it seemed, however, that the rules were different for infertile lesbian couples.

In the years following our decision to live a child-free life, the cryobank made the decision to allow gay known donors, and the medical institution that had denied us access to fertility services has become a leader in helping lesbian couples in Baltimore conceive. And my former employer— in part due to concerns raised by me and other lesbian employees—has since changed its benefits package so that fertility treatments are covered for lesbian couples. But these changes came too late for us.

Two years later, I was talking to my friend Leslie about my "choice" not to have children. Leslie had shared an office with me at my first job out of college and we had become very close. She witnessed my fertility struggles from the very beginning of my first marriage. I told her, "I'm quitting my job. I've decided to go back to school. I'm thinking about getting a graduate degree in child psychology. That way I can still help and support children even if I never have my own."

"Umm-hmm," Leslie said.

"And I figure a Ph.D. is going to cost me about what it would have cost to get pregnant anyway," I joked.

She didn't laugh.

I hoped I would eventually embrace a child-free life with my partner. Perhaps we would come to enjoy being able to travel at the drop of a hat, to have quiet dinners and romantic late night talks, to live our lives with each other.

"And one day," I said tentatively, "maybe one day, I will be able to adopt, when my heart is open…and when I can find an agency that will work with gay couples."

"You know, I just don't buy this," Leslie responded.

"What?"

"This whole child-free business. You've always wanted to have children. Yes, it has been really hard and I can't believe that the cards have been so stacked against you. But this is not the Harriette I know. You usually fight harder when faced with a challenge. I just don't believe this is the end of this story."

Her statement spurred me to action. Surely there had to be individuals who were willing to help us achieve reproductive equity—I became determined to find them. In 1995, I had joined a listserv for lesbian moms. Sitting at work, I had typed the terms, "lesbian" and "mother" into a search engine and up popped a link for a "lesbian moms list." The listserv was composed of a few hundred women from around the world who were lesbian or bisexual mothers. These women had conceived or adopted children either during previous heterosexual relationships or within same-sex relationships. The list also included women hoping and planning to become lesbian mothers.

I now began telling these women about my struggles and inquiring about other online support and advocacy agencies. Through this listserv I also found online support groups for women with PCOS who were trying to conceive, for infertile lesbians, and for overweight women who were trying to conceive. We shared tactics for finding open-minded practitioners, strategies for handling the stress involved in dealing with infertility and discrimination, and methods for boosting fertility and successfully riding the emotional rollercoaster of infertility treatments.

a supportive network

The women on these lists became cheerleaders when I was feeling downhearted; they became legal advocates when I needed help to bolster my arguments with benefits coordinators or insurance company representatives, fitness and health partners, and comrades when I needed someone to share in my righteous anger. These women helped me believe again that my dream of motherhood was as much my right as a lesbian as it had been when I was married to a man. Through these networks I eventually put together a new team of doctors to aggressively treat my medical conditions and who supported Pat and me in our desire to have a child. We were also referred to a local cryobank willing to process sperm specimens from our known donor with no question about his sexual orientation (we processed enough sperm for eleven months of attempts, which cost about $4,500). Through these grassroots support networks, we also found an insurance loophole that made each monthly cycle of fertility treatments cost us $850 per month rather than $5,000.

In June of 2003, we joyfully began trying to conceive our child. The first month was exciting: Pat and I would drive together to pick up our "swimmers" from the sperm bank and deliver them to the fertility center, a sign that read, "Baby on Board" taped to the car window. But despite a combination of oral fertility medication, fertility monitoring—including ultrasounds and ovulation predictor kits—and perfectly timed inseminations, we could not become pregnant. After our fifth failed attempt, our fertility specialist called. She was concerned that the oral medication I was using was not strong enough and that our next step was to move to fertility medication by injection. Each month of injections would cost between $600 and $1,200, in addition to insemination costs. Our credit cards were now nearly maxed out with fertility treatment costs, and we didn't know where we would find the money or the emotional resolve to move on to the "injectable cycles." We definitely would not be able to afford IVF (at $12,000 per month, not including medication) because my insurance company would not cover any of the costs. We simply couldn't afford to get pregnant.

We opted to try one more month of the less expensive oral medication, and then we would call it quits. Eight days after that insemination I started vomiting and my breasts were so sore I could barely place my arms at my sides. At twelve days after that insemination, blood work confirmed *struggle →* that I was pregnant! And two weeks later, we saw the tiny beating heart of *success!* our baby on a black-and-white ultrasound screen. Ten years in the making, our son's heart had begun its lifelong rhythm.

I have been, and always will be pro-choice. Since the moment my partner and I watched our son's flickering heartbeat, I've struggled with my pro-choice stance. I maintain that I am pro-choice, but anti-abortion, opposed to abortion as a method of birth control...but I subscribe these beliefs to myself only. After the experiences my partner and I have had, of outside forces dictating if and how we could conceive our child, we know the necessity of providing access to choices.

My mother, who passed away in October 2006 at the age of eighty-three, was a devout Catholic. Despite her strong belief in the church's doctrine, she would tell anyone who would listen that "church and state have no business messing around with a woman's body and her right to choose." This from a woman who had birthed seven children, whose children had provided her with twenty grandchildren, twenty-nine great grandchildren, and one great-great-grandchild.

My son was delivered via planned C-section at thirty-eight weeks gestational age, after months of weekly ultrasounds and non-stress tests, as well as a short stint of bed rest. Although I had dreamed of him for so long, fought for him for so long, nothing had prepared me for how much I fell in love with Harrison the moment I laid eyes on him. When I looked at him for the first time, I realized that when I was a naive 16-year-old, my longing was for him. I was not only meant to be a mother, I was meant to be *his* mother. I am so grateful to have been granted the constellation of blessings and hard work that led him to us.

Harrison is thriving. He loves to play in mud puddles and run as fast as he can down grass-covered hills. He has the most beautiful crooked smile, like he's always plotting his next mischievous endeavor. Feisty, like my mother, he sometimes has temper tantrums and loves to scream at the top of his lungs for no good reason. Other times he is gentle and soft-spoken, just like my dad. Harrison has inherited my stubborn streak (although I like to call it "strong will"), and has Pat's sense of humor (his giggles are contagious). Harrison shares our donor's love of music: he spends much of his day dancing and singing and tapping out rhythms with his feet. He says "please" and "thank you" without being prompted. He can identify all of the primary colors, recite the alphabet, count to 30, and can read over 400 words (at the age of two and a half). He is always well-dressed and well-fed, has more books than any child I know, and understands implicitly that he is loved by me (his Mommy), by Pat (his Momma), by our donor (his Uncle Jason), and by a host of our friends who make up his incredible chosen family. He is blessed, as are we.

But our story does not end there.

Our lives felt like a fairy tale in those first few weeks. Yes, we were exhausted (during the first week of Harrison's life Pat was so exhausted that she would fall asleep and snore for a moment each time she blinked). But we had become the family of our dreams. We settled into an ongoing cycle of nursing, diaper changes, nuzzling, and sleep. I returned to work five weeks after my son was born because, as a graduate student, that was all the maternity leave available to me. Pat remained at home to care for our son.

When I began falling asleep at work or behind the wheel of my car and experiencing tingling on one side of my face and trouble speaking, my internist thought I was having strange postpartum symptoms. When my hearing started to disappear, a CAT scan identified two tumors, one in my ear and another in the frontal cortex of my brain, which were responsible for my symptoms. Two weeks later, when my son was just four months old, neurosurgeons removed a large meningioma from within the left side of my skull. Six months later, a second tumor was removed from my inner ear, leaving me deaf in my left ear.

Pat adopted Harrison as his "second parent" when he was ten months old. After reading the glowing letters written by our friends in support of our family, the judge happily deemed Pat a "legally fit and proper" parent for Harrison. I burst into tears in the courtroom. We fell into a comfortable rhythm of daily life, all our affairs circling day and night around our precious Harrison; however, the orbit between me and Pat became ever wider.

Perhaps it was the stress of caring for a new baby while dealing with multiple health challenges, or maybe it was my struggle to simultaneously work toward the completion of my Ph.D. while parenting an infant, or maybe it was the sleep deprivation and the fact that my partner and I stopped having sex after our son was born, or maybe it was all the years of battling against outside foes that had led us to finally turn on each in their absence. Whatever the reasons, we ended our ten-year marriage the month after my mother's death.

My ex-wife and I are working hard to remain the best parenting partners we can be for Harrison. We have made the choice, for now, to live separate lives while continuing to care for our son, and perhaps rekindle the friendship and mutual support that helped us create him in the first place. In many ways, my premonition of single motherhood so long ago has eerily come to pass.

I'd thought that if I did become pregnant that our child should have a sibling by birth or adoption. But at age thirty-nine, with a complicated medical history, adoption would be a challenge for me: I would face difficulty passing the physical screening many adoption agencies require. My physical health also prohibits my becoming pregnant again. Moreover, the costs of medical and fertility treatments have not left me enough money for the costs involved in adoption or surrogacy. Therefore, for the foreseeable future, Harrison will be an only child.

There are moments when Harrison and I are running through the park on sunny days, when I see siblings playing together and a wave of sadness and rage rushes over me. Our favorite park is nestled within a mostly upper-middle-class, mostly white neighborhood where we don't always fit in with the crowd. I've overheard mothers talking amongst themselves about private schools and nannies, about choosing to be stay-at-home moms, about which fertility treatments have helped them acquire their current second or third or fourth pregnancy, or about how they thought they were finished having children and then, "oops!" I frequently just keep running, chasing Harrison as he heads for the tallest grass-covered hill or the largest mud puddle.

For today, the sun is shining, my son is stirring from his nap, and the playground is calling. For today, my choice to be his mother means embracing with gratitude the miracle that is Harrison: a child born triumphantly out of a battle for choice. And for today, at least, this is enough.

MOTHER'S DAY IN THE YEAR OF THE ROOSTER
by Ann Hood

MY DAUGHTER GRACE was born in the year of the rat. "Very clever," our Chinese nanny, Ju Hua, told us. "Very special." Those born in the year of the rat are sharp-witted and funny. They are charming too, and considered good luck. The Christmas that Ju Hua was with our family, she had her husband in Beijing send Grace a gold charm of a small rat hanging on a chain. "Very special," Ju Hua explained. "Special present for a special girl."

Four months later, Grace died from a virulent form of strep. She was five years old. Ju Hua and her daughter had moved into their own apartment by then. When they heard the news, they came immediately. Ju Hua's face was stricken, her crying uncontrollable. "That girl," she said. "So special."

Grace had been studying Chinese at school, and even after Ju Hua left us, Grace would visit her and practice Chinese. "Her pronunciation so good!" Ju Hua would tell me when I picked Grace up. They had cooked together, fried rice and dumplings and the pork dish Grace liked so much. Smelling of garlic and sesame, Grace would wave goodbye to Ju Hua as we drove away. Then she would sing me a Chinese song, or count to twenty in Chinese.

That April day when Grace got sick and I rushed her to the emergency room, as they whisked her to the ICU, the doctor ordered me to help keep the oxygen mask on her face. "Grace," I said, trying to hide the fear that had gripped me, "count to ten and then you'll be in the room where the doctor can make you better."

Squirming under the oxygen mask, Grace began to count: "*Yee, uhr, sahn,*" she said in perfect Chinese, "*sah, woo, lyo…*"

When Ju Hua visited us after Grace died, she told us that her own mother had lost a child, a 6-year-old boy. He had become sick very suddenly, like Grace, and he had died in her mother's arms as she walked miles to the doctor. "My mother never forget this," Ju Hua said. "But if he didn't die, I would never be born."

There are so many cruel decisions parents have to make when their child dies. The funeral director requested a sheet for the coffin, and I sent the cozy flannel one, pale blue with happy snowmen, that had just been put away with the winter linens. They needed clothes to bury her in, and I carefully removed the tags from the new Capri pants with the ruffled hem and the pink shirt that Grace had picked out but never got a chance to wear. We could, we were told, place anything we wanted in her coffin, so my husband Lorne and I gathered her favorite things, the things that comforted her: Biff, her favorite stuffed animal; Cow, the green blanket decorated with cows; her purple leopard lunch box; her glasses; notes from each of us; crayons and paints; and the gold rat on the chain that Ju Hua had sent for her from China.

I cannot say for certain when the decision to have another child happened. I do remember sitting alone on a summer afternoon in the room we called the Puzzle Room, a room where Grace and my son Sam and I had spent many afternoons listening to Nanci Griffith CDs and working on jigsaw puzzles, sitting there as the hot afternoon stretched endlessly and hopelessly before me, and thinking about how my arms ached to hold Grace and my entire body longed for the buzz of activity that used to surround me just a few short months earlier. It was that same summer that my husband and I camped out together on a beach in Maine and he said, "I have the craziest idea." "So do I," I told him. That was when I put words to it. "Let's have another baby," I said. And he said yes. Then we cried. A light from a lighthouse kept swinging past us, illuminating everything.

First, my husband had to have his vasectomy reversed. Then, I had to have my hormone levels checked. I was forty-four years old, and I did not expect good news. But the doctor who everyone told us could help make it happen, said that although I might need a little hormonal help, I could indeed get pregnant.

Once a month, my husband and I drove to New York City to the doctor's

Park Avenue office where Lorne masturbated into a cup and I was then inseminated with his sperm. Each time, the doctor was optimistic. Lorne's sperm were great—good swimmers and plentiful. I ovulated on schedule and had good mucous. We'd had babies before. We could do it again.

But after four months without a pregnancy, the doctor added Clomid to the protocol. Now I went for an intravaginal sonogram, my follicles were counted, and then we went to New York. Four eggs. Six. But no baby.

By March, I was having tests to see if something was going on. In June I had surgery to remove a benign polyp. By fall Lorne was injecting me with Pergonal at almost $2,000 a month, and it was producing fewer follicles than the Clomid, and I wasn't getting pregnant. In the past, I had gotten pregnant easily and fast. Now my hormones were going crazy, I had a new pimple every day, the shots hurt, and I was obsessed with every twitch and pang I felt from my head to my toes: was it a pregnancy sign or premenstrual? Everyone has read about or knows someone who has gone through fertility treatments. It is an emotional nightmare, fueled by false hope and the promise of a treatment that will work. Add grief to that and the cycle gets even worse.

One day, a friend told me that she knew how to get a baby in Russia, fast. It involved spending time in Finland. It would cost around $40,000, before bribes. The baby was a girl. She had red hair.

Another friend stopped by and told me that she could get children from Hungary. Not babies, but 2- or 3-year-olds. She could even get twins. Or siblings. It would cost $60,000. Plus donations to various people who would help along the way.

Some people urged me to give up the idea altogether. I heard stories of women who had a child after losing one and forced that new child into the role of the dead one. I heard of mothers dressing their new baby in their dead child's clothes, making them swim or dance or whatever the other had done. It isn't fair, I was told. Fairness was not something I believed in very much then. If things were fair, a healthy, intelligent, 5-year-old girl wouldn't die. If things were fair, a family who helped others, who lived a good life together, who loved each other, wouldn't be torn apart like this.

By this time, I knew that bringing a baby into our household would help all of us. It would help ease the burden of our grief on Sam, who was only nine years old and read our emotions each morning like barometers. It would bring back the noise and laughter our house had lost. It would fill my empty hours. Babies make you do things for them. They get you up and they get you moving. A baby's smile, I knew, could change everything.

I had spent almost $25,000 and I was out of expendable income. I realized that in the time that had passed, with the money I had spent, we could already have a red-haired baby from Russia, or 3-year-old Hungarian twins. One day, on the three-hour car ride home from the fertility doctor in Manhattan, I told Lorne exactly that. "I'm broke," I said. "I'm tired. And I'm a wreck." Relief washed over his face. With adoption, there was definitely a baby at the end of the process. "Let's see if this insemination worked," he said. It didn't. Lorne and I decided to stop the fertility treatments and focus on adoption instead. What I knew as soon as we made that decision was that in a year we would have a baby.

For the next few months, I had coffee with women who had battled Central American governments, rescued children languishing in Russian and Romanian orphanages, lied, borrowed money, corrected cleft palates and crossed eyes and weak hearts, lost babies they had held, named babies they never got to see, traveled thousands of miles more than once, all in pursuit of a baby.

"I don't know if I have the emotional stamina for this," I told Lorne after hearing my friend's story about three failed adoptions in Guatemala and over $100,000 spent. She did, finally, have her daughter. But still.

"China," Lorne said. "Everyone I talk to who adopted from China, it went like clockwork."

One afternoon I watched a mother at Sam's school pick up her daughter, whom she had adopted from China. I sat in my car and watched that little girl leap into her mother's arms and I drove home and emailed that woman. As it turned out, she lived two blocks away from us. "Come over for coffee," she said, "I'll tell you all about it."

Walking home from her house, Lorne squeezed my hand. "Let's start," he said.

Within a week we were sitting in a crowded room in an adoption agency in Boston, signing papers, collecting information, beginning the journey that would lead us to China and a baby girl.

I spent the month of April 2004, filling out paperwork for the adoption. It was exactly two years since Grace had died. We collected legal documents—birth certificates and marriage certificates and divorce decrees from our earlier marriages. We got fingerprinted and checked out for criminal records. Friends wrote recommendations, attesting to the strength of our family, our marriage, our stability. A social worker came to our house three times, poking in our closets and interviewing all of us, even 9-year-old Sam. Yet this process was the calmest, most focused thing I had done in two years. I had a purpose and I moved toward it with a doggedness I had forgotten I possessed.

What I didn't know was that while I filled out papers in triplicate and made appointments and arranged for a home study, a woman in Hunan, China, was giving birth to a baby girl she could not keep. Over a hundred thousand baby girls are abandoned every year in China. Some place the number at even higher than that. In Hunan, as in other provinces, infanticide is not uncommon. Some women give birth with a bucket of water by their beds; if the baby is a girl, she is drowned. Other women walk for miles from their village to have their baby somewhere that no one knows them. Baby girls are left on footbridges and in parks, at police station doors and orphanage entrances. They are left where their mothers know they will be found. It is illegal to abandon a baby in China, so they are left with no notes or pertinent information. In Hunan, a family who has a girl is allowed to have a second child. But that second child has to be a boy. Therefore, most of the abandoned baby girls in Hunan are second or even third daughters.

Almost a year to the day after we began our adoption process, we were on a plane to China to pick up our daughter. Six months after we filed our documents with the Chinese government, our phone rang. "It's Stephanie from China Adoption with Love, and I'm looking at a picture of your daughter." Somehow, through all my tears, I heard the words *healthy* and *beautiful*. We begged for more information. The ride to the adoption agency in Boston was only an hour away, but we couldn't wait even that long for news of this baby. Her Chinese name was Lou Fu Jing: Lou was the last name given to all the babies in her orphanage, which was in the city of Loudi; Fu was the name given to all the babies in her orphanage because it meant luck and it was given to counter their bad luck; Jing was the name the orphanage gave her—bright. She lights up a room, someone wrote on her referral papers.

The name we gave her was Annabelle, Grace's middle name. We had briefly chosen Mamie, and Daisy, and argued over Talullah. But we loved the name Annabelle, and we had loved it enough to almost give it to Grace as her first name. It honored Grace, we decided, without burdening the new baby.

Annabelle had been found in a box at the orphanage door, early in the morning of September 6, 2004. They estimated her age as five months. Most of the babies found abandoned are under two weeks old. Many of them still have their umbilical cord stump. No one will ever know what led Annabelle's mother to leave her there after five months. Perhaps she had not wanted to give her up at all. Perhaps a male relative waited until the baby was not nursing as much as a newborn does and then took her from her mother. Perhaps they tried to hide her in the system—a forbidden second or third daughter—and were caught. The penalties for this are huge, often involving many years' salary or loss of medical care for the entire family. Perhaps her mother died. Perhaps her mother got pregnant again and hoped for a boy.

We will never know what led to Annabelle being dressed in blue pants, white socks with blue flowers, a thin coat, being put into a cardboard box in a city that was most likely not her own. Around Loudi, there are dusty roads and fields of kale and sweet potatoes. Women walk with bamboo poles across their backs, one head of kale or a sweet potato in the baskets at the ends. They take this meager yield to a market miles away to sell. It is not green or beautiful there. No mountains or sea, no glittering architecture. It is not the China in glossy magazines. It is poor and rural and the women there sometimes abandon their baby girls rather than drown them.

We will never know Annabelle's story. We only know this: the date they gave her as her birthday—determined by the age they guessed her to be on September 6, 2004; chosen as an even number because even numbers are lucky—that birthday is April 18, the same day that Grace died. Annabelle, like me, was born in the year of the monkey. Monkeys are intelligent and are known to have a great sense of humor. Monkeys and rats are said to be the best of friends.

Annabelle arrived home on April 6, 2005. It was the year of the rooster. In Chinese astrology, there is improvement in difficult situations during rooster years. They are a time to seek emotional solace. One of the hexagrams of the I Ching that symbolizes the middle third of a rooster year—the time when Mother's Day falls—is the image of a small trickle of water flowing from a rock as a container below it slowly begins to fill. It is called, "The humble power of the smallest."

"They mark them, you know," someone told us before we left for China. "The mothers brand the babies they abandon. It's a sign of love."

We had heard stories about babies being found with a yam, a sign of how valuable the baby was. We had heard of a note left that simply said: "This is my baby. Take care of her." We had heard of one baby found with a bracelet around her wrist, and another with a river rock to indicate she was from a town near water. But this branding was something new.

The group of ten families with which we traveled to China, all got our babies at the same time, in a nondescript city building in Changsha. Changsha is the capital of Hunan Province, and it is four hours from Loudi and the orphanage. We were shuffled into a waiting room where we could see, in the hallways outside, dozens of babies on their way to meet their new families. A group ahead of us, babies in their arms, walked past. A new group arrived and were led to another waiting room. There was a lot of noise and then more babies appeared. "That's Annabelle!" I said, as a woman holding a confused baby wearing threadbare purple feetie pajamas rushed past. Others in our group spotted their daughters, too, and soon we were running out of that room after our babies. We followed everyone into a conference room, and suddenly our names were called and our babies were in our arms. Ten minutes later, crying and stunned, we were back on the bus with our new daughters. Soon, people were lifting pant legs or the cuffs of sleeves to show the small scars on their babies. "They mark them," one mother said, spreading her new daughter's fingers to reveal a scar in between the index and middle fingers.

On Annabelle's neck I found a thick rope of scar tissue, round and small. Later the pediatrician examined it and frowned. "Don't get upset," he said, "but this almost looks like a burn that has healed."

A month after Grace died, I had my first Mother's Day without my daughter. Sam and Lorne carved a heart out of wood, sanding it smooth as if they could ease the pain in my own heart this way. They threaded the wooden heart on a dark red ribbon, and it still hangs from the rearview mirror of my car. Lorne also gave me a book he made, with pictures of Grace and descriptions beneath them of what Grace and I had done together: cooking, reading, laughing, walking hand in hand. It was the worst Mother's Day I could imagine. Here was Sam, my son, offering me a heart. And here was the empty chair, the silence, my own heart, broken.

Each subsequent Mother's Day brought new pain—the passing of time without watching Grace grow up, the burst of spring blossoms in our garden mocking my loss. I was a daughterless mother. I had nowhere to put the things a mother places on her daughter. The nail polish I used to paint our toenails hardened. Our favorite videos gathered dust. Her small apron was in a box in the attic. Her shoes—the sparkly ones, the leopard rainboots, the ballet slippers—stood in a corner. I kept her hairbrush on a shelf in my closet; the fine strands of her pale blond hair were still tangled in it. As I walked out the door, I still sometimes paused to bury my nose in her powder-blue jacket, as if I might find something of her there.

Three Mother's Days later, I am sitting in my kitchen singing to Annabelle. It is raining, and I am singing the old Lovin' Spoonful song, *You and Me and Rain on the Roof*. I am singing to Annabelle and she is grinning at me, a big toothless grin. When Annabelle laughs, my heart soars. When she presses her hand into mine, or rests her head against my chest, or falls asleep in my arms, I feel myself slowly, slowly coming back to life.

Sometimes I touch that small round scar on her neck and I wonder about the woman who might have put it there. I wonder if she walked down those dusty roads I saw in China, past the endless fields of kale, cradling her daughter in her arms. I wonder if she cried when she placed her in that small box. I wonder what words she might have whispered to her.

On Mother's Day now, each year, I think about Grace. And I think about this woman I will never know. I, of course, thank her—and I praise her strength in doing this seemingly impossible thing: giving her daughter to me. She will never know that I have her daughter because I lost Grace. She will never know the road I traveled to get her.

Annabelle lifts her arms to me, and I pick her up.

"Mama," she whispers.

"Daughter," I whisper back.

DONATION

by Ashley Talley

MY MOTHER AND I have been speaking in numbers.

We know that HCG levels determine pregnancy. In the beginning, 50 is good. A reading above 25 makes you a mother, but below 5, you are not. After three weeks, you should reach 1,000. When your HCG level is 1,000 early on, you can picture your wide, white-mooned stomach. You can buy pants with elastic ovals in front from the maternity store at the mall and maybe stick a few paint swatches with names like cherub pink and mountain bluebell in your purse. When you have a 1,000, you are winning.

Fifteen is not good when you are hoping for 100 and picking out names. Low HCG numbers make you cry. Low HCG numbers make you wonder if you did something wrong in your life, if somewhere along the way you failed a test you didn't know you were taking. Fifteen is nowhere. With 85, or even 70, possibility exists, but at 15, your arms are still empty.

We have become mathematicians, scientists, and experts on the percentages of possibility: fertility rates, hormonal drugs, eggs, sperm, cycles. Before, we knew that the first baby created through in vitro fertilization was born in 1978 only because we remembered it from *Jeopardy*. But now we spit out facts like: 1984—birth year of the first baby resulting from egg transfer. 40,000—the estimated number of children born through assisted reproductive therapy last year; or 15,000—the dollars my mother and her husband spend on each round of fertility treatment.

My mother is forty-seven. She has been pregnant five times in her life, but I am an only child and, ironically, the result of the only pregnancy she didn't plan. After finding out she was going to have a baby as a 20-year-old junior in college, she chose to postpone graduation and marry my father, a fun-loving, football-playing frat boy. Three years, one child, and one miscarriage later, they went through a mostly amicable divorce, and Mama devoted the next fifteen years of her life to me. Our world never seemed small nor our lives unfulfilled, and I understood the word "family" to mean a planet of two people, a woman and a girl, who didn't need the orbits of second husbands or distant relatives, and certainly not of other children, to make it spin happily through the universe. Though she dated very little during my childhood, I never heard Mama mention being lonely.

When I left for college, she began a tumultuous relationship with Forrest, a man I met before she did through the martial arts classes we both took at our small town's karate studio. He was an artist twelve years younger than her, blond and sweet-faced, closer to my age than my mother's. A mutual friend, also in that karate class, introduced them at the gym, and they fell in love slowly, over old movies and gourmet meals. From the beginning, I knew he was a complicated person, introverted yet friendly, passionate yet occasionally passive. Though I didn't really come to know him then, and perhaps don't even now, I could tell that he was good and he was kind. Though the next few years of the relationship's turmoil often challenged that estimation of his character, I trusted and believed in those two qualities completely.

When my mother loves, she loves hard, and the first time that Forrest broke up with her, she became a depressed and despondent woman I didn't recognize. During the subsequent breakups, I helped her sweep the shattered pieces of herself into piles she could reconstruct later, but every time she seemed mended or nearly happy, Forrest came back into her life and the cycle began again. Finally, after five years and a thousand ups and downs, he said to her the words she had wanted to hear all her life. "I love you. I want you to be my wife and the mother of my children." And with this definitive declaration, that on-again, off-again relationship turned into the most stable and happy of marriages, missing only one aspect to make it complete for my mother: a child.

Mama is one for five in her attempts to have a baby. That's a 20 percent success rate, only marginally lower than the 26 percent of couples who have a child through in vitro fertilization, which was the first infertility treatment she and my stepfather tried. Since that initial attempt, they have moved on to assisted reproductive technology and egg donation, which have significantly higher success rates. In what now seems a strange and complicated twist of events, my eggs were the first my mother used to chemically conceive.

Lately, Mama begins phone conversations with news like, "You know Courtney Cox is pregnant, right? She's thirty-nine. Julia Roberts is pregnant again, too, and John Edwards's wife had a baby at fifty. And I heard the other day that Geena Davis got pregnant at forty-eight. And she had twins!" I don't think my mother ever thought very much about any sort of biological expiration date until she met and fell in love with Forrest. But now I imagine she must feel possibility moving further from her reach with every passing second.

My mother is the person I'm closest to in the world, but our lives have often moved in opposition to one another. The more she trusts her choices, the less I seem able to believe in my own. Just as her life was falling into place—an engagement, a beautiful new Victorian home, an unexpected but hoped-for pregnancy—mine seemed to be falling apart. I realize now I resented her and Forrest for the hands they held in public and the private way she whispered to him during a play or church service. Love notes meant for his lunch bag ended up on the kitchen table, and the boxer shorts and lacy bras that appeared in our shared laundry annoyed and embarrassed me. Mama got pregnant naturally at the age of forty-three, a few months before the huge June wedding she and Forrest had planned for three hundred guests. Still bearing a certain amount of Southern Baptist guilt and fearing the months counted backward by their friends and very traditional family, they were married secretly and quietly by Mama's best friend's father, a judge who was the first person outside of my family to hold me after my birth.

I was in New York for the weekend of the ceremony and didn't know about it until afterward. Mama swears she told me and that I chose not to change my travel plans. "You said you already had your plane ticket," she tells me when I ask her about it. "Of course I told you Mr. Slayton was going to marry us that weekend, but you said you already had your ticket. I would never have kept something like that from you."

I have no recollection of learning of the ceremony, but by now, Mama and I realize that many of our memories are murky and convoluted, distorted to suit the way things turned out. But I do remember the annoyance and detachment I felt toward her and Forrest's relationship, and it's possible I could have been so blasé toward this incredibly important event in my mother's life that I chose not to cancel my unexceptional weekend plans.

In any case, a few months after that quiet March ceremony, Mama had a miscarriage, and she walked down the center aisle of the church on the arm of her father, beautiful, happy, and a little desperate, for what she's told me, "You'll understand when you meet someone you really love. You'll want to create life with them."

definition of love

At that point, my life seemed far from any understanding of love, and miles from the idea of procreation. After my college graduation and a stint as an editorial intern with a travel magazine, I moved back to our small town, ostensibly to teach ninth-grade English at the high school I attended and where my mother still taught—but mostly to move in with my boyfriend, a beautiful anomaly of a man whom I never really understood. Forrest and Sean could not have been more different. Where my boyfriend was strong in will, my stepfather was strong in heart, and each had faults the other one lacked. My mother was always wary of Sean's charm.

He was a college dropout who regularly beat me at Trivial Pursuit, a former model who had become a roofer. He read philosophy books for hours before meeting me at bars for tequila shots and dancing, where he bought beers and told jokes to men whose faces he would later shatter in the parking lot over imagined or exaggerated insults. Though he lacked much softness, I appreciated his intensity, intelligence, and passion. But after we moved in together—a step my mother warned me against—those tequila shots turned into Budweisers before noon and the Nietzsche tomes became heavy objects thrown angrily against a wall. By the time I acknowledged the alcoholism, drug use, unfaithfulness, and emotional abuse, things were broken that could not be fixed, and I realized he was not someone with whom—in my mother's measure of real love—I could ever create a life.

When the world came crashing down on me late one night in early July, my mother was on a belated honeymoon, and it was my father, in town for Independence Day, who saw the bruises at my throat and wrist and went with me to gather my belongings from the house I shared with Sean. I went to Mama's house that morning to be alone; the rooms were quiet and empty, with the gray light of dawn filtering through the curtains. I called the house where she and Forrest were vacationing, but when she answered, I hung up quickly and hiccupped short breaths between sobs. When I called back hours later, I was calmer and I explained what had happened.

"Well, we'll come home," she said, and even in her thick, sleep-filled voice, I noticed her "I" was already firmly a "we."

"No," I said. "It's fine. I'm okay." My voice maintained a calm I didn't feel.

"We can pack up right now and be there in five hours," she offered repeatedly.

But I found myself unwilling to express to her the terror of the situation I'd just experienced or to even show her the desperation and loneliness I was feeling in those moments. "No, I'm fine. Enjoy the rest of your honeymoon," I told her, getting off the phone quickly. I was angry at my mother for not being there exactly when I needed her most, and I wouldn't share this grief with her. I wouldn't even show her the injuries.

Like the long sleeves I wore for weeks, the faces I put on that summer were meant to hide or distract from the reality of my life. If my mother laughed at a family dinner, I turned away and gazed to the floor stonily, and if she tried to have a serious conversation with me, I smiled at her gravity and walked away. "Whatever, Mom," I said, using a nomenclature I knew she didn't like and rolling my eyes like a 13-year-old brat. "Just chill out." I kept the emotions I was feeling as carefully hidden as the rough scabs and fading bruises on my skin.

I turned away from Mama as I never had before or have since. I felt she had taken away my family, that small orbit that before had meant mother and daughter, and I accused her of callousness, selfishness, and inconsideration of my feelings. I would not accept or even try to understand the shifting groundwork in this woman who had always been my stability and my home. I was floating through my own world, untethered and scared, and though she had supported me through four years at Brown, six months in Europe, and another five in Alabama, she seemed to have let go. She could not hold me, or would not. The strength of connection that had always bound us, perhaps since it was a physical cord umbilically attached from her body to mine, seemed to have disappeared, and I felt its absence as absolutely as an amputation.

I moved to Philadelphia with my best friend, and stayed at another girlfriend's house when I visited home. We still talked nearly every day, though I kept my half of the conversation mostly surface. "Work's fine. Yeah, we saw a movie tonight. I don't know when I'm off for Christmas. How is everybody? Great." But after long, strained months during which she tried to reconnect with me, my iciness slowly melted, and I went to her, as I always have, with my questions and fears. Things returned to normal between Mama, Forrest, and me—or perhaps life just settled into what it would become. I knew that, above all else, my mother still wanted to conceive a child with her husband, and they were already in touch with the Duke Fertility Center by the end of that year, 2003.

Oddly, neither my mother nor I can quite remember when I became involved in her quest for a baby. Mama locates the conversation during the brief time I lived in Philadelphia, perhaps over the weekend that she, Forrest, and some other family members came up to see me in a production of *Steel Magnolias*, where I played Annelle, the devout Christian hairdresser portrayed by Darryl Hannah in the movie. In the final act, after a quick change when the stagehands stuffed a large pillow under my dress, I walked on stage nine months pregnant, pushing at my lower back and softly rubbing my stomach, the way every movie-mother-to-be does. My family laughed and clapped at my performance, but I recognized the falseness and absurdity of the situation. My mother desperately wanted that swollen thrill of pregnancy I was portraying onstage, but my own life, so unsettled and nomadic, was far from its actuality. I felt like a girl playing a woman, a daughter pretending to be a mother.

Mama says my role in her attempt at pregnancy arose not long after that performance, but my most vivid memory of it is a few months later over scratchy phone lines between Southeast Asia and her house in southern Virginia. After saving up money from my office job in Philadelphia, I moved to Kuala Lumpur, Malaysia, in January of 2004 to live with my aunt and uncle. I spent the next months exploring the region and managed calls home every week or two. But still, neither Mama nor I is certain who first brought up the idea. Neither of us seems willing now to claim its instigation; this ambiguity lends a sense of inevitability to the situation.

Her older sister wasn't able to have children, and Mama always said she'd be willing to be a surrogate if Gwen wanted her to. Perhaps it was during one of these discussions that the topic of donation was first broached. "Well, could Gwen donate eggs to you guys, or is that not how it works?" I asked uncertainly.

"No. Women over forty have something like twenty-five percent of the chance of having healthy, viable eggs as women in their thirties, and I think it goes down about the same into the twenties. Most egg donors are in college, I think."

"Yeah, I remember those weird ads in the college newspaper offering thousands of dollars for eggs. It's so strange." The phone line, so many thousands of miles long, was silent; it seemed wrong to attach monetary value to this life my mother wanted so badly to create. "Well, Mom," I said, "I'm only twenty-four. I mean I could do it if you guys needed someone."

There must have been a pause there; long, breathy seconds when we both adjusted to the idea and the choices it would involve. I pictured Mama's face and Forrest's and my own. I thought of a puzzle with pieces that necessarily overlapped to form the right picture. Ideas of heroism or altruism or redemption passed through me but never settled into reasons or motivations I could clearly say. But during those long moments, everything seemed to settle in, rightly, between us, and the strange construction of this new idea came to me to feel something like another type of cord— a link not just between me, my mother, and this unformed child, but also between the person I had been and the person I could be. The baby, the girl, the daughter, the sister, and the mother. I can't say exactly what

Mama thought of the plan, though we agree neither of us questioned its plausibility.

For weeks after that, as Mama and Forrest continued to make plans with Duke's fertility specialists, there was a repetition of variants on the same conversation. "Are you sure, Ashley?" she would ask over and over. "Because you don't have to. I don't want to put any pressure on you." I remember short, weighty pauses, when I ran my fingernails along the creases in the dark wooden floors of my aunt's house. It was still so outrageous an idea, particularly from our distance apart, almost directly across the world from one another, that I didn't really know what to say.

Because then, and even now sometimes, the whole thing seemed like science fiction, a strange, futuristic plot twist dreamed up by Rod Serling. I was offering to donate eggs to my mother, which would then be injected with her husband's sperm and implanted in my mother. She would carry and deliver the child, and they would have a baby with the closest possible match to her own DNA. She would have her dream then—and her family—and perhaps then one of us would be tethered to something strong and rooted.

"No, Mom, I'm sure," I told her in different ways, again and again. "I wouldn't have offered if I didn't mean it. I don't have to do much, right? It's just…I mean it's just like some shots and a short…procedure, right?" My vocabulary didn't include a lexicon with which to talk about these events, and neither did my emotions. I could only express things in the negative: "No, I'm not scared, I'm not unsure, I'm not nervous. I don't think I'll feel weird or care later or have issues. No, I don't want you to use someone you don't know." I found it difficult to define the reasons behind my choice, and without this vocabulary it was hard to reassure Mama of my certainty.

I didn't know how to say it, but some small, locked part of myself was sure the decision was right. I wanted to offer this gift to my mother and her husband; this tangible chance at life was certainly the ultimate present. I like to give thoughtful gifts—I've knitted scarves, arranged weekend getaways, handpainted wineglasses for Christmas presents—but I sometimes wonder if my offerings are more selfish than altruistic. I wonder if I confuse gratitude with love or I desire recognition and affirmation of my goodness over real esteem. I continually seek approval, and in some ways, perhaps this procedure was to ensure that my mother, whose opinion has always mattered most, never doubted me and was always a little indebted to me.

Looking back now, I also wonder if my choice to donate eggs to my mother and stepfather had little to do with the conception of a child or the creation of a new family. That spring of 2004 I was living a life of flux. I seemed to be between so many things—jobs, relationships, homes—and I was looking for some footing or grounding in my life. I needed something to hold me somewhere and this process provided a connection not only to people, but to a place. To complete the donation project, I had to be within a few hours of Duke for the regular exams and procedures, and by living in my mother's house, I didn't have to pay rent or explain to a roommate what the vials in the refrigerator were for or why I stuck a needle into my stomach daily. For all my gypsy ambition, I realized I wanted to be needed—moving back home and helping my mother have a baby offered me a temporary purpose as I struggled to find my own.

One aspect of the project that preoccupied me from the beginning was the math and chemistry of the whole thing: if I'm half my mother and half my father, and if the baby is half my DNA and half Forrest's, then one fourth of the new life we're creating is chemically my father. I pictured my dad's loud, stubborn strength, his rollicking energy and raucous stories, and then I thought of my stepfather's deliberate way of going about the world, of his soft, cheerful voice and artist's hands. What sort of person, what face, would emerge from such strange roots? The branches of this family tree were tangled and complicated, and I've learned since then that many health systems don't allow daughter-to-mother donation because of such complexities. But as we navigated the twisted corridors of Duke Hospital on my first visit there, the situation didn't feel outlandish or wrong.

Mama and Forrest led me into the narrow, dim waiting room of the fertility center, and greeted Teresa, one of the head nurses, by name. I filled out long forms about my health and family history, and then we were taken into a small room with a table and four chairs. Dr. Price, an awkward but polite young physician, went over the basics of the process with us. I felt my mother glancing at me from time to time, trying to gauge my reaction to the information.

the science In his nasal southern accent, he explained the drugs we would be taking and their various effects in readying my mother's body for pregnancy, temporarily suppressing the functions of both our ovaries, and eventually, hyperstimulating the egg production in mine. He mentioned the single shot of HCG I would be given when an ultrasound showed I was ready, and he emphasized the importance of a strict schedule and timetable for administering the drugs. The normalcy with which he and his assistants treated and talked about these procedures reinforced my decision, and when Molly, a pretty young nurse whom we all liked, took us to another room to show us how to give ourselves the shots, we might have been in a cooking or yoga class for all the ease and humor involved in our lesson. As we stuck saline-filled syringes first in oranges, and then in the pinched-up skin of our stomachs, Mama said, "Maybe this is something you'd like to do. Something like Molly?" I had recently mentioned perhaps going back to school for medicine, and at that moment, with a future we thought would be filled by the miracles of science, working with infertile couples seemed a natural, suitable option.

"Yeah, maybe so," I answered, feeling the harmless liquid spread beneath my skin as I pressed the end of the syringe toward my body.

Over the next months, Mama and I made the hour-long trip to Durham several times a week, undergoing numerous physicals, blood tests, and ultrasounds. Egg donors normally go through a psychiatric evaluation with the hospital's clinical psychologist, but because I was not an anonymous donor and had discussed everything with my mother and stepfather, Dr. Price said we could forego that technicality.

One of the major decisions we were asked to make over the extended consultations with various experts was whether or not we would tell the child about its origin. After a lot of discussion during which we all tried to silently gauge what the other two were thinking, we decided that we wouldn't tell the child unless it—he, she, possibly they—found out on its own. In fact, we decided to tell no one about the procedure, which made for some interesting explanations to friends about the syringes in the backseat of my car. That choice felt right to me, though, because I did consider what we were producing as Mama and Forrest's child. "I'm not having the baby," I said on multiple occasions. "I'm just helping out with the biology." *→ physical, not emotional*

[margin note: privacy = child's shot @ normalcy]

The biology and chemistry turned out to be fairly complicated in itself, however. My mother and I became smart in ways never required by our literary occupations. We learned to say sub-q for shots given just under the skin, and IM for the intramuscular ones that had to be injected by another person. We understood that progesterone prepares the uterus for pregnancy, Lupron stops ovaries from producing eggs, and Follistim stimulates egg production. We knew that the single gonadotropin shot I took had to be perfectly placed because it cost over $2,000. Like Marines, we began to use acronyms with ease: IVF, ART, HCG numbers, and that awful bloated feeling of OHSS. We knew the value—monetary and emotional—of estrogen patches and alcohol swabs and needles and birth control pills and regulated cycles. We would have been brilliant addicts, had we been another type of women, knowing as we did the exact angle at which to inject ourselves and the softest part of the lower back to inject each other.

But, as with anything one does over and over, these once-foreign practices became part of our household routine. There was nothing unusual to walk in the kitchen and see my mother's pajama top pulled up and Forrest behind her, wincing more than she was, as he tried to give the IM shot where it would cause the least pain. In front of the refrigerator, I would quickly and painlessly jab in the syringe of hormones, just above the waistband of the black pants I wore to my waitressing job. It was nearly summer by then, and I was determined not to let what was happening at home affect the rhythm of my life. I still went out drinking with my friends after work and lay by the pool, slightly swollen in my bikini from the daily injections of Follistim. Though I wasn't seriously dating anyone, I knew that I couldn't have sex until after the retrieval since I was off birth control and extremely fertile—we hoped.

When an ultrasound showed that my eggs were numerous and ready, they set a morning in late May for the retrieval—a procedure during which the eggs are extracted through a long needle that is inserted into the follicles of the ovaries. I don't remember much of the experience, especially after the IV was in my arm and anesthesia fogged my consciousness. I know I was ready for it though, after feeling discombobulated, swollen, and slightly crazy for several months. I was ready to regain my own balance. Since beginning the donation process, my moods had been erratic and I was easily irritated. I had also stopped taking the antidepressants that had helped me through the previous months, and the more time went by, the more stirrings of that old resentment toward my mother and her new life began to reappear. Again, I felt myself untethered, without a real home, now with a body and temperament I couldn't predict. By the day of the retrieval, I was ready to be done.

The last thing I remember before totally going under was holding my mother's hand and crying. I couldn't tell her then why I was crying, and even now, I don't have words for the emotion. I am the sort of woman who cries at movies and weddings, on tragic occasions and beautiful, moving ones, too. But the tears that day were not from any feeling I could pinpoint or name. Perhaps, in my drug-induced state, I saw the lengths I would go to for gratitude and reassurance. Maybe I pictured a tiny face with tiny lips that did not call for me. Maybe I was happy for Mama, or relieved for myself, or scared of the way life would be from now on. But I honestly cannot translate those tears into something explicable and relatable. I was just holding my mother's hand and crying.

I remember nothing of the procedure itself, though it is supposedly very painful if the anesthesia wears off. The nurses gave me pills for any residual pain, and I slept in the backseat on the way home. I had arranged to meet an old friend from college in Baltimore for a baseball game the same afternoon, and I wouldn't let the idea go, even after my mother's worried cautions. The retrieval had been successful, yielding twelve or fifteen eggs, and Mama and Forrest, tentative and thankful, gave me their car and gas money for the six-hour drive.

"You know how much this means to me, don't you?" she asked me, tightly holding my body against hers before I left. "You know how much we appreciate all you've done for us." There were tears in her voice, but all I did was nod, get in the car, and drive away.

I shouldn't have gone. I was bloated, chock-full of hormones, and I think I yelled at Andres more than I spoke to him. We were walking along the Inner Harbor toward Camden Yards when, after another irrational outburst, I finally explained what had happened that morning. He stopped me on the sidewalk. "Wait, wait, what? You did what? Is that why you've been so weird for the past couple months?"

"I haven't been weird. I just haven't been able to tell you—or almost anyone—what's been going on, so I sort of feel like I've been leading this double life," I said. "But I'm really glad I did it," I told him when he pressed me about my feelings toward the situation. "I was happy to be able to help them, and it didn't really affect me that much. I mean, I'm glad I did it, but I'm glad it's over too." As before, I couldn't tell him exactly why I had chosen to donate my eggs, but I assured him over and over that I knew it was a good decision.

After hours of Darvocets and driving, I nearly got sick that night on the way to Georgetown, but something drove me to continue the weekend trip we had planned. I needed to assert my independence from the situation my mother, her husband, and I had just gone through; I needed to step away and let the rest happen to them and not to me. I was happy about what I had offered Mama and Forrest, proud that I could help them gain something so monumental, but now I needed the story to be their own. I wanted my involvement to be over and my life to go back to normal. I was ready to wholeheartedly take on the role of daughter, and leave that strange, murky question of "mother" far behind.

complex emotions developed

I was traveling again a few weeks after the successful fertilization and implanting of several eggs. I was heading south this time when Mama called me crying. She tried to talk but quickly handed the phone to Forrest.

"Hey, Ashley," he said in a voice I've never heard rise above calm. "Teresa just called and the pregnancy test came back."

He was quiet for a second, but with Mama's reaction, I felt like I didn't even need to ask the question. "And, well, it's complicated you know, like all this stuff is. She's technically pregnant, but the HCG numbers are really low, and they think it's just a chemical pregnancy."

I sighed slowly and said, "Well, there are still some frozen eggs, right? So they can use those, right, and try again?"

"Yeah, yeah. I'm not sure when that will be, but we're not giving up!" His optimism tried desperately to crawl over my mother's tears, and I guess he mostly succeeded because when she called me back a few hours later, her voice was clear and stable.

"I guess it's not true what they say, is it? 'You're either pregnant or you're not.'" She laughed and I tried to join her. "There is an in-between!"

That fall, I moved to coastal North Carolina and began graduate school. In September, Mama and Forrest used the final three fertilized eggs from me that had been frozen earlier in the spring. They waited tentatively for the numbers again and were finally sure enough to call and tell me they were pregnant. A few months went by, hopeful and thankfully uneventful, until I was eventually ready to believe it myself. We were all so happy through Thanksgiving and early December, and they planned a special Christmas Eve dinner to tell their parents. Envelopes addressed to Grandma and Grandpa waited on their fine china with tiny ultrasound pictures inside. While Mama and Forrest clutched each other's hands and I stood in the doorway with my best friend, our family opened their cards and various animal-like shrieks erupted after a few minutes of confused silence.

"Look at that!" Forrest's mother shouted to his father. "That's my grandchild! My first grandchild. Look at that!"

As they moved around the table, hugging and congratulating one another, I turned to my friend and asked her which bar she wanted to go to that night. When my grandmother came over and put her arm around me, she asked, "And how do you feel about being a big sister for the first time?"

I shrugged off her embrace, smiled widely without teeth, and said something noncommittal. "Yeah, that's crazy isn't it?" I grabbed my coat and bag, refusing the bread pudding and coffee Mama was offering, and my friend and I left for Hill's Tavern. No one else knew of my involvement in the pregnancy and, walking away again, I tried to deny the connection, too. A part of me wondered if all the years ahead would be like this. Was my place in this new life and new family that of a bystander? Would I always be on the fringes now, a shadow in the doorway, waiting to leave? How would this child consider me as it grew? Was it simply biology I had helped my mother with, as I assured her? My knowledge of the truth behind this new baby rendered the whole celebration absurd and a little heartbreaking, but I hoped I was the only one who felt that way.

Three days later, Mama had a miscarriage. She cried on the couch for several days, and I sat in the chair beside her, feeling weird, guilty, sad, and, in a small way, relieved. It was not a person I had known or a life I had felt, though technically, perhaps, it should have been. I did not know how to grieve for a death that was not quite death, from a life that was not quite life. I didn't know where to put the child in my own story—and so I stepped away and tried to distance myself from what I could not talk about or understand.

To me, it felt like both a failure and a victory. I felt responsible, in an irrational way, for the failure of the pregnancy, as though my eggs weren't quite good enough to survive. Perhaps it was one too many glasses of wine, I thought, or the cigarettes I still smoked sporadically that killed this thing that would have been a person. In another way, though, a piece of me was glad that we would not have to deal with the questions and complications that would inevitably arise as the child grew up. We would never have to consider what the words "mother," "daughter," and "sister" actually meant in relation to us.

But the feeling that I had let Mama and Forrest down, that I had failed in a very basic way, overrode my relief, and after a few months we agreed to begin the process all over again. During the spring of 2005, I began the drug cycles once more and made the two-hour drive north to Duke several times. On one of those visits, I was asked to sit down and talk with Julia, a vibrant, friendly psychologist employed by the Fertility Center. She was surprised that I hadn't had to go through the battery of tests on our first go-round, and she insisted that it was necessary this time.

Julia was young and earnest, and after I went through a basic series of psychological and personality tests, we sat in an office and chatted like friends. I was lulled into the conversation, never thinking that it was anything more than a formality. She was particularly interested in my history of depression—"Just situational," I said, waving it away. "I'm fine now."—and in that moment right before the last retrieval when I had cried without explanation. I thought I came across calm, informed, and sure of the choice I had made and was making again, so when Julia told Dr. Price that she could not, in good conscience, allow me to donate eggs, I was stunned and irate. I felt that I had been duped and betrayed by this woman, and my anger was so potent I wrote a letter the next day to the head of the Center, complaining about her overly easy manner and what I judged to be her gentle manipulation and unwarranted duplicity.

Looking back, I realize that my anger was mostly misguided. I was mad that this choice I had made, willingly and with open eyes, was being taken away from me by a person who had no real relationship to the situation. She removed my role in Mama's quest, effectively severing my connection to the new family my mother was working to create. But really, why should I have had such a direct part in it? I'm sure I knew deep down that Julia was right to stop the donation process, but I resented the confiscation of my choice in the situation. I wanted the right to give this gift to my mother and to be a part of the transformation of my family. But this was a new family, and I did not need to help create it to remain a part of it. I never fully considered the weight my decision might come to bear upon myself, my family, and the new life we were trying so hard to produce, and I understand now it was the choice I didn't make, couldn't make, that was ultimately the right one.

I recently found a journal from the time of the donation process and came across this paragraph: "I find myself unwilling to analyze my situation too much—unwilling to make any sort of actual decision about how I feel, but I guess that's okay—that's how life happens, right? Without our careful orchestration, without even our vaguest say-so." I agree with this past self, I think. Often it's not the choices we make but the events we cannot control that determine the course of our futures. I like to believe I have power over my life and its paths, but I know that sometimes you need to close your eyes, throw up your hands, and take what comes. And that's a choice, too.

Two years after my last visit to the fertility clinic, my involvement in Mama's effort to get pregnant has ended, but she and Forrest are still trying. They have reached their final attempt now, having maxed out credit cards, borrowed from her parents, and taken out a second mortgage on their house. They are using eggs from a donor they will never meet, and they still give shots, take pills, and visit Duke with methodical regularity. Mama is positive when she talks about it even now, sure somehow, that if you want something badly enough, if you make choices and sacrifices to get it, then it will become something you can hold.

SUMMER, 1959

by Carolyn Ferrell

MY MOTHER AND HER SISTER push the old green VW Beetle from the shed down the cobblestone drive. This is their chance to escape the drudgery of Mutti's home, the endless polishing of wood and washing of wool and cooking of dust. The sun is high and behind them, the house stands empty. Maike, newly out of the *Pedagogische Hochshule*, wears a pantsuit and sandals; my mother wears a dress, a gift from Maike, one of the first store-bought outfits she has ever owned. (*You can have this and more, if you work hard enough!* Maike promised, as my mother modeled the butter-yellow shift in the mirror at *Karstadt*.) The women maneuver the car into the street while clouds overhead drift smoothly out toward the Baltic. Though this is midsummer, the air reels with autumn crispness. The engine refuses to start, and so the women get back out and push the VW toward the street's decline. There is something inelegant about this labor, but my mother and her sister don't care. They don't care how they look or what the neighbors think, most of whom have always been deeply suspicious of Mutti's daughters. *They* know that the neighbors know that Mutti doesn't approve of this VW (she often calls it a piece of junk while chatting in the garden with Frau Mortorf). But what does that matter? Maike drives it with obvious pride. Mutti herself drives a used Karmann Ghia, a reckless piece of car that barely gets her to and from the center of the Heikendorf, where she teaches elementary school. She earned that Karmann Ghia, just as Maike earned the VW—but there is something awful, of course, about a daughter claiming the prize in much less time than it took the mother. (*Will Maike and Elke ever know what a struggle my life was?* Mutti asks Frau Mortof as they shake their heads in the twilight.)

At the decline, my mother and Maike give the VW a final push, jump back in, and descend the hill. Frau Mortorf opens her curtains and shakes her head. Look at that—the one girl merely seventeen and her sister no more than twenty-two, and a teacher at that! The height of *Unverschaemtheit!*

My mother and Maike wave to Frau Mortorf's window as their car zips by, its motor finally engaged! *Auf wiedersehen, Frau Mortorf!*

They brake at the bottom of the hill to embrace each other and apply lipstick in the rearview mirror. They can't stop laughing. After a minute or so they drive off. My mother and her sister have to make good time if they want to make the festival at Flensburg, which will be starting in a matter of hours.

* * *

Long Island,
November 2006

This was in the late 1950s. I was a student at the Pedagogic College where they trained teachers. To be honest, I was pretty mediocre. My teachers often let me slide when I mentioned that Maike Schmidt was my sister. She was the shining star; the teachers expected me to do well because of her. And I did do well in Germanistik. But basically I slid.

Maike had received her degree and was already teaching in a school. She was not married. My sister was not like other women. Germany in the 1950s, you have to understand.

I wanted to quit school. I wanted a job. I wanted to move out so badly. My parents had just gotten a divorce and Mutti used me as a sounding board. She complained all the time about Papa and his women—I couldn't take it.

I came out of a generation where there were no choices for women. There were no choices for girls. I wanted to work. I wanted to have my own money. There weren't even choices for boys. My brother, the highest in his class, was taken out of school to work on the farm. He did all the work Maike had done as a young girl.

After the war, we had mostly food from the farm, but not much. We owned no clothes except that which we sewed. Our sewing was lousy. The seams in our dresses were all off.

Back on the farm refugees sometimes showed up at our door, begging for something to eat. Sometimes a small group of Jewish girls would appear at the door and simply sing for food. They wouldn't say a word, they would just stand in front of you and sing together for something to eat.

There was always hunger, deprivation. Old men like my father singing American pop songs only using Nazi words instead of the English lyrics. People all around saying: Why can't we just forget?

After she divorced Papa, Mutti moved us all to Heikendorf. A small brick house. She moved the kitchen into the basement because she needed the space for six children. She did that by herself.

I was never good in school. But she insisted.

But then, in the summer of 1959, I met an American G.I. and we began writing letters to each other.

Mutti at first knew nothing.

* * *

In the 1950s, everyone was a hitchhiker. My mother's two sisters traveled across the continent using only their thumbs: Switzerland, France, Italy. Now that Maike has the VW, she and my mother can travel in style.

One hour after they depart the sleepy village, the women take a detour through the streets of nearby Kiel—a foolish thing, considering how expensive gasoline has become. They have been through these streets dozens of times—ever since Mutti moved them to the small brick house in Heikendorf from the large farm in Muessen (which, to her chagrin, Papa had gambled away). For my mother and her sister, there is nothing like the freedom of Kiel, especially on a day like today, when something indefinable is in the air. The trip is an extravagance; it will now cost Maike and Elke their lunch money.

But what does it matter? They are free. They *will* make it to Flensburg.

Sometime later—after more singing and laughing and getting lost— they stop the car outside of Rendsburg; Maike jumps out to use the bushes for a bathroom. At first they think they are alone on this stretch of highway, but then my mother notices a tall dark hitchhiker standing off to the side, under a large road sign which shades him almost completely. My mother honks the horn. Maike, laughing in embarrassment, runs back to the car while adjusting her pants (and new girdle underneath). Behind her, fields of yellow flowers, *Rapsfelder*, bend in the roadside breeze. The hitchhiker emerges from the shadow and smiles. The women see he is black.

But his face is *so* sympathetic. My mother goes for the lipstick.

The stranger waves awkwardly, then removes a military jacket from the duffel bag slung across his shoulders.

So, Maike says thoughtfully. An American soldier.

But a handsome one at that, my mother adds, rolling down the window.

* * *

You have to understand. I was ambivalent for so long—I had such mixed feelings. There was no one thing. Finally I just up and ran away to the airport. While I was there I sent Mutti a postcard telling her how sorry I was. My handwriting was a mess. A woman befriended me, took me to the jet. And then a stewardess placed me in my seat. I couldn't stop crying. But in spite of that, all the time I was thinking: what would my friends say if they could see me now?

After Mutti discovered the letters I had been receiving from Bob, she went down to the Post and insisted they not give me my mail anymore, which they did. I realized I would have to get Bob to send his letters to my friends. So they got his letters and passed them on to me, but Mutti found out about that as well. My friends left me in the lurch.

I used to call him collect. Before Mutti made that fuss at the Post, he used to send me letters with money—the first money I ever had. I bought a striped dress. I bought a pair of high-heeled shoes. I remember thinking: I never had high heels before.

I kept on spending the money he sent when in reality I was supposed to use it for a ticket. Finally he got mad and accused me of using him. But it was the first time I'd had any money. You have to understand.

I had to get away from Germany. We had no food in the house. I remembered when Bob and I met, how we wound up dancing at the music festival in Flensburg—it was heaven. There was no one thing that made me leave, only that I wanted more of that day in Flensburg.

After that festival, we wound up taking him with us to meet Mutti. She liked him well enough. Then he returned to his base and stayed about six more months in Germany. It was only after he returned to America that Mutti interfered with his letters to me. She stopped thinking of them as harmless.

I took the plane all by myself to America. He met me at the airport in New York. I remember thinking how disheveled he looked. He was tired. I'd been crying on the entire journey. His was a cool reception.

I remember thinking: but what of our letters? Nearly two years of letters, from Germany to America. There was so much romance. In them he said he couldn't live without me.

* * *

The soldier apologizes, telling them he knows it's unusual to pick up a complete stranger—back home he would never do such a thing—but would they consider taking him along? They don't know him from Adam, he admits, but really. He wouldn't hurt a fly.

My mother, fluttering, is unable to say a coherent word and simply holds the car door open for him.

They introduce themselves—another awkward moment—and immediately Maike starts the VW without any trouble.

My mother tries not to look at him, and he tries not to look at my mother. The trip to Flensburg goes by incredibly fast; the old car is on wings. The whole time, Maike is the only one talking, practicing English which she'd perfected from student trips to England. My mother, on the other hand, is embarrassed by her English and thus contents herself with stealing glances at the handsome soldier. *Why would he think they would be afraid of him? He looks as gentle as a lamb.*

They arrive at the festival by afternoon and park at a beach where musicians are busy setting up their equipment. A phonograph plays through ancient loudspeakers, Peter Alexander and his syrupy songs on eternal love; all around, young people mill about, distributing fliers and talking and smoking and singing. The air is warm. The soldier at once asks my mother to follow him down further along the beach, where they can be alone and maybe find a spot to dance. Maike laughs, a little out of jealousy, but urges my mother to go. The soldier promises to bring Maike back something to drink, a soda pop or something, whatever they drink over here in Germany. Maike grins dourly and waves them on.

My mother follows this handsome stranger along the crowded stretch of beach, where at every step, newer, flightier throngs of teen girls and boys dance and laugh and chuck the fliers to the ground. In the distance yachts glide through the harbor. Closer by, gulls dive in and out of garbage bins. Eventually the soldier finds a somewhat secluded dune—only one other couple there, lips to lips—and pulls my mother into a makeshift sort of dance.

(My mother wants to ask for a *limonade* but wonders if it is the right moment. With the music playing, his eyes sparkling. This is, after all, love at first sight.)

The soldier whispers in my mother's ear, tells her how lovely she looks, that she is the loveliest in all the land—he whispers under the drone of the loudspeakers, Peter Alexander crooning, "*Ich weiss, was Dir fehlt…*" the soldier's breath on my mother's cheek is like a miniature fire, a roasting anticipation of love, and just when my mother thinks she can handle no more, when she feels she is about to combust with happiness, the soldier steadies her with his hands, looks her in the eye and says, *All I'm doing is trying to find a way out.*

My mother nods, not understanding.

He is, of course, talking about the army, the subject foremost on his mind, but my mother can't really know that. She doesn't understand most of his words, though what she has comprehended thus far has electrified her. She wants to hear more—no one has ever told her that she was the loveliest of them all. *Ich weiss, was Dir fehlt*—my mother swoons to the music and to the eyes of the handsome soldier and suddenly loses track of the world—of Maike, of Flensburg, of Heikendorf, of Mutti. She wants to be a fairy tale for the rest of her life.

He whispers again, *I need a way out. That's all I'm fighting for.*

And my mother gazes dreamily into the eyes of this glorious stranger and sings along with the song on the loudspeaker: *I know what you are missing.*

* * *

*You have to remember. This was the fifties. Someone once said the word "orgasm"
in Mutti's presence and she went berserk. This, after having nine pregnancies.*

*Bob took me from the airport to a hotel in Brooklyn, a true fleabag hotel.
My first impression of America. When I pulled back the sheets, bedbugs scurried
everywhere. He left immediately for work, and I was alone. The subway was
next to our window. Everywhere you heard women and children screaming. We
stayed for a week. I was so lonely, I didn't dare venture out. I cried every day
out of loneliness. Soon I told him: we can't live like this.*

*We went to his mother's apartment in Brooklyn, which was stuffed with fur-
niture and roaches. She was married to Bill, a drunken philanderer. After each
of the births of my first three children—in 1962, 1963, and 1965—Bill found a
way to tell Bob that their skin was too light, that I must have had an affair. And
Bob actually asked me whether that was true.*

But when could I have found the time for an affair?

*After I arrived in America I was immediately pregnant. It was taken for
granted that we would have a family, though at first Bob didn't want to get married. He wanted to live together and raise children. He didn't consider marriage
necessary, but I insisted.*

*So. 1961. We rented an apartment on Avenue I. Roaches everywhere. We
had nothing, no furniture. Bob controlled all the money. What he liked to do, for
fun, to keep me from crying, was go for long drives. I always wanted to stop
somewhere and walk. But he never stopped.*

*Mutti's letters came all the time. I was so unhappy, I couldn't speak the lan-
guage, I had no one besides him. And he didn't want to hear about Mutti. All
that was left behind.*

*Going back to Germany was no longer an option. I told myself, I did this to
myself, I have to stick it out. I had fought for my freedom so ferociously. There
was no turning back. You have to understand. There really was no choice back
then.*

*I had given up opportunities—the Pedagogische Hochschule, the chance to
be a teacher like Maike. Having my own money. I was totally dependent on him,*

for everything. It was just like being in Germany with Mutti.

One day Bob said to me, "It's time for you to go to work." What do you mean? I asked. I have a home now, I can do whatever I want.

That's how I had always imagined it. That was what was always told to me: marriage, home, and children.

But soon Bob took me to fill out an application as a nurse's aide.

* * *

Dancing barefoot in the sand, my mother and father concentrate on the lovely racket of their own breathing. *Would they know, as evening slowly came on, as the wind picked up heft across the water, as some of the ships furled their sails in the purple dusk—would they know that I was not far away, following their every step?*

Before my mother left Germany, Mutti had warned her: if you ever have children, we won't acknowledge them. By "we" she meant herself, my mother's brothers, and my mother's father who, though not directly in the picture, nearly died when he learned that his favorite daughter had run away to be with a black man.

After my mother became a mother, Mutti would send endless reel-to-reel tapes to the apartment in Brooklyn and then to the house on Long Island. Every inch of her voice burst with the hard nails of her tears. Mutti would narrate her suffering in great detail, how there was nothing left for her to live for, how my mother had destroyed the hopes of the entire family. What had she worked all her life for, Mutti wailed into the tape, if all she got in return was a selfish, selfish daughter?

Would my parents know I was there already, on that day in Flensburg, looking back toward the future?

* * *

That first year, before you were born, was the worst.

* * *

Eighteen years later, in a mall parking lot in Massapequa, Long Island, in the middle of a pitiful afternoon, I'm supposed to be in love.

I'm sitting in the front seat of Rob Richman's souped-up Chevy, listening to his boyish tears, feeling guilt sweat from my skin. Rob is spoiled, self-indulgent; but I can no sooner walk away from him than I can fly to the moon. In his most urgent voice he tells me that he wants a baby, that he wants us to marry, that he can't live without me. He does not apologize for punching me in the ribs just the day before, in front of my mother's house, the one she bought after her divorce. He does not say he's sorry because today is different from yesterday, and with Rob, the wisdom has always been: *don't look back.*

I'm supposed to be in love; indeed, everyone thinks I should love him, especially a few of the popular girls at school who've never taken an interest in me until now. How often do you get a guy who is clearly so crazy about you that he'll follow your every move? *I wish I could be loved like that,* one of them (until recently an archenemy) tells me as we sit in the library, flipping through college guides.

And Rob does follow me: throughout the hallways at high school, to the library, to the door of my best friend's house. To orchestra rehearsal, to concerts, to classes. To parties, to practice rooms, to corners where I think I'm alone. There he is, in love. The only choice I have is to reciprocate.

And until this afternoon, I have done a good enough job. But today, something makes me jump in his car, the way I usually do after every single school day, rain or shine, and borrow his wisdom. Right to his face I announce that I'm leaving and not looking back.

Because until this afternoon, it didn't seem to matter much that his parents hated me. A month or two before this, his father had politely let me in their house, led me to the closed door of Rob's bedroom, and then quietly ordered Rob to "get this nigger the hell out of here."

Until this afternoon it didn't seem to matter much that I knew that Rob's own mother has stood crying every day at her cash register at the Grand Union Supermarket, bemoaning the fate of her beloved boy, the straight-B student. To her everything has always been plain as day. *A girl like Carolyn? With a German mother, no less! What else could she be after but a home and a husband?*

I will use him, she believes. I will get pregnant and ruin his name.

I am trouble, his father tells him. That's what their kind is like.

Now all that is moot because I'm leaving and never looking back.

The rest of the afternoon is spent driving in circles around the shopping mall parking lot, where Rob continues to cry and beg and wheedle; he attempts to crash into a huge trash bin, but he loves his souped-up car too much to actually carry out such a threat. After an hour he drives over to Marjorie Post Park in Massapequa, the place where all the indiscreet high school couples make out. He puts his arms around my neck and wails. He tells me his parents never loved him, that they never expected anything great from him. Sadly, his older brother Mike is the success. Married at twenty, with a child on the way now at twenty-one, and a scholarship to Nassau Community College in hand, Mike is his parents' golden dream.

Rob grabs me by the shoulders. *Why can't you expect something from me?*

A little while later he drives me back to my old neighborhood, to the house where I lived for fourteen years with my parents and siblings. I barely recognize the place. *We could move back here*, Rob suggests timidly. The house and lawn are neatly manicured but shabby all the same. Someone has told me that since we moved out four years ago, it has been burglarized five times. This neighborhood, full of black people who stand at their curtains and watch for the next thing, frightens Rob to death.

He takes off for the other side of town, the white part. At the gates of Amity Beach, early evening stars pave the sky like brilliant bricks. *I would be the best husband, I promise. I'd never make you cry.*

I roll down the window and stick my head out into the chill air. I swear I can hear the sound of laughter somewhere far away.

You can go to the community college. We can go together. Why do you need to go away to college?

He knows I won't wait for him. The college I have chosen is an hour away from here—in Rob's words a "sleepaway college"; he knows I won't look back. I won't visit, I won't write. I won't dream of his fairy tales, the future he imagines for us. When he suggests, as he does that afternoon at the beach, that we move in with his parents and give our love time, I almost vomit.

Rob will not stop his tears—he expects them to get the job done, despite my stony face, despite the fact that I have opened my door and am already out on the sand. This whole afternoon *isn't* what he has bargained for. People at school tell Rob he resembles John Travolta from *Saturday Night Fever*, and he loves hearing that. He loves hearing he is a catch, that he would be voted Most Attractive Male if it weren't for all those black fool boys who turn the teachers' heads. He loves worshiping me until I can't take it anymore, me, his first dark-skinned girlfriend. On days when he isn't crying, Rob plays drums and smokes pot and lines his bedroom walls—much to his mother's chagrin—with Playboy centerfolds.

You don't love me! You've always used me! My parents were right!

He is the first white boy I have ever dated.

A man and a woman walking nearby stop and stare at us, perhaps taken aback by the screaming. *Don't go, please don't go! I'll kill myself if you go!*

But I do move on, closer to the water's edge, where I look up once more at the clouds drifting across the brickway of stars. I can just make out the studded silhouettes of my parents as they touch each other's hair with their hands. A gentle gesture, one that will rarely come again.

Rob comes charging after me, not caring if this couple will try and stop him. But they do nothing but stare. *A baby would make everything all right! Why don't you love me?*

* * *

Once I begged Bob for a pair of nail scissors, then another time a tube of sunburn cream. We had gone to Coney Island and I was so burnt. I was homesick. But nothing. He refused to buy me these things. It took months before my personal effects were shipped—via boat—from Germany. Mostly books, some clothes. I read Goethe when I wasn't crying.

* * *

For a few weeks after that day, I will not know how to leave Rob. Eventually June rolls around; on my graduation day I see him, to my great shame, standing in the bleachers on the school lawn, cheering me on. My teachers have pretty much given up on me—this in spite of the fact that I've been accepted to Sarah Lawrence College on a full scholarship. They see how Rob tails me. They notice my textbooks scarred with his name.

But when my teachers ask, I don't talk about Rob. I tell them I am planning to become a writer, that I've dreamt of becoming a writer since I was a little girl, when my mother handed me a brown marbled notebook and told me to put my poems in it.

In reality, it would take that evening, and another boy—a tall, muscular thug who crashes my best friend's graduation party—to finally drive Rob away. At the party, this thug will get a little drunk and hurl insults at Rob; later on, he will dispose of my boyfriend in a good old-fashioned black-boy white-boy fistfight. My best friend's father (who has been on the phone with his mistress and has gotten sick of our interruptions) eventually comes outside from the basement bar and kicks the three of us out.

Rob walks to a local Carvel, where he calls his mother to pick him up. The next time I see him is in the middle of a later night, when the police are called to escort him from my mother's house, where he is weeping on the steps.

But for now, I am saved. As I drive the thug home, he kisses me on the neck; I am now his. He doesn't cry or wheedle. He simply states the facts in that kiss. He fought for me. I should be his. It is only fair.

Luckily the thug is not interested in marrying or having babies. *There are places you can go*, he will whisper in my ear, as we sit on the couch in the den of his house and listen to his parents scream in drunken rages. His fingers will twirl the lock of hair just behind my ear. *If I gave you a baby, you wouldn't have to keep it.*

In the background, oblivious to everything else, his parents travel up and down the stairs, throwing glasses, bottles, car keys at each other, cursing the day they ever met. His mother has just lost her job of eighteen years at Grumman Aerospace where she worked as a secretary. His father's landscaping business flourishes, despite his non-stop boozing.

But the thug's fingers will remain in that caress, his eyes will remain on me, almost until the day I leave for Sarah Lawrence. *Trust me, baby. There are places you can go to get a baby taken care of. If that's ever the case.*

* * *

I worked as a nurse's aide until I was five months pregnant. Only after David's birth in 1965 was I finally diagnosed with severe anemia. I kept fainting with each pregnancy and was told I was simply tired. One doctor told me everyone fainted, that I was not special.

At the hospital, I met doctors who hated me. One of them, from Poland originally, called me a Nazi. He got the other doctors to dislike me as well.

I stayed on, working with a kind nurse, a woman from the West Indies, Mrs. Henry. She helped me because I still couldn't speak the language well. When I got home, I gave all my earnings to Bob. He then gave me $10 a week for expenses. Food. Clothing. Medicine.

Bob moved us out to Long Island after the roaches became too much. They were actually crawling in your crib at Avenue I.

We got the house in spring of 1963. The real estate agent told me, "This development is just for colored people." But the house was like a dream come true.

Even though I had no money for plants, I found seeds, and started a garden.

I had one baby after the other. I had to rise each morning to make Bob breakfast at 4 o'clock. Even when I came home from the hospital with a baby. Breakfast at 4 was just one of my jobs.

On North Ronald Drive I was the only mother who stayed home. Mostly the other women on the block—all black women—were nice to me. But they all had jobs and they needed a babysitter. I would say yes, and then some would leave their kids with me for days. They took advantage, but they were never mean.

Sometimes I would get a note in the mailbox—"You think you're so special." People would lose their houses in the blink of an eye. But many of them saw me as lucky, because Bob was the provider. And not everyone on the block was married.

Once a relative of Bob's came out from the projects in Brooklyn and called me "Cinderella."

But if you had to name my story, it would have to be called, "No Choices."

* * *

Everyone could have one. Every cheerleader, every homecoming queen, every honor student, every plain-old average girl. All you had to do was look in the phone book. The 1977 yellow pages of Suffolk County, or Nassau County; it was all the same. If you didn't look in the phone book—if you were too country to do so, or too poor to know better, or so utterly uneducated that you actually believed you should keep the baby, then that was your own damn fault.

But everyone had an escape hatch. Everyone had an opportunity. This is what made us different from our mothers. We could escape a lifetime of bitterness just by lying on a doctor's table in the space of a lonely gray afternoon.

* * *

Three children in bottles. Three children in diapers. I used to go into the bedroom and cry. Bob would come in—"What's the matter?" I would say I didn't know, then I would say, "I need a break!"

"From what? You don't do anything around here."

All around me women went to work. I wanted to as well, and soon filled out an application at a local factory. They wouldn't hire me because of my language.

A friend from Brooklyn once asked me, "Why don't you get a tubal ligation?" But I had no idea what that was. One of the neighbor women on Long Island advised me to use a douche after sex. That way I could stop the babies. But I was afraid to try.

Things changed when my fourth baby was born in 1969. Bob got sick with the mumps and had to leave work. We had no money for a while. Then he took me to the local community college and signed me up. I didn't even know my own social security number. But in 1971, I went back to school. And that was my real beginning of my emancipation.

* * *

My mother and my father didn't notice Maike approach them on the sand. The light was nearly gone. They both sat up and giggled, completely giddy. My mother's dress was ruined with wrinkles. There was not a trace of lipstick on her lips.

Maike worried about making it back home that night. They could not afford a hotel. And what of this G.I.? After she had been so nice to him, a perfect stranger? He hadn't even bothered to buy her a *limonade*.

Time to go, she whispered to her sister, turning in the direction of the car.

* * *

One professor raved over the first essay I handed in. I'd written about my brother Uwe, who'd just died in an equestrian accident. The professor told me I was such a good writer. I couldn't believe my ears!

Though he had put me in school, Bob made sure to tell me: You can't make it without me. He was beginning to have regrets.

But then. I got a 100 in Anatomy Lab, and a 98 in Physiology.

It was so hard for me. I would put the last baby on my bed with a lot of toys and close the door. Then I would open the dictionary and write words down. It was so hard for me, the education. But I would go to bed at night and think about formulas in chemistry.

I remembered Mrs. Henry. How I used to admire her. But becoming a nurse was like a dream to me back then.

I was realizing how you grow when you get schooling. I thought: my God! The world is opening up!

It's not that I didn't enjoy having my babies. I did. But I suddenly saw myself as a nurse.

There is nothing like emancipation.

* * *

Another eighteen years go by. I am driving my small son out to Long Island to Grandma's backyard, where he will kiss her many times and read many books in her lap and sing along to all the German songs she remembers from her childhood.

In another few years I bring my new daughter to join in. By then I am a little over forty years old—twice the age my mother was when she first had me. I am a writer, a professor of creative writing at my alma mater, and married—happily—to someone I met in graduate school.

What if my parents had seen me back then? What if they could've heard me cry out, like some sort of heady savior? If I'd reached my arms toward the stars where they most certainly sat, and shook them hard? What then?

The children help Grandma tend her garden; this is her day off from the hospital, where she works full time in the ICU. She has worked as a nurse for more than twenty years and now dreams of teaching nursing to others. She has even gone back to school to earn credits toward a bachelor's degree, though the grandchildren are taking up more and more of her time.

Ben gets a small patch to call his own, a circular area of earth around the sour-cherry tree where he and Grandma plant a few petunias. Later, he helps his baby sister Karina slide down an old plastic slide to get into the wading pool, where they both shed the morning dirt in water that cascades over the edge and into the grass.

And even later, after lunch and baths and early pajamas, my mother takes out her book of German children's songs and points to the pictures and begins to sing, the kids curled up in her lap on the chaise longue. And there is no sweeter sound, no sweeter picture—but all I want to do is interrupt her. I want to ask my mother if she remembers that large cherry tree in Mutti's backyard. I once climbed it when I was visiting Mutti for the summer. I remember experiencing the worst stomachache after a day in its limbs, indulging in the fruit, attempting to talk to the crows that were eyeing me from the gooseberry bushes. The tree was a true majesty, looking out over rooftops at the Baltic Sea, at the very beach where Mutti used to make the girls swim every morning before school, rain or shine.

She believed it would build character. She believed it would save them from something she refused to define in terms the girls would truly grasp. Women just needed to be saved, she would say. Not only from men, but from the world. Leave it at that. (At which her daughters would laugh and call their mother hopelessly old-fashioned.)

But what did that laughter matter? Mutti brought her daughters out to the rolling surf each morning before school and ordered them to swim in and out at least two times. Despite their complaints, their constant begging to be allowed back home, to sleep in, just this once.

She was so old-fashioned, the girls moaned, stepping their feet into the icy water. Why didn't she listen to them, why didn't she forget the past, why didn't she just let them live their lives—just this once?

A NORMAL WOMAN

by Kate Maloy

WHEN I WAS ELEVEN, my mother gave me a brochure that explained menstruation, largely through diagrams. She asked me later if I had read it, but that was the extent of our conversation until I was almost fifteen, when she sent me to the family GP because I hadn't started to menstruate. Awkwardly, she explained ahead of time that he would have to examine me in quite a personal manner. I don't recall her words, only her reluctance to meet my eyes. She was never at ease with girl talk or any other form of intimacy.

I went to the appointment by myself. It was summer and the doctor's office was an easy walk from our house. Everything is still there in my mind's eye—the weather (sunny), the walk (tree-lined, alongside broad front lawns), what I wore (pale-blue shorts and a sleeveless blouse with matching stripes). I was sun-brown, skinny, scared, and completely incapable of asking anyone, my mother or the doctor, the questions which I urgently wanted answered. It was 1959. Sex and reproduction were veiled in euphemisms. A girl's menstrual period was her "friend" or, conversely, "the curse." The clinical names for genitalia were more shocking than the bluest profanity. Adolescent boys had no control over their runaway "urges," so girls were expected to keep things from "going too far." My father once handed me an issue of *Reader's Digest* with a pointedly bookmarked article entitled "Even Nice Girls Get Pregnant." We were big on reading about life issues in my family, much less big on talking about them or expressing the emotions they stirred up. My father apparently didn't even know how late my first period was, or he wouldn't have worried that I might miss subsequent ones.

Given all this silence and indirection, I was hopelessly ignorant about my body and had no idea where to go for information. If I didn't have periods, could I ever have sex? Would I ever really be a woman? Was I even plumbed right, or was something missing or askew inside me? I couldn't ask my friends, from whom I was determined to hide my predicament. They didn't seem to notice when I kept quiet during slumber-party discussions of sanitary napkins and leakage and cramps—perhaps because I readily jumped into related conversations about breasts, bras, and boys.

Dr. Koenig offered little help. He questioned me about my body before the examination, but even he was oblique. Eyeing my chest, as if trying to see through the stripes that covered it, he asked if there were "anything there." Mortified, I whispered, "Yes." There wasn't much, but enough to justify my answer. I don't remember what else he asked me, and I don't remember the examination. Neither do I remember an injection, but I know he gave me one because I began bleeding a few days later, without warning. I do remember that the doctor, speaking not to me but to my mother, by phone, called this "priming the pump."

Apparently this induced period satisfied the two of them that everything was in working order. It didn't satisfy me, because I still didn't menstruate without someone at the damn pump handle. Still, I didn't complain. I couldn't allow myself to plead, for I couldn't reveal the depth of my anxiety. Surely I was a freak.

It's hard for me to believe today that I was so timid on the one hand and so stoic on the other. For years I lived alone with my fears and my conviction that I would never be normal, would never marry, would never have a child, would remain forever outside the hot and heavy rounds of love, sex, and romance. My insistent hormones finally proved me wrong about sex, if nothing else. I still thought I would never be a mother.

* * *

I operated on this assumption all through my twenties, until a dramatic episode turned everything around. It started with abdominal pain, which I dismissed until I could barely move and everything I ate lodged like glass in my belly. I remember going to dinner with a friend and his parents and eating only salad and still finding it hard to sit upright. My friend's father, a surgeon, noted my discomfort and insisted that I see a doctor. I did, and he referred me to a gynecologist, who prescribed pain pills but couldn't identify the source of the problem. When it persisted, he scheduled me for exploratory surgery.

I lived in San Francisco and worked at a publishing company on the Peninsula. One day, the pain got so bad at my office that I had to leave. I drove myself home with some difficulty, only to realize that I'd left my pain pills behind. Panicked, I called a friend and coworker who also lived in the city, and she said she'd bring them to me. She couldn't possibly get to my apartment before six, so I lay down and tried to relax. I began visualizing the pain. I gave it a color, a size, a texture, a sound, a temperature—and it began to fade. I even fell asleep before my friend arrived.

That, I soon learned, was a stupendous feat of self-hypnosis, for the cause of the pain was an ectopic pregnancy, implanted in my right fallopian tube and exerting steadily increasing pressure as the embryo grew. On that worst day, as I waited for my pills, the tube finally ruptured. I know this because the nature of the pain changed immediately. It was no longer as sharp, hot, or focused; it remained intense, but it was more diffuse.

I went in for surgery several days later. Afterward, I woke to a nurse standing next to me in the recovery room. She said, without preamble, "You were pregnant." I was groggy, and my belly must have hurt, but all I really felt was soaring delight. From then on, my periods were regular as the moon.

* * *

Everything back then—the absence of periods, the fears and secrecy, and then the stunning fact of a pregnancy—primed not only my menstrual cycles but my passions. I was almost thirty but felt giddy as a young teen. I was finally a normal woman! I'd have to buy tampons, maybe even Midol! I'd need birth control, too, at least for the time being. By the usual clock, I was already past the age for a first child, but that didn't bother me. I *would* be a mother one day. It didn't matter how long it took.

It took until almost the last possible moment. I was a restless person, given to trading jobs and locations every few years. I'd moved often as a child and had attempted to stop this perpetual motion by marrying halfway through college. The marriage proved disastrous, though, and when it ended I went on the move again, traveling from Maine to California by way of Boston. I worked as a cocktail waitress, a dinner waitress, a copyeditor, a production editor. Nothing held my attention for long. I had a lot of growing up to do.

It now seems likely to me that my anxious and largely silent adolescence had left me unsteady in ways I never thought about. I continued to keep my most troublesome emotions to myself, as I had done then, and I tended to react to events in my life rather than to reflect upon them. I had plenty of friends and sufficient lovers, but in fact I kept very much to myself, more by habit than intention. I perfected a seeming openness, but it was a disguise I wasn't even aware of adopting. I could talk easily—and even eloquently—about books, ideas, emotions, and experiences, but I never let my self-doubts show, sometimes not even to myself.

At thirty-three, I finally began a relationship that would lead to a long-term marriage. Five years later, after our extended shakedown period, I got up early one morning, mixed chemicals and urine in a test tube, and watched in disbelief as a brown ring gradually formed in the solution. The ring meant I was pregnant. It wasn't by design, since my husband was unsure about having children, but I instantly gave in to joyful anticipation. This was early in 1983. At thirty-eight, after years of running every day, I was in great shape. I would sail through pregnancy and labor; I would be a mother at last. Soon my husband was eager, too.

* * *

The first indication of a problem came as I lay on my back and felt the sliding pressure of the sonar scanner trace the longitudes of my abdomen, which was just beginning to grow round. I craned my neck to the right and watched the shapes within me take form on a monitor. One of the shapes moved—my *child*. Later, I was advised not to call the fetus a child, but, as I lay there, that is exactly what it was. No advice ever changed that perception. I had formed vivid images of this baby. I'd imagined its weight and warmth, the grip of its hand around my finger. With my genes and its father's, it would be fair and blue-eyed. Given talents and bents on both sides of the family, it could have a gift for music, writing, medicine, teaching, drawing, photography, auto mechanics, carpentry, law, or philosophy. Or it could just as well be a soccer player, a puppeteer, a politician. Seeing the bearer of all this potential move inside me before I could even feel that movement made my pregnancy all the more real. It cemented a bond; it made me a mother.

I kept my eyes on the monitor, mesmerized by the baby's head, limbs, spine, and bug-size beating heart. I remained more fascinated than worried, even when my obstetrician told me we'd have to postpone the amniocentesis. The baby and the amount of amniotic fluid were smaller than normal. That didn't necessarily mean anything—maybe I'd just gotten my dates wrong—but it would bear watching. I was unsettled but not seriously worried by what was probably a minor variation from the norm. Even at thirty-eight, my chances of having a healthy baby were strong—better than 1 in 120, at least for Down syndrome. I never saw any numbers for an out-of-the-blue anomaly.

I had to go back twice more before they were able to perform the amniocentesis. The test at that time was usually done at about the sixteenth week of pregnancy, when there is enough fluid to grow the cells for fetal diagnosis and also enough time for a second-trimester abortion, should the test results, which took three to four weeks, prove abnormal.

I was just over eighteen weeks pregnant when they finally did the test, and they still got only a minimum of fluid. Then it took longer than usual to grow the cells. When the results finally came in, I was nearly twenty-four weeks along and had been feeling the baby move for at least a month. I was getting bigger all the time, and everyone knew I was pregnant—not just friends and family but clients, neighbors, and acquaintances.

By then I was terrified about the outcome of the test, so, with my husband teaching, and unavailable, I called for the results from a friend's house. I stood in her kitchen on a warm day in May, looking out the back door and listening to a disembodied voice at my ear saying, sadly and kindly, something about extra genetic material on the long arm of chromosome number two. They didn't know what it meant; it was exceedingly rare. So far, they had found no similar case on record. But it was not, the voice emphasized, an actual trisomy. In other words, there wasn't a whole extra chromosome in the second pair, just a larger-than-normal one paired with a normal one.

I had invested so much in the reality of having a child that I couldn't fully comprehend a threat to that reality. I felt the nightmare disjunction we suffer when disaster, in a single incomprehensible moment, wipes out cherished expectations. I fiercely resisted the blow. I tried to understand what the doctor was saying and tried to ask intelligent questions, but I clung to my expectations. Given ambiguous news, I grasped at every reassuring speculation and rejected the dire ones. I even remember wondering why my friend looked so shocked when I told her what I'd learned.

* * *

Geneticists analyzed my DNA and my husband's, but they found no explanation there. We both had normal chromosomes, which meant that the baby's abnormality was the result of a spontaneous duplication of genes that no one could explain. It was not a consequence of our ages. It was likely to cause severe mental and physical handicaps, but this was at best an informed guess. The guess could be confirmed only if the literature contained another case like ours, in which the effects of the abnormality were known.

Ten days after my phone call from my friend's kitchen, medical literature yielded nine other cases of a partial trisomy on the second chromosome. My husband and I sat in the office of the geneticist who had led the literature search. I can still see her pretty, sharp-featured face as she explained that only one of the nine cases was close to ours in the amount of duplicated material, its location on the chromosome, and the fact that it was spontaneous and not inherited. That baby died twenty days after birth of multiple heart and kidney defects and would have been severely retarded had she lived. If we continued the pregnancy, our baby—also a girl—would almost certainly have all or many of the same defects, if she even survived until birth.

I remained largely numb as the geneticist delivered this news, though I sensed I couldn't sustain my suspended state for long. Perhaps I was trying to delay the full impact when I looked across the desk at her and said, "It must be hard for you, telling people this kind of thing." She gazed back at me as if from a great distance, without the least comprehension. Her indifference was like a slap, and I barely made it out of her office and into the sunlight, with my husband holding me up, before I heard a high-pitched, animal noise that seemed to come from someplace far away—the sky, perhaps. It was several seconds before I understood that it was coming from me.

* * *

During our wait for the DNA analysis and the literature search, we knew we might never have any more definitive information than the amniocentesis had yielded. As time passed and our anxiety grew, we slowly understood that we were going to end the pregnancy, with or without the certainty we waited for. The decision could not wait upon the facts, because the facts might never come in.

The choice was in one way a foregone conclusion. What I expected to do—based on conversations about this eventuality, my pro-choice political stand, and my moral conviction that abortion was sometimes the best of the unfortunate options available—was what I did. But my thoughts about abortion, conceived so long before my child was, did not save me from having to make the decision anew, as if for the first time, in the midst of awful pain. My reasons took on the shape and specificity they could never have in the abstract. This was a real child, whom I loved. I refused to take the considerable risk that she could never live an independent or pain-free life. I could not subject her to the likelihood that her existence, by my admittedly subjective standards, could barely be called a life. Many would consider me arrogant for imposing my will on my daughter, but there was no escaping that. I had to decide one way or another and could not consult her. It was not an arrogant but an agonizing choice; not the right thing to do but, to me, the less wrong.

Now, as I look back, I am acutely aware of how inadequate facts, arguments, and circumstances are to convey the impact of that choice. I'd have
thought that the need to make a decision would act as a balm against the
emotional sting, but it doesn't. Nor does it bring resolution or acceptance.
Necessity takes care of practical needs, permits action, tidies up the room
in which the mourners mourn. It does not stand and weep with them or
help them to come to terms with loss. My rational, civilized parts—those
that made arrangements after weighing odds and information—func-
tioned as if by rote when deeper and more ancient parts were urged awake
by pain. Those are the parts that truly characterize the ordeal.

The pain was most intense at night, when sleep escaped me except for
restless, dream-filled scraps. I was haunted by my child, who still moved
but was already a ghost inside me. Each tumble and kick would take my
breath away. I would hold my belly, try to cradle the baby, and cry endlessly. It is terrible to carry a doomed child beneath your heart.

I began to avoid being seen in public. On one occasion, guided by my
civilized self through the aisles of the grocery store, I met an acquaintance
by the dairy case. She told me cheerfully how well I looked and how
becoming my pregnancy was. My impression of that moment is that my
surroundings went gray; color drained from butter wrappers, cheeses, and
containers of fruit yogurt, and only the harsh fluorescent lights stayed
bright. I said nothing, and I could not smile, but my acquaintance did not
appear to notice. From then on, I felt like a fraud in public, my womb a
tomb, nothing about me what it seemed.

The day before I checked into the hospital for my abortion, my husband and I sat together with our hands on my belly and said goodbye to
our daughter, both of us weeping uncontrollably. I didn't think I could
survive the consequences of my decision—the procedure, the loss, the
emptiness.

At the hospital, we were escorted not to the maternity wing but to the
older part of the women's facility, far from the joyous new mothers and
their beautiful, wailing infants. I changed into a gown, and my obstetrician gave me a saline injection that would kill the fetus (the child) and
induce abortion. Then he squeezed my foot sadly and left me to face what

would come.

Every natural process was distorted and betrayed. Love had to destroy its object out of love. Birth became death; I went through labor to deliver a dead child. That labor was full of contradiction and alienation. No cheerful nurses attended me or explained the frightening process that the saline had set in motion. They waited at their station in the hall. No one ever examined me. Even when I was well into labor I was told it was too soon for anything but mild cramps. My husband's presence was essential, but there was little he could do. Physical intensity and emotional stress consumed me and entirely separated me from him. Caught up in that terrible labor, I felt outcast and powerless. After it was all over, my formerly solid self seemed to dissolve, and all I could do was bleed and weep. I never saw the baby. I only felt her slip out of my body.

* * *

My rational ideas about abortion and my firm political convictions in favor of individual choice had not prepared me for a primal state in which reason was subordinate to imagery, association, and feeling. I felt morally defiled, guilty, forced into an association with the death of what I loved and wanted. This frightened me—and then I became afraid of the fear, thinking I had betrayed my ideas and had lost hold of principles that were part of me. I was a feminist. I believed in each woman's right to choose what happened to her own body, and I'd have been outraged, as I agonized over my own choice, to be told that it wasn't mine, after all. Why, then, was I feeling guilty? Why was I seized at three or four every morning with a mindless, numbing terror? Why did I insist that people I didn't know well be told only that we had lost the baby, not that I had undergone an abortion?

I couldn't tell what I was ashamed of—the act, or my feelings about it. I was furious at the thought that people would judge me. My prochoice allies would support my act but scorn my anguish as gratuitous self-punishment. They would see it as an implicit capitulation to those in the right-to-life camp, who would condemn my act but approve of my guilt, regretting only that it had not prevented what they would call my crime.

I had been compelled by every instinct and belief to consent to death for the sake of love and life, both of which now wore more changeable faces. I'd had to submit to a dilemma whose terrible ambiguity left me no possibility of control or rightness. I'd been forced to accept the enormous irrationality of random catastrophe. Above all, I'd had to make a decision beyond my knowledge or powers about someone else's fate. In each unwilling submission and choice, I recognized my own mortality and limits.

After I came home from the hospital, a group of women from my husband's workplace offered to visit and help, but I declined. My pain and moral anguish were too personal to share with relative strangers. I had learned the hard way that no clear-cut right or wrong, yes or no, was possible. My dilemma had been lit only dimly by the sparks and beams of the public battle over reproductive choice. That battle took place in an abstract world of black and white, whereas I lived among shifting shades of gray, feeling completely unprepared to sort them out.

* * *

I mourned for a long time after the abortion, well past the point at which some of my friends thought I should simply move on. I knew that the patience and sympathy of others often wears out long before grief does, but it hurt me nonetheless. What's more, the only way I could imagine moving on was to get pregnant again and finally bear a healthy child.

Time was running out, but I still didn't conceive for two more years. There was no definitive explanation for this, just as there had been none for the absence of periods earlier on. I've often wondered whether that first problem was psychosomatic, since by my teens I had long absorbed my mother's lack of pleasure in any aspect of being female. She was emotionally distant, not given to physical affection, and crushingly bored with life as a housewife and mother in the fifties and sixties. When I was fourteen, she even told me that she should never have married or had children. I suspect this is why it took the shock of a medical emergency to establish my menstrual cycle. I think my body held out for years against even my humiliating sense of freakishness, for I'd learned at practically a molecular level that there were no rewards in womanhood.

My extended inability to conceive after the abortion seems less likely to be the result of subconscious self-protection, though I'm sure I repressed a great deal of anxiety. My friends' apprehensions were right there on the surface, not in their words but in their expressions, in their carefully edited responses to my determination to conceive again. I knew they feared another devastating loss for me, but I was sure that lightning wouldn't dare strike a second time—or a third, if you count the ectopic pregnancy. All I had to do was *get* pregnant, and I couldn't understand what was taking so long. Motherhood had become an obsession. Nothing else could make me feel whole after being so torn apart by disappointment and loss. At some level, out of conscious reach, lay the other component to my obsession, and that was the question: *How could a normal woman have conceived such a drastically abnormal child?* An acquaintance had brought this right out in the open when she said, "Oh, how awful. It's like you're carrying a monster." I was so confounded I couldn't speak, but I didn't have to. She had put into words exactly what had been lurking unacknowledged in my own mind.

* * *

I didn't start feeling afraid until I finally did conceive again—and then anxiety broke through in moments so vivid that they had to have come from some subterranean well just boiling with dread. Had this dread erupted sooner, I might have lost all courage and given up.

My stress broke through at night in dreams of loss and sorrow. During the day, it interfered with my ability to concentrate and it created terrible tension at home. On one occasion, my husband and I fell into a baseless, crazy argument that flew rapidly out of control. We shouted and railed at each other, neither of us listening, each of us simply exploding with anxiety. I fled the room with my hands over my belly, as if I could block the baby's ears, for I was certain that if it heard this row it would be marked for disaster. I ran upstairs to my office and shut the door, my heart racing, tears overflowing—and then I heard a voice say, clear and strong as anything, "This baby is perfectly fine."

I still don't know whether the voice was an actual auditory phenomenon or a strong artifact of my imagination, but I believed it utterly in that moment and for days afterward. As the date for amniocentesis neared, I lost some of that belief and became increasingly susceptible to terrors that seemed to snatch at me from every direction. Soon, however, I noticed that reassurance quickly followed fear, as it had done after my fight with my husband. I began having marvelous, comforting dreams, some of which carried direct, unmistakable messages about the baby. In one of these, he lay peacefully on his back, smiling and kicking his chubby legs and gazing at me with blue-sky eyes full of floating clouds. In another I saw the image of Quan Yin, a revered figure in Buddhism who denied herself nirvana in order to help the struggling mortals of this world. In my dream, she took the form of a 700-year-old wooden bust I'd seen at a museum where I worked as a freelance writer; I took to visiting her each time I went in to deliver or consult about work. Mounted on a pedestal, in the center of a large hall lit by clerestory windows, she seemed to float in the shadowless, ethereal light. She never failed to give me peace.

* * *

The amniocentesis went perfectly this time and the results were good. I was carrying a "normal male." I wasn't even surprised by then, just elated. Normal child, normal mother.

I did sail through pregnancy this time. I never had morning sickness. I kept on running until at least six or seven months along. I had no spotting or bleeding or anything whatsoever to set off alarms. My water broke the day after my due date, and I went through eight hours of labor without anesthesia. I wasn't going to drug my son.

When he was finally born and placed directly on my stomach, I was surprised by how hot he was. Of course, yes, he carried the heat of my body into the world with him, but I had never thought about this. I was surprised, too, that he was so quiet. He gazed at me, seeming alert and curious, with eyes so dark they were almost navy blue. In quick succession I saw in his face my mother, my husband's mother, various aunts and uncles. Resemblances flowed across his features like pale lights and then were gone. Then he looked like himself, a brand-new person, entirely unique.

* * *

At this writing, my son has just turned twenty-one. It turns out I was right about many of the features I had thought a child of mine might have. He is indeed fair and blue-eyed. He's a gifted musician, an excellent writer, and, like his late father, inquisitive about the meaning of life and the grand puzzle of human behavior. Above all, however, he is steadfastly himself, with passions and traits that surprise me. His ear for his own drumbeat has sometimes led him widely askance of expectations in school, at home, or among friends. As a result, he has endured long stretches of isolation and alienation, has suffered judgments and disapproval from many directions, has made dangerous mistakes, and has sunk into depression yet refused prescription drugs. Just now, though, he is happier than he's been in five or six years, and he believes that none of his pain or sadness has been without purpose. He holds his own, with increasing clarity and strength, and he is sometimes startlingly wise. I am proud of him and love him beyond words.

In light of his struggles, though, when I now think about the torture of having had to decide my unborn daughter's fate, I realize that every decision about every pregnancy either ends someone's fate or sets it in motion with no guarantee that it will be benign. Bringing another human being into a world teeming with trouble and glory is just as momentous a choice as ending a pregnancy, perhaps more so. The only escape from such immense responsibility is never to get pregnant at all, and that's not a sure thing, either.

But this is just the way of things. Nothing is ever sure, and sometimes, with no warning, life will bring us more than we feel we can handle. In such a case, the important thing is not to do the right thing, since we can't ever see the long-range consequences of any act or decision. The important thing is to be as true to ourselves as possible under the circumstances.

THE DECISION

by Katie Allison Granju

I BEGAN TO SUSPECT something was very wrong the day I could no longer walk across the library at the law school where I was a first-year student. Ten weeks pregnant, I had been fighting excessive fatigue, loss of appetite and night sweats for almost a month.

"Relax," my midwife told me. "You're just having a rough first trimester."

I was inclined to believe her. At age twenty-seven and in perfect health, I had no reason to believe anything more than extreme morning sickness was plaguing me, and that was no big deal. Three years previously, pregnant with my son, I had felt so good that I had even wished for a little first-trimester yukkiness so that I could feel "really pregnant."

Still, the nagging feeling that something was going wrong grew stronger with each wretched day. The afternoon when I found myself collapsed in a chair in the law library brought the situation to a head. A classmate had to practically carry me to her car so that she could drive me home, where she insisted on taking my temperature: 104 degrees.

Within hours, I was admitted to the maternity floor at a local hospital, where I spent the next eight unhappy days. Each afternoon, just to make sure that all was well, the obstetrician would perform an ultrasound, showing us the tiny *beep, beep* of the fetal heart and the jerky movements of a glowing human jumping bean. We began calling the baby "Peanut." My doctor was puzzled as test after test failed to determine the cause of my illness. He brought in an infectious disease specialist, who tested me for everything from HIV to malaria.

On the sixth day of my confinement, as I was lying miserably in my hospital bed, watching a rerun of *The Andy Griffith* show, both of my doctors entered my room, closed the door and turned off the TV without asking. Now I knew for certain that I had been right: something was terribly wrong.

I had an acute, primary cytomegalovirus infection, popularly known as CMV. The disease is not generally something to worry about...unless you are immuno-compromised, which I wasn't…or pregnant. CMV, we were told by the obstetrician, is very dangerous to a fetus, particularly in the first trimester. It is a leading cause of congenital neurologic impairment, severe physical anomalies, devastating mental retardation and infant fatality. Really, we were told, we should consider our "options."

CMV in mom causes baby to have problems

Suddenly, I, a person with all her grandparents still alive, a person who had never even been to a funeral, was faced with death. Not only was I faced with death in the abstract, I was faced with The Decision. Consulting with my sweet, 26-year-old husband, a man similarly unschooled in the ways of mortality, I was charged with handing down a judgment as to whether Peanut would continue to leap and hop about in my womb and ultimately, be born alive. With a somber face, the doctor uttered the words that were to become so familiar to us over the next weeks, "No one can make this decision for you. Only you can decide."

Only, I couldn't. Not without more information. And maybe not even then. We immediately became experts on CMV and its potential sequelae. I stayed up all night for days after the diagnosis, reading medical literature and searching the web for answers. None were forthcoming. The best information available told us that if we carried the pregnancy to term, there was approximately a one in four chance that an infected baby would be affected by the CMV in some way. I was paralyzed with grief and indecision.

As an ostensibly pro-choice woman, I realized that I was not actually "pro" anyone ever having to make a choice like this. Although no one wanted to offer an opinion as to what we should do, everyone had an angle. My doctor answered my questions honestly and told me that if his wife or daughter were faced with a CMV diagnosis in the first trimester, he would definitely encourage an abortion.

The minister whom a friend sent to see me was gentle and kind. Yet, she assumed that I was crying because I had already made the obvious decision to have an abortion and was grieving. She offered to set a time for a memorial service after the abortion to "celebrate and remember." She even showed me the feminist liturgy she had photocopied for just such an occasion. I found her point of view strangely repulsive and without intellectual honesty. If the life I would be taking was worthy of religious

value of the life

remembrance and ceremony, how was it possibly mine to take? There are no memorial services for appendectomies or squashed bugs. Only for people.

I was hesitant to share my dilemma with a certain close relative because I feared her unbending anti-abortion stance. Of course, she immediately realized the decision with which I was faced after someone told her of my diagnosis. She telephoned me to instruct me that, although abortion is wrong, sometimes God realizes that the time is not right for a particular soul to come into this world. Considering the circumstances, she opined, no one could blame me for whatever decision I felt was right. Her stunning hypocrisy angered me. Despite her stated views, she was conveniently able to allow for choice in this issue when the woman in question was someone she loved.   → situations change views

As days passed and I wrestled with my conscience, I realized that I was petrified of the physical procedure itself. My doctor assured me that he could perform the abortion at the hospital. I wouldn't have to sit in a waiting room at a clinic. I told him that, although I realized that most first- and early-second-trimester abortions are performed under local anesthesia, the only way I could face this would be knocked out cold. He agreed. I knew that I could be admitted to the hospital, drift gently off to sleep and wake up, relieved of this problem forever. I would never have to think about it again. This sounded both tremendously appealing and completely horrifying.

When I envisioned the actual opening of my womb and suctioning of its contents, the same primal instinct kicked in that would have allowed me to single-handedly rip the lungs out of any man who laid a hand on my little boy. What kind of mother would allow her defenseless offspring to be taken from the very bosom of maternal safety and warmth? I felt sick, and wept yet again.

My father tried to reason with me, pointing out the lifelong ramifications of my decision. He was terribly worried that I would be forever shackled with the responsibilities of caring for a severely ill or disabled child. He fretted that his big plans for his own child would be sucked away forever by a draining responsibility from which I could never escape. many people are encouraging abortion.

I, too, was seized with these fears. I secretly believed that I simply wasn't up to the task of mothering a child with serious health and developmental problems. What would that do to our other child, whom I already knew and loved? What would it do to my career goals? Our marriage? And what about the baby? The thought of seeing our tiny baby suffering, perhaps hooked up to tubes and wires in a neonatal intensive care unit, caused me almost unbearable psychic pain. I imagined a future in which our mentally retarded and physically handicapped 13-year-old child would endure the cruel taunts of other teenagers.

looking out f/ herself

I began to wonder if I was being selfish in even considering giving birth to this baby. Would anyone choose for herself the life that this child might face? Were my own fears about a relatively minor surgery and future guilt good enough reasons to bring forth a human being who would have to live with the consequences of my own cowardice? I tentatively decided that motherhood is full of tough calls and hard decisions, both in the name of love and in a child's best interests. This must be one of them, I thought. I would do what was best for all concerned.

looking out f/ the baby

I telephoned the hospital and weakly scheduled the procedure for the next day. The admitting clerk who took the call easily misunderstood my vague instructions and thought that I was coming in for labor induction of a full-term, healthy pregnancy. "Congratulations," she said brightly. I corrected her mistake and her tone grew dark, almost menacing. She told me to meet my doctor at the labor and delivery wing at 6:30 a.m. sharp the following morning. She abruptly hung up.

There, I thought to myself. I have done the right thing. No turning back. I felt like someone had drained all the life from me. I sat in a darkened room for the next several hours, absently rubbing my still-flat belly and murmuring maternal expressions of comfort to no one in particular. Later that evening, my husband and I discussed the choice that had been made. I attempted stoicism. He reminded me that we had a friend coming over to bring us supper, as many kind people had done throughout my illness and convalescence at home. I roused myself enough to get dressed and out of bed.

Our friend arrived and we all ate together. I told her of my decision and the reasons behind it. She listened quietly and then asked if she could tell us a little about her brother, who had died recently at the age of nine. She recounted a tale of extraordinary courage on the part of her parents, her sister, herself, and especially, on the part of a little boy with Down syndrome named David. This child and this family had lived through all of the things I feared when I considered birthing my own baby, including David's eventual early death. Still, the joy and love of his brief existence had canceled out all of the pain, fear, and hurt. No one who knew David had any regrets. Our friend showed us his photograph: a beautiful and smiling tow-headed little boy, obviously mentally retarded.

[handwritten margin note: friend's anecdote abt herself ↓ changed narr.'s mind so she made the "harder" decision]

Neither do I have any regrets about the decisions I made after that discussion. I never arrived at the hospital the next morning. I canceled the abortion and after a pregnancy alternating between exhilaration and despair, gave birth to my daughter, Elizabeth Jane Chevillard Granju on August 15, 1995. She was born ten days early weighing 6 pounds and 11 ounces. She was born infected with congenital cytomegalovirus and had two seizure episodes in her first year. Since that time, however, she has been physically and developmentally normal in every way. She is also a strikingly beautiful child, with shiny dark hair, olive skin, and a lithe, elfin figure. Jane's epilepsy could conceivably worsen and she is at risk for neurologic problems and progressive hearing loss until she leaves childhood behind. Still, she is remarkably healthy. *[handwritten: Yay!]*

Many people want to extract a moral from this story. Pro-life friends tell me that Jane is my gift from God for making the right choice. They want to hold my baby up as their own personal anti-abortion poster child.

Pro-choice friends attempt to use Jane as a cautionary tale for why choice should be the focus of the debate, rather than abortion itself. After all, I was able to carefully consider each of my options and ultimately, have the final say. This wouldn't have been possible in another political context. My own views have become less reactionary and more cognizant of the complexity of the abortion issue. I continue to fear the slippery slope that we head down when we deny women the right to choose when and how we bear children. Many abortions do indeed "stop a beating heart," as the bumper sticker says.

However, I will not allow Jane to be used as a crucible for the views of any person or group. I know that I would love Jane just as much if she had been born severely disabled. I do not, however, deny the relief I feel that she is so radiantly well. I am deeply aware that I was graced with this experience, which has allowed me to see that the blessing is sometimes as much in the struggle—from which I have learned so much—as in the outcome.

NO STONE UNTURNED
by K.A.C.

THE PASTA ROLLED in the boiling water. "I think it's done!" my 7-year-old declared as he peered into the steaming pot. The phone rang. "Sheesh," he grumbled, "why do telemarketers always call when we are fixing dinner?" As I stirred the pasta, he brought the phone over to me, grinning as if he were delivering a secret prize. "The caller ID says *California!*" He was sure it was his oldest brother phoning from college.

Although the voice on the other end of the phone was warm and familiar, it was one that I had not heard for a number of years—the nurse coordinator from the hematology clinic where we had taken our oldest son as a young child. She apologized for calling during dinner hour on the East Coast, but said she had an urgent favor to ask me. A young woman had come to their clinic looking for information and support. Suzanne was a genetic carrier for hemophilia who, after feeling for years that she would not have any children, had recently married and decided that she would like to start a family. Her memories of growing up with an older brother who had hemophilia had left her feeling anxious and uncertain about passing on the trait. However, after visiting a summer camp for children with hemophilia, her perspective had changed. Today children with hemophilia can ride stunt bikes, play soccer and baseball, and dream of any career. With preventive treatment and the safest drug technology available, an individual with a bleeding disorder can have a full and active life that defies the sedentary, restricted, and shortened life spans of the past. This was very different from her brother's experience. It gave her hope for the family she planned to begin. Still, Suzanne had some doubts. How would she feel when faced with the reality of a challenge she could only begin to visualize, amidst the orbiting emotions of a pregnancy?

The nurse told me Suzanne was now over eight weeks pregnant, and was awaiting prenatal diagnosis of the fetus. I was remembering how agonizingly long the wait for these results could be, sometimes over two weeks, when the nurse asked if I felt comfortable talking to Suzanne and her husband about my own experience.

I could completely empathize with Suzanne. There is a delicate and difficult balance between wanting to celebrate a pregnancy, and waiting to find out if a future child may be affected with a serious genetic disorder. They were looking for support beyond what the clinic could offer professionally; they wanted to talk with someone who knew what they were going through. I immediately offered my support in whatever way would be most helpful. The nurse suggested I contact Suzanne at her work that evening to arrange a time that we could talk over the weekend.

"If there were ever a couple who could handle a challenge like this, it would be you two," my husband and I were told many times by family members and friends offering reassurance after our son was diagnosed with hemophilia. I was not sure what to think about this odd comment. Their confidence seemed rooted in our shared interest in science and health; my clinical training as an emergency medical technician and degree in health education, and his degree in physiology and skill in research technology.

While waiting for her husband to join our conference call, I felt an immediate connection with Suzanne. We acknowledged the sensitivity, the intimacy, of what we would talk about.

"I've never discussed my entire reproductive history in one sitting," I admitted, "Outside of all the medical history forms you have to fill out at the ob-gyn office."

"We appreciate your willingness to share your experiences and thoughts with us, over the phone, never having met each other..." she said. I mentioned the bond I have with members of the hemophilia community, incomparable to any other in my life. I knew that our discussion would be a mutual opportunity, though I did not realize how much I needed, and would benefit from, the process myself.

* * *

When our son was born, we lived in a small cottage alongside a raging stream in Vermont. I was twenty-five years old and my husband was twenty-six. We had been married four years and felt ready to begin a family. My older sister had a seven-month-old son to welcome the second grandchild, his new cousin. She offered to support us in the birthing room, and nurtured us with a wellspring of love, experience, reassurance, soothing piano music, and banana bread. Her knowledge about new-borns, post-partum recovery, and the wide new world of parenting sus-tained us in the first several days of our son's life during a snowy March. By the warmth of the woodstove, we experimented with techniques for changing tiny diapers, successful breast-feeding, and giving a first bath. We felt secure in the new dimension of our lives, feeling a love unknown to us prior to holding this extraordinary baby boy.

Our lives came to an abrupt halt five months later, when bruises in the shape of fingerprints emerged along his tiny ribcage. We had just returned from an extended visit with family in California. During our trip, we delighted in watching our infant son roll over and sit up for the first time, all in the company of loving relatives who were eager to hold the newest baby in the family. Back home, I was changing my son on the braided rug in my father's kitchen, when he commented about the light bruises around his ribcage. My father's physician-trained instincts told him something was not right. He suggested that we take him to our pedi-atrician right away.

At the hospital laboratory, they had difficulty finding a vein to draw blood. Overnight, after numerous needlestick attempts, our son's rapidly bruising arm swelled to twice its normal size; when he woke up in the morning it looked like a sausage. We took him to the emergency room right away, where they immediately admitted him to the hospital. After a day of consultations, intravenous tubes, hemorrhaging, lab results, and blood transfusions, we were finally told, in the middle of the night, that our baby had a serious and rare bleeding disorder.

"Are you aware of any history of bleeding in your family?" the physi-cian asked. "No," we answered anxiously, standing next to our son's hos-pital crib.

He then confirmed from our son's chart the fact that there had been complications with his circumcision, requiring additional sutures to stop the prolonged bleeding. We remembered.

"This is perhaps one of the most classic initial symptoms seen in hemophilia," he said.

Our baby asleep, we spent the hours until dawn on the phone with concerned family members trying to explain what we had just learned.

My husband had read about hemophilia the previous summer in a novel about the Russian royal family at the turn of the century. I had heard the term "bleeder" in my emergency medical technician training while in college. It was difficult for us to comprehend how the term "hemophilia" could redefine our lives overnight. Slowly, we began to sort through the haze of our bewilderment to find ways that our lives had not been changed. We quickly learned that our son would not bleed to death from a cut, a common myth. The missing protein in his body would cause him to bleed longer, not faster, with internal trauma to muscles and joints. We were told the "fingerprint" bruises on his ribcage were classic symptoms found in infants with hemophilia who were held securely. I immediately thought of all the relatives who had held him on our trip to California. Soon we discovered a far more grim, though fortunate truth in the timing of our son's birth. The blood products used to treat his disorder—severe factor eight deficiency (hemophilia A)—had received a mandate by the FDA in March of that year, the month he was born, to be heat treated as a safety precaution against HIV contamination. Had he been born any earlier, requiring treatment with blood products any sooner, he would have been infected with the HIV virus. The next several years would painfully reveal the extent of the tragedy of the HIV contamination of the blood supply—and the resulting devastating loss of thousands of lives within the hemophilia community.

Our confidence in managing our son's diagnosis grew at a rapid pace, as did he. When he began to crawl, we discovered how vulnerable his knees were to painful bruising. We added extra padding to his clothing to protect them. When he began to pull himself up to stand, we had to eliminate sharp corners he could fall against. We became hypervigilant in trying to prevent falls or bumps to his head, knowing the serious consequences of a bleed resulting from head trauma. Many happy times were spent, for everyone, entertained by an inflated rainbow-colored stacked-ring walker on wheels. Not only could he bounce entirely cushioned, he had bumpers to keep him a safe distance from anything too threatening. Knowledge and persistence became our greatest tools in advocating his needs within the healthcare system. When a swelling developed between his brow while he slept one night, changing his toddler features dramatically as the morning progressed, we brought him to the emergency room. They quickly infused into his vein the missing protein his body desperately needed to stop the internal bleeding. There were several exhausting emergency room visits where his pain persisted and our nerves frayed, as his tiny veins eluded the needle. A major bleed in the largest muscle of his slight little body placed him in the hospital for a week over his fifth birthday. His grandfather stayed with him continually, to play endless games of Candy Land, while my husband and I juggled our work schedules.

Our son became adept at using crutches. His childcare center had to redefine the parameters of outdoor playtime. There were parts of the climbing structure, the fireman's pole and a high tower, that became off limits. We met with the staff there, to negotiate limits and safety concerns, and relieve anxiety. We debated the benefits and drawbacks of having our son wear a helmet all the time. We did not want his experience to be too different from any other energetic child getting ready to enter kindergarten. In an effort to try to normalize our lives, we began to explore options to reduce the number of regular trips to the emergency room. We wondered about being trained to give him the IVs ourselves at home, and the idea of treating him preventively before a bleed would begin. The hemophilia clinic was just beginning to design a training model for home infusion therapy. We benefited from the additional expertise of close friends, a couple who had trained as medical technicians and offered us on-call guidance and reinforcement on weekends, on the rug at school, or late in the night. When we were unable to feel the proper tension of our son's vein after puncturing his skin, to know that we had accessed it correctly, our friends would offer us their arms. We would then experiment on their veins, to spare the excess trauma on our son. We began to feel a greater sense of control in our lives.

Eventually, we began to consider the idea of having another child. We knew many of our family members and friends assumed that we would not have any more children, but what we had learned from our son in the five short years of his life convinced us that we should follow our original plans to have a larger family.

Planning my second pregnancy was very different from the first. Knowing that I was a carrier for hemophilia A did not leave much room for carefree spontaneity. I read everything I could find on natural ways to influence gender determination during fertilization. Having a daughter meant the possibility of having another carrier, but not the disorder itself. We were working with one-in-four odds to conceive an embryo with the mutation, meaning that we had a 75 percent chance of averting it. We researched the options available for prenatal diagnosis, along with their associated risks. My husband and I agreed that if we were able to get pregnant again, we would have the most effective screening done so that we would have critical information ahead of time. After that, we would have to determine what to do with the information.

Despite all the anxiety, I was pregnant within a short period of time. Now the stress shifted to the timing of prenatal diagnostics. We found that eight weeks of anxious waiting for the procedure did not compare to the agonizing two-week wait for results.

We were visiting my family over the holidays when we received the phone call. Nothing could have prepared me for the weight of the news. As I collapsed in tears on the staircase of my father's home, alongside the same raging stream where my husband and I had lived earlier, I felt overcome by countless memories of trauma our young son had experienced. His tears, his questions, and his pain flooded my head. I thought of the funerals I had attended of adolescents and young men, all sons of the women in my local support group who were born before my son, who had struggled valiantly, incomprehensibly, with HIV/AIDS. I could not find the resolve or hope within myself, at this time, to feel optimistic about having a second child with hemophilia.

In the days leading up to the termination of my second pregnancy, the intense sadness I experienced was unprecedented for me. The sorrow continued for months afterward. I found solace in my work, in the company of Alzheimer's patients whose unconditional appreciation of my familiar smile each day, as they struggled to remember who I was, reminded me of the opportunity to be present in my actions, rather than search for past memories or future thoughts. I knew I had made the right choice, and did not feel regret. I did, however, feel the loss.

Several months later, newly pregnant, I found myself waiting out the weeks before prenatal testing once again. During a staging ultrasound at six weeks, it was clear that the pregnancy was not viable. No fetal heartbeat could be detected. The miscarriage required another clinical procedure, in order to preserve my chances for future pregnancies. My body and will were worn out.

This time I found refuge in volunteer work for a statewide education and advocacy organization dedicated to hemophilia. I was asked to assume a position on the board of directors after the representative from our chapter died of AIDS. The grace and strength of the individuals I had the opportunity to work with, as they managed the complexity of their hemophilia and HIV status, was a constant inspiration. My energy was refocused through the determination I felt in advocating for the needs of the hemophilia community.

Within a few months, we were ready to try once again. Time passed swiftly through the early stages of my fourth pregnancy. By now we were familiar with the tests that finally told us I was carrying an unaffected male fetus. We were elated by the news, grateful for the opportunity for our now 6-year-old son to have a sibling. My colleagues within the hemophilia community were excited and relieved for us. The sense of peace I experienced throughout the remaining months of my pregnancy was a welcome change.

The hemophilia advocacy board met in an office building shared by Planned Parenthood. I remember an occasion when, visibly eight months pregnant, angry pro-life protestors shoved graphic placards in my face. My resolve deepened. I glared back at them, unshaken, knowing that they had *no* idea what my experience had been. How could I begin to describe it for them? Was it any of their business? I had made my own decisions about life's complexities, not for political or religious reasons, but for *my* body and *my* family. It was *my* right, *my* choice.

My mother offered to accompany us in the birthing room at our second son's birth. From his first breath, she saw the strong resemblance he shares with her father, my grandfather whom I had grown up with. She held him close, whispering lovingly, and told him about the legacy he brought with him and the one he was joining. Our son's calm demeanor as an infant would develop with him. We knew that his experience would be different from that of his older brother. He would face his own challenges. He would define himself through his strengths and grow by understanding his weaknesses, just as we had observed in his brother. We were grateful for another opportunity to develop as parents, to enhance our reference point on the world through the eyes of a second child. He would grow to be one of his brother's greatest admirers.

When we relocated again, I left my career to stay at home with my children and devote any spare time to volunteer work within the hemophilia community. Meanwhile, rising liver function tests confirmed for us that our oldest son had contracted hepatitis C through contaminated blood products he received as a toddler. The initial round of heat treatment against HIV had missed the non-A/non-B hepatitis virus, later identified as hepatitis C. While the implications of this infection were not clear then, the consensus was to be as proactive as possible in seeking treatment, particularly in children who were otherwise asymptomatic. Our son would help to blaze the trail in single-therapy treatment for sixty weeks. Enduring both pre- and post-liver biopsies made him quite a warrior at ten years old. He managed to take it all in stride, for the most part, with his quick wit, curiosity, and stubborn will.

My volunteer work led me to accept a position on the board of directors of a national organization representing hemophilia. Once again, I was replacing a director who had succumbed to AIDS.

I was approaching my thirty-eighth birthday when my husband began to carefully probe the idea of having one more child. At the same time, I was being encouraged to consider a nomination as president of the national organization. If elected, I would be the first woman to serve in this role. Neither proposition was easy to consider, though somehow I found the energy and conviction to do both. Fourteen years of experience with hemophilia and biotechnology left us both feeling the impact of our lives having been enhanced and redirected in ways we could have never predicted.

We made arrangements for an additional sample to be obtained in what would be my final experience with prenatal diagnostic screening. Having already identified the specific mutation that our son and I shared in his laboratory at work, my husband had confirmed definitively with all my sisters that no one else in the family carried the mutation. I was a carrier through spontaneous mutation. My husband's curiosity about the mutation itself would guide him in recognizing precisely what to look for in the genetic screening. He would be able to determine the results, in what had previously taken two weeks, within a few days.

This time, the call came from my husband. When he began by asking me to sit down, I felt my heart pound wildly in my chest. It felt surreal for both of us. "We can do this," he said with a lilt in his voice, "we are very used to boys." He said that while he was sorry we wouldn't have the chance to have a daughter, we would have another son who did not have hemophilia.

My oldest sister's eyes have shown me insight and strength for as long as I can remember. They were as wide as I had ever seen them when she kept us focused in the birthing room one last time. "This *must* be his head!" she said. Her immediate connection with our youngest son was magnetic. Together they share a talent in art, supervisory skills, and contagious curiosity. This sparkling-eyed "little man"—fondly named by his dad—completed an unlikely threesome of brothers, each seven years apart. Our eldest, after recovering from his middle-school knowledge and embarrassment of how it all happened, is now seasoned in infant care and gadgetry. Our middle son, relishing being an older brother himself, nurtures his younger sibling with great interest, patience, and affection. For his part, the youngest provides his brothers with endless amusement and adulation.

There are no shortage of adventures and celebrations for the brothers to share: traveling across the country, first steps, track meets, Disney World, recitals, frosting cookies, music, kindergarten visits, college applications, trips to Maine, fishing, the prom, graduations, stone walls, concerts, sailing, studying French, houseboating, and leaving home for college. One of the strongest bonds they share, unique to each perspective, has been their awareness and sensitivity of hemophilia.

I cannot imagine my life without hemophilia. I think of conversations in support groups, clinics, and meetings, where generations of families spoke about the legacy of passing on hemophilia, and the mystical link with English and Russian royalty at the turn of the twentieth century. I contemplate my personal experience with a spontaneous incidence of the disorder, occurring in one-third of all cases, cementing its timeless presence from a reference in the Bible to today. I find it all fascinating: the history, the legacy, and the science.

"This is *my* hemophilia, not *yours!*" my son said to me. I remember the look of exasperation on his troubled teenaged face. He had asked me to give him more space in our home by not making hemophilia a constant focus. I had seen this struggle for ownership coming for years. The opportunity to process my own personal challenges of being a carrier had been wrapped securely in my volunteer work. Now it was time for me to back off, and focus my energy on helping him navigate through the emotional and physical changes happening as he grew into a young man's body. He was both ambivalent and angry about having hemophilia. Life was confronting him with more pressing concerns.

Our son had relapsed with hepatitis C before he entered high school. Research continued to support an aggressive approach, this time with a combination drug therapy that had a 40 percent response rate. The grueling side effects of the therapy seemed acceptable when compared to the long-term effects of advancing liver disease. We encouraged him to consider the option of taking a year off between high school and college to complete the draining, one-year drug therapy. He would then have the stamina to pursue a personal goal of running cross-country all four years of high school, an unthinkable pursuit for an individual with severe hemophilia only a generation ago. Sailing through the single-drug therapy as a 10-year-old was a strong indicator of his body's ability to respond to antiviral therapy. It was not, however, a predictor of how he would fare in a combination drug course nearly ten years later.

The regimen was wrenching for him most of the time. Weight loss, nausea, insomnia, and fatigue were often daily struggles. He tried to cope with his thinning hair gracefully, despite how it enhanced his gaunt stature. In his darkest and lowest moments of battling depression, it was often the strength of the bonds with his brothers that would carry him through. In the end, it was the resilience he had developed from living with hemophilia that helped him endure, and prevail over, the elimination of hepatitis C infection from his body.

* * *

After I spoke with the couple from California, a couple of weeks passed before I received a handwritten card in the mail. I had been thinking of Suzanne every day. They had found out that the male fetus she was carrying was affected with hemophilia. She explained how the gravity of this had hit them both harder than they were prepared for. I remembered one of the final thoughts we had shared at the end of our near two-hour conversation that Sunday morning.

"I know this may be difficult for you to answer. I am wondering what your feelings would be today, if you were in my position, knowing what you do about hemophilia, about having a child with hemophilia?" she had asked quietly.

"I cannot imagine my life without our son," I said with great emotion, tears filling my eyes. "I have watched him grow in his comfort and acceptance of having hemophilia. It doesn't define *who* he is, but instead has helped him to recognize his own insight, strength, and compassion." I mentioned the gift he has been to my life.

Suzanne's note described their assurance in knowing they wanted to keep this pregnancy. They felt supported by the prospect of entering parenthood and the world of hemophilia together with their son. When we had the chance to meet a few months later, she glowed in her pregnancy, beauty, and energy. The four of us, husbands included, talked warmly about the exciting adventure ahead. We shared family photographs, our son's college entrance essay, and hugs.

Several months later, while attending parents' weekend at my son's college, I had a chance to visit the couple once again. As we climbed the stairs to the second floor of their house, I was eager to see their 4-month-old baby. Lying on his back in the crib, he greeted us with an excited grin, happy eyes, and tiny kicking legs. His soft, sweet smell and snuggly little body were irresistible to me as I held him close. His mother described the details of his first emergency room visits, IV needlesticks, and infusions of factor. I nodded and remembered, as I touched the small hard swelling in his cheek, the remnant of his first bleed. We talked about the amazing growth and changes that happen every day with infants, and the emotional drain of seeing them prodded by needles. Each of their faces—parents and baby—showed that they were flourishing. It was a wonderful sight. Later in the weekend, as we pulled away from my son's apartment building after saying goodbye, one of my sisters commented on how impressed she was that I seemed to be holding myself together so well. "Nope, " I said quietly as the tears flowed, "I'm not sure if it will get any easier."

* * *

My knee throbbed as I pressed down on the clutch. I touched it with my left hand and felt a small hard lump. I had banged it against the corner of a cupboard the night before. I can be described as a "symptomatic carrier" of hemophilia, with a factor eight level that hovers around 30 percent. I smiled and thought of my first son, as I often do, and my link with him through this minor, little bump. Considering the number of major, larger bumps he has faced in his life so far, I know that he has many more ahead. We both now have twenty-one years of experience in diagnosing and managing the physical pains associated with hemophilia.

We are currently charting new territory together, with my son living on an opposite coast attending college. He is realizing the demands of college courses, the necessity of time management, and the responsibility that comes with greater independence. In our frequent phone conversations we discuss the complexity of serious relationships, managing monthly budgets, ordering medical supplies, and nutritious recipes. I continue to recall the pang in my heart when I had to say goodbye to him the first time we left him at college. I balance the pain of this memory with the image of him waiting at the airport for me that same year; his tall lanky body and long hair sticking out from underneath a knit cap, holding up a sign with the word "MOM" scratched on it in ink. When he saw me coming toward him he held it up, waving it back and forth, before flipping it over to read "WOW." He had the same crooked, impish grin that day—ingrained in my mind from the time he was hospitalized in a cage-like crib at five months old, with his tiny swollen arms restrained and taped with IVs. His grin through the bars that night seemed to tell us that not *everything* had changed, and things would be all right.

Protecting his body from injury requires a vigilance he is mastering well; protecting his heart will require a different kind of vigilance, one that he must discover for himself. Just like his brothers.

THE STORIES WE TELL

by Katherine Towler

WHEN I TURNED THIRTY in 1986, my sister gave me a T-shirt that featured a cartoon woman, one hand held dramatically to her cheek, mouthing the words, "I can't believe it. I forgot to have children." At work the following week, I attended a meeting with my coworkers, all women. Making small talk before we got down to business, one of them asked me what I had received for my birthday. I can still remember the looks on their faces when I described the T-shirt, my favorite gift. There was a moment of stunned, disapproving silence. Finally one of them said, "That's horrible."

At the time, I lived in Manhattan and was single. It wasn't just that I had forgotten to have children. I had forgotten to get married, too. My coworkers were sophisticated, urban career women, not the sort who would be expected to react as they did. But the T-shirt and I had crossed a line, mocking the sacrosanct notion of children as the ultimate fulfillment.

I did not set out to be a rebel. I am essentially a shy, private person, given to introspection. In most situations, I do my best not to get noticed. Somewhere along the way, however, it became clear that I was not like most other people. I did not want to have children. Though I saw nothing rebellious in this fact of my nature, others seemed to find it, if not rebellious, then at least subversive—or odd or sad or just plain inexplicable.

A friend recently told me the recurring fantasy of her adolescent years; she used to dream about being the mother of five boys. An only child, she wanted to have children and lots of them. She did not imagine her future husband. He would come along at the appropriate time and did not matter too much one way or the other, but she could see those five boys. "A basketball team," she said. "That's what I wanted."

When she asked me if I had ever had such fantasies, I was stumped. I played with dolls when I was young and liked dressing up, pretending to be a grown-up woman, but I cannot recall ever imagining the children I would one day have. It wasn't a part of my landscape, a part of the story I told myself.

* * *

At the age of eight, I used to sit on the living room couch with a copy of *Reader's Digest*. I would stop when I came to the brightly colored pages of the ads and make up stories about the people in the pictures, giving them names and relationships and concocting elaborate scenarios. They might be from Ohio, where my grandmother lived, and have a farm with lots of animals; maybe there had been an accident with a piece of equipment and someone got hurt. Now they were all running in from the field to get help. They were a ways out of town and there wasn't time to wait for the ambulance, so the father took the injured child and set him in the backseat of the station wagon. It would turn out to be only a broken leg, nothing major—my stories usually ended happily—but there were some tense moments getting to the hospital.

I have a vivid memory of myself at this age, turning the pages of the magazine, mumbling the words out loud. It wasn't enough to think the stories. I needed to say them to make them real. Like the books I read, my inventions were as real to me—if not more so—than the daily events of my life. The actual world, where I was forced to confront such agonies as gym class and other children my age, was a place full of frightening experiences completely beyond my control. The stories I created were mine, as were the books I read. Here I was master of everything, free to make it come out the way I wanted, free to become someone else through the pages of a book.

I became a writer on those afternoons when I sat on the couch with *Reader's Digest* and gave the two-dimensional people in the ads roles to play and plots to enact. Or maybe I was already a writer, and it was then that I fully recognized, for the first time, the depth of my desire to tell stories. The recurring fantasy of my adolescence was that I would grow up to live in a garret, where I would write brilliant poems and novels. I would not make much money. This went without saying and was the price to be paid for giving my life to art. I did not care about money or possessions. I wanted only the chance to write.

* * *

We all tell stories. We trade information, get to know each other, provide entertainment, make sense of a senseless world, laugh and cry through the telling of stories. What is gossip, the oldest form of communication, but telling stories? Yet the most significant stories often remain unspoken, hidden away. These are the stories we tell ourselves in the privacy of our own minds and hearts about who we are and who we may become.

The story I was telling myself when I turned thirty and wore my I-forgot-to-have-children T-shirt around New York was this: I would never meet the right man. This was the year when *Newsweek* magazine came out with an infamous article declaring that a woman who was single at thirty had only a 20 percent chance of ever getting married. The odds were stacked against me, the experts said, and I was inclined to agree with them, not so much because I trusted their forecasting. No, it was more that I wasn't at all sure I wanted to get married.

In this, as in my lack of desire to have a child, I was aware of being distinctly different. My single friends were desperate. They scanned the personals tirelessly and went on seemingly endless chains of blind dates. They talked about almost nothing else. Consumed with the longing for love and companionship, with the great hope of beginning the adult lives they had imagined, they were also terrified that the time for having children would pass before they found a partner.

One of these friends, a woman named Betsy, showed me a collection of baby clothes she had purchased. She laid the tiny things out on the bed in her studio apartment, darling little hand-knit sweaters and hats, a miniature pair of denim overalls. She was not seeing anyone at the time and was not planning to get pregnant until she met the right person. The articles of clothing lying there, waiting for a baby to fill them, were heartbreaking.

I felt compassion for Betsy. She was so unhappy, so filled with longing for something she knew should be part of her life but that she could not make happen. At the same time, I was perplexed. I could not imagine going out and buying clothes for a baby that did not show any signs of existing. How could anyone have such a tenacious desire for something so abstract? I understood that to my friends, the husbands they wanted to find and babies they wanted to bear were not the slightest bit abstract, but to me, it all seemed like nothing more than ideas, ideas that did not especially interest me.

* * *

Various people questioned me about my single state. Robin, a friend from college, was especially blunt and persistent.

"Don't you want to meet someone?" she asked.

We were sitting at her kitchen table after work one day. Robin had recently been married and wanted everyone to share her bliss.

I shrugged. "Not really."

"Don't you get lonely?"

Yes, I did get lonely, but I did not want to admit to this. It was loneliness that drove me out on occasional dates and led to brief, ill-fated affairs. I shrugged again. "I want to write. I don't see how I can write and be married."

She looked annoyed. "Of course you can write and be married. You think that there's a finite amount of energy, but it's not like that. If you let somebody into your life, you'll have more energy, more to give."

"Maybe," I said, quickly changing the subject.

The truth—and it was a hard truth to acknowledge, to myself or others—was that I was happiest when I was alone, seated at my desk, writing. Everything else in life was simply what came before writing or after it. Going through a day at work, meeting a friend for a movie and dinner, talking with my mother on the phone, taking a run along the river, all of it was simply what I had to do in order to make an appearance of being part of this world and to fill the time between the concentrated bouts of writing. My real life was elsewhere, however, in the pages of my journal and short stories and a fledgling novel.

When I was thirty, the choice seemed clear. I could give myself to writing, or I could give myself to another person. Robin tried to point out that this story I was telling myself, this story I clung to, justifying my choices, could change, but I scoffed at the idea. I did not understand then that the story I told myself was an evolving one, that nothing, not even my own understanding of myself, would remain fixed as I grew older.

* * *

For the better part of a year, my cousin tried to convince me to meet the upstairs tenant in her rambling old house in Newton, Massachusetts. We had so much in common, she said. I resisted, until one weekend when I was visiting, a snowstorm hit, and there was no possibility of going anywhere. "I could call Jim and see if he's home," she said hopefully.

"All right," I said with a certain resignation. What did it hurt to meet someone?

It turned out I was the fifth woman she had introduced to Jim. There he was, in the one-bedroom apartment upstairs, in his thirties, a psychologist with a slim, athletic build and neatly trimmed beard, alone. She couldn't stand it. He had to be perfect for someone.

Jim was, I quickly learned, a gentle man with a quick, sharp sense of humor and wide-ranging insight and knowledge on everything from bluegrass music to geology. He made his own jams and jellies and canned them. He read voraciously: fiction, memoir, history, and philosophy. He owned a cabin in Vermont where he planted a huge vegetable garden. We did, as my cousin had promised, have much in common. Among these things was the fact that neither of us wanted to have children, and it was this knowledge that made it much easier, a year and a half later, to say yes to marriage.

I don't remember when Jim and I had our first conversation on the topic. In my memory, the understanding that he didn't want children was simply there, a part of him I recognized and knew from the start, though of course he must have explained it at some point. I experienced it, at least in retrospect, as an essential piece of his makeup, something I absorbed about him as much as discovered, and was both relieved and the slightest bit disappointed to find. I had harbored a minor hope that, if I was going to meet someone, he would persuade me to have children, making the decision for me. I would wake up one morning and find that I was a mother. I would become like everyone else in the world. But in another part of myself, larger and more certain, there was an overriding sense of relief. I was off the hook. I could give up being alone, but I didn't have to become a parent.

We were both thirty-five and convinced, when we met, that we would never marry. The business of trying to find someone was too messy and discouraging and draining. It was easier to give up the idea altogether. Somewhere around thirty, we had both decided we would remain single. Done with wasting our time on relationships that didn't go anywhere, we were determined not to wade back into those waters unless we thought it would lead to commitment and marriage. Otherwise it wasn't worth it. We were dubious that the person who could convince us to change our minds would come along and, having made our peace with this, remained more or less content in our independent lives. For me, there was the consuming focus of my writing and the freelance business with which I supported myself. For Jim, there was a demanding career as a psychologist and the clients to whom he gave so much. With the decision to get married, with great trepidation, we traded our old story for a new one.

* * *

"You probably believe that you've finally met the one other person in the world who was meant for you," the priest said. "This is total nonsense, of course."

We were to be married in the Episcopal Church and, as part of our preparation, met with the priest for counseling. Had I heard him correctly?

"You could have ended up with countless other people," he went on. "The truth is that before this you weren't ready. You didn't meet the 'right person' because you weren't ready to take this step. Now both of you are ready."

His words were shocking. He was supposed to affirm the great wonder and romance of the step we were about to take. Instead, he threw cold water on it, but I recognized, even as I resisted hearing what he had to say, that he was right. The story we were currently telling, that at our more advanced age, against all odds, we had miraculously found each other, the one intended for each of us, was only part of the truth. There was also the truth that we were both stubborn, independent types, late bloomers who took a long time to come around to being able even to imagine each other, let alone make the decision to accept and attempt to love each other.

The transition to being married was not an easy one. Jim and I had to learn to give up some of our coveted independence and control. Saturdays were no longer an oasis of free hours we could spend as we liked, without consulting anyone. What time we went to bed at night made a difference to someone else. Gone were nights of staying up all hours with the lights blazing and music playing. We had to learn to take each other into account in making decisions about everything from what to have for dinner to buying a house. Sometimes I wondered if I would get more writing done if I were still single, if it would all somehow be easier. Eventually I came to see that maybe I would write more as a single person, but the writing would not be as good. Life might be easier, but it would not be as rich. Every once in a while, I think about what might have happened if I hadn't met Jim, and we hadn't both been ready to take that step. The vision of that other life, as a single person, haunts me. How much I would have missed, how much I would have lost. From Jim and with Jim I have learned so much. There are the simple things that have made my life fuller, like planting and harvesting our own potatoes, and the more profound, like learning to truly love.

No doubt people who have children think the same sorts of thoughts. How much they would have missed without having children, how much more impoverished their lives would be. No doubt they look at those who are childless and pity them for what they don't know they lack. My old friend Robin was one of these. I was inching toward forty, with no signs of becoming pregnant, when I visited her, emboldening her to ask the question directly. "Are you and Jim planning to have children?"

"No."

A pained look came over her face. "Are you sure?"

"Yes."

"Before we had kids, I was worried about what would happen with me and John," she said. "I thought I wouldn't be able to love him enough and love the kids. But it's not like that. Having kids only made our love stronger. It magnified the love."

I should have simply agreed with her and said no more, but I felt compelled to defend myself. "I can't make a living and write and be married and have kids. The kids would be too much. I just know this."

She gave me the pained look again. "Think about it."

The connection to our earlier conversation was not lost on me. I had made room in my life for Jim. Why couldn't I make room for children, too? This time, though, I was sticking to my story. Without the tug of that longing for children that so many others felt, without any desire on the part of my partner, it simply didn't make sense. Being a mother is not in me. I know in my heart that I would be a resentful mother, that my emotional and psychological makeup are such that it has taken everything I have to produce the writing I have produced. I have struggled to find enough left over to give to a marriage. I doubt there would be enough left over to give to a child.

* * *

A couple of years after Jim and I were married, my sister Leela, the one who gave me the T-shirt, called with the news that she was pregnant. There are three of us in my family—"the Towler girls"—as we were known as children. I am the oldest. Marie, the middle sister, has remained single and without children. Leela, eight years my junior and recently married, was looking like the last hope for our parents. To their credit, my parents never pressured any of us either to get married or to have children. I remember my father asking, once, "Have you and Jim decided not to have children?"

When I told him yes, that was the case, he responded, rather cautiously,

"I hope you've really considered this. You would make wonderful parents."

This is the refrain we have heard from many people, many times. We would make wonderful parents. I understand why they say this. We both enjoy children and are good at interacting with them. Jim has specialized throughout his career in working with children and adolescents. We are the sort of people who, to outward eyes, "should" have children because we would have so much to give them. I can't dispute this. In another life, one we are not leading, I agree—we would make great parents.

My father did not mention the topic again, and in the years since, has accepted, with graciousness and equanimity, the fact that we are not going to provide him with grandchildren. Now my little sister was stepping up to the plate.

When Leela asked me to be present at the birth of her first child, I was honored. I did not suspect she had an ulterior motive. I flew to Michigan ten days before her due date. It was unlikely the doctor would let her carry the baby to term because Leela is diabetic. The fetus of a diabetic is apt to gain more weight in the last trimester due to the higher blood-sugar levels. This, along with possible complications when a diabetic gives birth, makes doctors wary of letting the baby get too big. We hoped we had timed my arrival for just before the birth.

Leela met me at the airport, waving wanly when I spotted her at the gate. I tried not to show too much surprise at her size. She was huge, her belly so enormous it seemed miraculous that she could walk. In fact, she didn't really walk. It was more like a waddle, shuffling from one foot to the other, trying to balance all that weight on a frame that did not appear designed to hold it.

I went to hug her, but I succeeded in merely draping my arms over her shoulders, unable to get much closer. "You look great," I said, attempting to sound convincing.

"No, I don't. I look like hell and I feel like hell. If this baby isn't born by tomorrow, I'm going to kill myself."

Okay, I thought, so much for the beatific expectant mother I had been imagining.

* * *

"I'm exhausted," Leela said when we reached her house. "I haven't slept in three weeks."

"Why don't you take a nap?" I suggested.

"How can I take a nap when I can't lie down? Or sit for more than ten minutes without having to pee?"

"Why don't you try the couch? I could prop pillows around you."

"Right, like the couch is going to make a difference." She went stomping to the kitchen.

I followed her. "Do you want something to drink?"

"No, I do not want something to drink," she spat. "I want this baby to be born."

Leela's mood did not improve in the days that followed. On the third day of my visit, I accompanied her to her appointment at the hospital clinic. To her great relief, the doctor decided to prepare Leela to be induced, putting a gel on her cervix. The plan was to try this for a few days and see if the contractions would start on their own, but the response was instantaneous. Before long, the contractions were five minutes apart. Leela's husband, David, arrived from work, and we were ushered into a birthing room.

It was clear from the start that I had no business being in that room. Though I knew that Leela had wanted me there to support her and David, and simply to share the experience, I felt helpless and overwhelmed and ill-prepared. I had never attended a Lamaze class or seen a film of a birth. I had no idea what to expect, and no idea what to do. I had paid little or no attention to the pregnancy and childbirth stories I had heard over the years. I settled for being the one to apply the frequently begged for chap-stick while David said over and over and over, in a remarkably calm and controlled voice, "You're doing just great. Okay, breathe in. That's good. Now breathe out."

After more than twenty hours of labor, Leela's cervix had dilated to just eight centimeters. We had gone through a night and the better part of a day without sleep. Though Leela had finally agreed to drugs and an epidural, she was in such pain from the contractions that she was hallucinating, telling me she saw our dead grandmother at the foot of the bed. When I called my father from a payphone out in the hallway to give him an update, I began sobbing the moment I heard his voice, scaring him beyond reason. Every few hours, I went to the vending machines or the cafeteria. David and I ate bagels and cream cheese and candy bars and popcorn. I kept applying chapstick to Leela's lips and fishing ice chips from a plastic cup for her to suck on. David kept telling her to breathe. When the labor had gone on almost 24 hours, the doctor suggested it was time to consider a cesarean section. Leela came out of the haze of pain. "No. Give me more time."

I nearly burst into tears again. I avoided looking at David. Both of us would have done anything to convince her. I was ready to fall on my knees and beg her to have that C-section.

The doctor agreed to give her another half-hour to see if she would dilate more. Leela didn't understand, though we tried to explain, that it had been three hours since there had been any change. She thought it was fifteen minutes. The doctor, called away for an emergency C-section, left us alone for far longer than half an hour. The contractions came every minute, wracking her body. In between she fell asleep and snored, only to wake sixty seconds later, moaning and seizing David's hand, her hair plastered to her forehead, wet with sweat. I glanced at the window and saw that darkness was falling. It did not seem possible that we were going to go through a second night of this. Exhaustion and despair filled the air like a fog, surrounding the bed where Leela lay. In her delusional state, Leela was still clinging to the idea of the natural birth she had imagined, but David and I were long past imagining anything but an end to this ordeal. It had come to seem like simply a marathon of suffering. I could barely remember that there was supposed to be a baby at the end of this.

Finally a nurse arrived with two sets of green scrubs for me and David. "Come on," she said. "Rules are only one person in the operating room, but you've been here through all this. I'm getting you both in."

We made a procession down the hall to the operating room and there, at 7:09 p.m., John Towler Kausch was delivered by C-section after 28 hours of labor. He weighed 9 pounds and 1 ounce. David and I stood on either side of Leela, at the head of the gurney. A small plastic curtain was erected so she could not see what was happening below her waist. I could have looked over and watched the procedure, but I chose not to, until they lifted him into the air. He was so big, his arms and legs so long, his head so round, already so very much a person, so very much himself. It was impossible to believe he had been inside my sister's body. Everything about that moment was a glorious and fantastic miracle.

The next day, when I entered the hospital room and saw my sister propped up in bed, cradling Jack in her arms, I felt a tremendous wave of gratitude to Leela for her great act of faith in having a baby. It was as if she had done it for me, though of course she had not.

* * *

A few years later, Leela confessed that she had asked me to be there for Jack's birth because she thought it would convince me to have a child. "How did you think that was going to persuade me?" I said, laughing.

"I guess it wasn't the best idea," she said.

I love being an aunt, a role I seem ideally suited to play. Jack, now thirteen years old, sends me the poems he writes and always requests books as birthday gifts, though he does not think he wants to be a writer. He is learning Arabic and wants to be an archaeologist. Eve, his younger sister, plays the harp for me when I visit and demonstrates her ballet positions. She wants to teach music when she grows up. I have watched them go from being infants to toddlers to wonderfully articulate young people. I have shared the wonder and hope with which they have grown, with which they see the world, discovering, through them, wonder and hope again in myself.

I sometimes think that Jim and I just ran out of time. We weren't ready to have children when we got married, for the obvious reasons we gave and many others, ones we could voice and ones we could not. Now that I am fifty, those reasons seem to matter less. How many books I produce in the course of my career as a writer does not feel as crucial as it once did. I am more focused on the small moments, the simple pleasures that make life what it is. I am still most myself when I am at the desk, writing, but there's everything else I love, too—being in Vermont, when Jim and I work in the garden and take long bike rides on back roads, dinners of good food and wine with friends, and nights out at concerts and plays and movies. There's happiness in all of it. A missed day of writing is not the cause for anxiety, frustration, even anger, that it once was.

There have been times when I have revisited the idea of having children, when I have asked Jim, "Are you sure?" There have been times when I have watched a mother with her daughter, strangers on the street, and thought, "That could be me." There have been times when my period was late, and I have imagined that maybe, surprise of surprises, pregnancy would force us to become parents. There have been times when I listened to older women talk about seeing their children married, about the births of grandchildren, and felt a pang of regret, knowing I will not have these experiences. But these times have been few and far between. For the most part, it has been clear that, though it could have gone another way, this is the way it went for me, and it is right.

* * *

There are many ways to tell a given story. This story can be told as one about a choice not made, a path not taken. Framed by a culture where having children is the norm, it is a story about what I did not do. People feel justified asking the question: why don't you have children? I don't ask them: why *do* you have children? But I have not experienced this story as one of negation. For me, it is a story of embracing, at each turn in my life, what was best for me and what was best in me.

As a woman, I feel peculiarly compelled to defend my choice not to have children. I shouldn't feel this way. Perhaps just as no one truly makes a decision to have a child—it is too momentous and life-changing an event to be reduced to something that can be debated, pros and cons weighed, a decision arrived at—no one truly decides not to have a child, either. It is an evolution in a life as much as it is a decision, a recognition of who you are.

The story I have told, like the stories of many other women, those who have children and those who do not, is a story about accepting ourselves and the vast possibilities afforded by the accident of our time and place of birth. It is a story about finding the stories that fit us best. It is a story about growing into the lives we are given.

A COMPLICATED PRIVILEGE

by Elizabeth Larsen

I MET MY DAUGHTER Flora in the lobby of the Westin Camino Real, the grandest hotel in Guatemala City. At the time, I didn't question our decision to stay there. The low value of the currency meant we could afford a little opulence while we celebrated this momentous event. We spent the day before Flora was brought to us sightseeing in Antigua, the former capital of the Spanish colonial government that is today a rustically tasteful haven of cafés, textile boutiques, and bed-and-breakfasts. That night, back in Guatemala City, we waded in the pool and ran on the treadmills in the fitness center, where a polite attendant handed us plush white towels and spritzed the equipment with a flowery disinfectant. We splurged on room service and sipped the surprisingly fine Merlot stocked in the mini-bar. We became so absorbed in our books that we hardly noticed the sun setting behind the volcanoes that watch over the city. I wrote letters to Flora in a journal I'd bought especially for the trip. "We've been waiting so long to meet you—almost seven months!" the first entry reads. "Ever since you were seven days old and the agency emailed us your beautiful photos, we've wondered what you will be like."

Today, I reread that journal and clearly see what I was editing out of my rosy narrative: I chose the Westin because I unconsciously needed to pad the space between my anxieties about adopting a child I had never seen and the reality of the destitution most Guatemalans live with every day. Those same pages also tell me that I was more emotionally fragile than I was willing to admit.

hidden complex emotions about adoption

When Jonathan and I decided that our third child would be adopted, part of me felt guilty because I thought I was getting off easy. We had two boys. We wanted our third child to be a girl. I grew up the eldest of four sisters. My life—girls' elementary school, women's college—was built on a foundation of female companionship that I dreamed of for my own family. Instead of spinning nature's roulette wheel, I wanted the sure bet that adoption offered. That the longed-for daughter would arrive without the vomiting and labor pains and hormone rodeo seemed too good to be true. I simply could not imagine how waiting—what a useless word for such torture!—to love and raise a child who was already born would plunge me into a desperate depression.

emotional effects on parents?

So, when the elevator at the Westin chugged toward the lobby, I was propped up by Zoloft and adrenaline. When Jonathan pointed the video camera at me and said "Here's Mommy waiting to see Flora for the first time!" I looked at the lens, and for the sake of my child, stifled the urge to yell, "Shut that damn thing off!"

Then the doors slid back. I remember noticing the rose marble floors and the opera house drapes and wincing. I was naked and sweating when I met my sons in the sterile fluorescent glow of a hospital birthing room. Now I was facing Flora's foster mother, Maria, a stout Guatemalan woman with a 6-month-old baby riding at her side in a woven sling. As they bent their heads toward each other and laughed—later I'd look at photographs of this moment to remind myself that Flora *could* laugh; for weeks her eyes grazed her new home with a blankness that made it seem as though all the color had been drained from her life—I wanted to be anywhere but in this grossly dolled-up public space where the bellhops and businessmen were taking in the awkwardness of the moment.

Our Guatemalan lawyer was, to our surprise, apparently out of the country visiting family. Our adoption agency in the U.S. had given us the phone number to his office and when we pleaded with his assistant, Lucia, to come and translate during the meeting with Maria, she said she wasn't available. My Spanish had fallen victim to my 40-year-old brain, which despite months of refresher lessons, couldn't fire up the words I needed when my class discussed cooking utensils or firefighting. Jonathan's was nonexistent. But I was somehow able to ask Maria to walk with us to the hotel's business center so that we could hire a translator. On our way, a gray-haired man in a suit stopped to shake Maria's hand. Later she told me that he was an adoption lawyer whom she used to work for. He owed her four months' salary that she knew she would never be paid.

The woman who ran the business center was feeding documents into a fax machine when we blew into her office. Seeing Flora, she stood up from her desk and shook hands with Jonathan and me. Then she nodded at Maria. I asked her if she could ask Maria a few questions about how to care for Flora: What time did she go to bed? How often did she nap? Did she eat solid foods?

The translator dutifully repeated my questions, but when Maria answered, she paused.

"She wasn't told that this was your pick-up trip," she said. "She thought you were only visiting."

As the realization sank in that she was saying goodbye to a baby she had bathed and fed and loved for six months, tears spilled down Maria's cheeks. She adjusted the stroller's back to the flat position to show us that Flora liked to take her bottle lying on her back. And then, her voice catching, she recited the prayer she repeated every night as Flora fell asleep, making the sign of the cross as she whispered. She explained that she and her husband tried to prepare themselves for the moment they had to say goodbye, but it was always difficult.

Worried that an impromptu farewell was too abrupt for both Maria and Flora, we asked her to join us for lunch in our hotel room. I have no idea what I ate, but I remember that Maria ordered fried chicken and gave Flora french fries, which she happily gummed throughout the meal. We talked and gestured about our families. We told Maria about our boys. Maria explained that her youngest son, who was not quite a teenager, had the same birthday as Flora.

Maria stayed until 8:00 that evening and I still believe that our ability to communicate is one of those examples, like the stories of mothers who lift cars off their children, of how in times of incredible stress, the body can push itself past its everyday limitations. Besides talking about her own children, I asked Maria if she knew Beatriz, Flora's Guatemalan mother. When Jonathan and I accepted Flora's referral, one of our first questions was whether or not Beatriz would want to meet us when we came to Guatemala. We had done enough reading to know that _any information about genetic and cultural heritage can be pure gold for people who are adopted_. We wanted our daughter to have as much as we could possibly get her, so that if she was ever interested in knowing more about her heritage, the process wouldn't be the paperwork version of an archeological dig.

Through our American social worker we had learned that Beatriz "would love to know us." Then, one week before our trip, our social worker had called and told me that a meeting would not be possible because Beatriz had gone back to her village and wasn't reachable.

"But she's from Guatemala City," I said. "Do you think he is telling us the truth?"

"It's hard to know," the social worker answered. "Some lawyers in Guatemala do facilitate meetings between a child's Guatemalan and adoptive families, but many are still uncomfortable with any degree of contact. I think it's impossible to know whether he's being honest or shading the truth to suit what he personally thinks is best. Maybe he just didn't want to tell us that Beatriz changed her mind."

I was so new to intercountry adoption—a subculture with so many adamant and conflicting opinions about the "right" way to parent that I was terrified *any* decision I made would be wrong—that I worried our desire to meet Beatriz was more about us than about her or Flora or the values of their culture. So I thanked the social worker for her time and hung up.

Now, sitting across a fold-out room service table draped with a crisp white tablecloth, I wanted to know more. What, I asked Maria, is Beatriz like?

Maria smiled. "*Muy linda*," she said. "*Muy cariñosa*." Very lovely. Very affecionate. We had a photocopy of a picture of Beatriz that was taken when they matched Beatriz and Flora's DNA, so I knew that she was beautiful. But this second detail stopped me. Maria had to be talking about Beatriz's behavior toward Flora. Did Beatriz visit Flora when she was being fostered by Maria? This thought comforted me. I wanted the experience of being nursed, bathed, cooed to—*loved* by—her first mother to be stored in Flora's cells. I asked if Beatriz had visited Flora while she was living with Maria.

"*Si!*" Maria nodded, enthusiastically. I explained that the lawyer's office had said Beatriz didn't have a phone number. Maria looked confused. Then she held up her cell phone and gestured that Beatriz's number was stored in her speed dial.

"Would she want to meet us?" I asked.

Maria shook her head. I think she said that it would be too painful for Beatriz to see us with her daughter. Maybe, I thought, the lawyer *was* trying to protect Beatriz. Who were we, with our notions of openness to intrude on her private sorrows? → difficult f/ Flora's birthmother

I looked at Flora, still working on a french fry. Maria had styled her hair so that two ponytails stuck out from the top of her head like miniature oil geysers. She was heartbreakingly dear, contentedly munching away with no idea of the shock and sadness that was to come when she woke up the next morning and Maria wasn't there to help her ease into the day. Suddenly, my happiness about Flora getting at least a tiny slice of Beatriz didn't seem so clear-cut. Somewhere not far from our bubble of lavish buffets and poolside margaritas, a woman was coming to terms with the fact that for all she knew, she would never see her child again.

We'd brought presents for both Maria and Beatriz. The agency had warned us to keep birthmother gifts simple because anything fancy like jewelry could lead to unwanted questions by relatives or friends who knew nothing about a baby. Worse yet, they could be misconstrued as bribes. For Beatriz, I'd bought a wooden heart and a second copy of the journal I was using to write about the adoption. I knew from the social worker reports that Beatriz could read and write—a true accomplishment in a country where 30 percent of adults are illiterate. (Maria signed all her documents with a thumb print). So we tucked a letter into the journal. "We will raise your daughter to love and honor you and to love Guatemala," it read. "If you want to see her or to meet us in person, we will come back to Guatemala."

As Maria was getting ready to leave, I opened the package with the journal and wrote our names on the back of the envelope. I knew that neither our social worker nor our agency nor our lawyer would have approved—I think because they worried that Beatriz would try to extort money from us or attempt to immigrate illegally—but I suddenly didn't care. Jonathan and I knew Beatriz's address and her national identification number. Why wasn't she entitled to the same information? helping the birthmother

"Please. Give. Beatriz," I said in Spanish to Maria. She nodded that she would. When she left, I was weeping. It was the first taste I had of the bittersweet joy and complex privilege that is the life of the adoptive parent.

* * *

I was in the shower when the phone rang on the morning of Flora's first birthday, so it was a bit of a shock when Pamela, our new *au pair* from Ecuador, rapped on the door and nervously explained that someone from Guatemala was on the line. I pulled a towel around me and raced downstairs, my wet feet stamping footprints across the carpeting. It was Maria, but unlike that weekend in Guatemala City when adrenaline had pushed my ears and vocal cords past their linguistic limitations, I couldn't make out a single word from the raspy tangle of syllables rapidly coming at me.

I pushed the phone toward Pamela. My hair was dripping down my back.

Pamela nodded her head as she listened, then asked Maria to pause for a moment while she translated.

"She's calling for Beatriz," Pamela said.

"That's Flora's Guatemalan mother," I answered.

Pamela's eye's widened. This clearly wasn't the kind of cultural exchange—nearly naked host mother, emotional foster mother, message-sending birthmother—she'd had in mind when she signed up at the agency in Quito.

"Maria said that Beatriz wanted her to call and thank you and Jonathan," Pamela continued. "She says that she knows she made the right decision. She's doing well."

I'm sure it was the combination of Maria's selflessness—foster mothers in Guatemala make at most $160 a month—and the proof that Beatriz was marking the milestone's of Flora's life that shattered me that morning. My shoulders slumped and my chin hit my chest as I wailed. Pamela put her hand on my shoulder.

"She is very emotional," she told Maria.

Worried about the rapidly skyrocketing cost of the call, I got back on the phone to say goodbye. I sent Maria hugs and kisses and love from

Flora, Jonathan, the boys, and me. I asked her to kiss Beatriz for us and to give her our love and to tell her that we talk about her all the time with Flora. I told her to tell Beatriz that Flora was thriving. That was all I could cram in before the connection cut back to the drone of the dial tone.

Maria called again six weeks later. But instead of bringing news from Beatriz, she explained that our lawyer had threatened to fire her if she called us again. (How he knew we were in contact is still a mystery to me. Did Maria or Beatriz tell him? Did our agency?) She suggested that she could keep her word to him by never calling us again, but that we could still contact her.

That night while I was changing Flora's diaper I sang, "Who's my girl?" pulling the tab taut across her stomach. She pointed at her chest and laughed, her dimples creasing into pinholes.

When we accepted Flora's referral, Jonathan and I were confused because all four of her names were the exact same as Beatriz's. We decided it was the efficient work of our lawyer—a detached decision made for the sake of the checkups, blood tests, court appearances, and paperwork that was to follow. So we changed her first name to Flora and made Beatriz her middle name. Now, as Flora was reaching up to tickle my chin, our reasoning seemed preposterous. Beatriz, I suddenly realized, had chosen Flora's name. Giving her child her name was the only gift she could offer, the one filament of connection between their tragically brief life together and an unknown future.

Jonathan walked into the room, flushed and sweaty from wrestling with the boys, who were now downstairs, happily digging their spoons into bowls of cold applesauce. I kissed Flora's cheeks and looked up at him. Having a third child had been my idea. Jonathan had only agreed reluctantly, after months of debate had made it clear that I would always regret it if we stopped at two. Now that the consequences of that decision—and I don't mean only the stresses of nurturing and supporting three tender souls, but also the complications of raising a child of a different race and culture—were more complex than we could have ever imagined, I felt horribly guilty for talking him into it. No matter how many Spanish-speaking caregivers we employ (after Pamela was done

(handwritten margin note)
Adoption
·· complex f/ parent
• child loses home culture
• double-takes fm strangers

with her *au pair* stint, we hired Mimi, a woman my age who was born and raised in Guatemala City) or how many trips to Guatemala we take, white American culture will be what Flora intuitively understands. Perhaps that will never bother her. But I can guess that the doubletakes we get while grocery shopping together may.

Jonathan smiled at us. "She's getting so big," he said. "She'll be talking soon." Ever since that first day at the Westin, his doubts about having a third child have been surpassed by his adoration for his daughter.

His grin fell as he noticed the tears on my cheeks. "Did something happen today?"

I nodded my head. I was too spent to tell him about Maria's phone call and how it made me question not only the ethics of our lawyer but also the legality of Flora's adoption.

"What is it?" he asked.

"I think Beatriz wants us to find her," was all I could say.

* * *

I was working on deadline the afternoon the searcher's email flashed on my computer screen. It was a month after we had made the decision to hire someone to find Beatriz and I was terrified that our good intentions would yield disastrous consequences. Many adults who have been adopted strongly believe that searching for birthfamilies is such a private and personal choice that it's not a decision that should be usurped by adoptive parents. What if this was a decision Flora ended up resenting? And what if we were wrong that Beatriz wanted us to find her? Perhaps the lawyer had been protecting her after all. What if the searcher inadvertently drew attention to her and put her in harm's way? What if our idealistic ideas about the importance of openness were inappropriate for Guatemala? Jonathan and I agonized over how to weigh our belief that to know one's roots is a human right against our desire to let Flora determine the course of her adult life and relationships.

In the end the scale tilted down on the side of two facts. First, because Beatriz had contacted us through Maria, we felt fairly confident that she would want ongoing information about her daughter. And second, the economic situation in Guatemala is so unstable that we worried that by the time Flora was old enough to make a choice to search, the trail might have gone cold. When we wired the money to Guatemala to pay the searcher, we told ourselves that if she found Beatriz, Jonathan's and my role was to act as placeholders. We would send letters and photos and—if it seemed like Flora could handle it—we would visit her in person. We would maintain the connection between Beatriz and Flora until Flora was old enough to decide for herself what she wanted from this relationship.

Our agency was supportive of our search, but counseled us that we shouldn't make contact with Beatriz simply because we felt guilty that we were raising her child.

What about grateful? I thought to myself. I didn't want Beatriz to be punished her entire life for a decision that in my heart I now knew was not truly a choice. Nor did I want my daughter to never know who in her birthfamily she looks like—or not be able to fill out the family history section of a health questionnaire. I didn't want Flora to wonder why Beatriz had decided to place her for adoption. I wanted her to have as many answers as she had questions.   Flora's roots

It doesn't take much effort to connect the dots and realize that almost every woman today in the developing world—whether she's Guatemalan, Indian, or Chinese—who places her child for adoption in a foreign country is buckling under some form of financial, reproductive, or soci-etal oppression. Making a decision in these circumstances is not in any way a choice. And that's where we get to what still wakes me up at night and makes me toss for hours about this choice we *were* able to make. Because try as I might to justify adopting Flora by telling myself that she was going to be adopted even if we had walked away from the adoption, and that life with a family is what every child deserves, I can't look away from one ice-cold fact: I was blessed with two sons and still ached for a girl. Because I am American and wealthy, I was able to get what I wanted, even though at forty years old, my biological options were dwindling. I didn't want to accept that my life could be bound by the limitations of biology. In my culture, we think of this as reaching for our dreams.

[handwritten margin note: birthmother's lack of choice makes adoptive mom feel guilty abt choice]

During our pre-adoptive counseling, Jonathan and I both hashed out our concerns about the ethics of choosing the gender of our child. We also discussed the potential hardships for a Latina child raised in an all-white family. We knew from reading the few books out there on intercountry, transracial adoption that many transracially adopted people feel internally like they are white descendants of European settlers because that's how they have been raised. But outside their families they're often at a loss because people expect them to intuitively understand what it means to be Chinese or Columbian or Haitian. They are also often unprepared to defend themselves against racism because their adoptive parents haven't experienced it firsthand.

We asked our social worker about the possibility of doing an open domestic adoption. Her answer was that since we already had two biological children and were only open to adopting a girl, we wouldn't be a very compelling family to an American birthmother. We never once considered foster care, nor did we give any serious consideration to adopting a white child from Eastern Europe. Our youngest son was only a year old when we started our paperwork and we wanted to preserve the birth order of the family. We also didn't want to take on the challenges of a child with a severe attachment disorder or fetal alcohol syndrome. (I don't mean to imply that this is standard in children from Eastern Europe, only that the stereotypes frightened us.) We wanted a healthy baby who had never spent even an hour in institutionalized care. Guatemala had lots of them. And it was easy to get to from the United States, which meant that we could go back often for family vacations. The choice, as we saw it, was clear.

Jonathan was often openly concerned about the ethics of intercountry adoption. "I just need to know that the child we adopt has no other options," he tearfully explained to our social worker. When I recently recounted this conversation to a woman who had been adopted from Korea, she questioned our agency for not going deeper into a discussion that could have potentially made us decide that intercountry adoption was not right for us. But the truth is, even if the agency had offered us a pamphlet or questionnaire or lecture Powerpointing recent criticisms about intercountry adoption, I wouldn't have listened—because I was so power-

fully absorbed in the force of my own wanting. If someone had told me
that a fraction of the $30,000 we spent on the adoption would have
allowed a poor Guatemalan mother to keep her child, I would have felt
guilty, but my decision wouldn't have changed. I was spending that money
because I wanted a daughter. Our agency told us they had carefully vetted
their Guatemalan lawyers to ensure that they were involved in adoptions
"for the right reasons." Even though I'm a reporter who is trained to ferret
out hidden facts, we did no research to assure ourselves that our agency's
evaluation of their partners was sound.

wanted a child badly ↓

never checked on the facts

* * *

The email from the searcher did relieve us of one worry. Beatriz *had* been
hoping we would find her. She thanked us for making it possible to watch
her child grow up and confided that the decision to place Flora for adoption was the most wrenching of her life. She missed Flora, prayed for
Flora, and wanted her to know that she would always love her and that
not a day passed when she didn't think about her. She said that before the
adoption she was a bubbly person. Now she kept mostly to herself.

→ Beatriz's ♥

Beatriz told the searcher that she'd seen only two photos of Flora. I
knew that Maria had over two rolls of shots we'd given her for Beatriz and
that—prior to our search—the head of our agency had hand-carried a
photo album to Guatemala that she was going to give Beatriz through our
lawyer. I still haven't been able to bring myself to ask Beatriz if she ever
received the wooden heart or the silk journal with the letter we wrote her.
Because, while I can't be angry with Maria for not passing along the photographs—she couldn't endanger her job—I don't want to know for certain that she kept our present from Beatriz.

It's one thing to imagine a woman in a faraway place grieving for her
lost child. Before we found Beatriz I did this daily. I pictured her
despairing that she would never see her daughter again. But as soon as an
image of her sobbing into her pillow or asking the lawyer for photos of her
child entered my mind, my brain concocted a counter-narrative, a story
where Beatriz was healing from her loss. A story where not having to raise

the child I tucked into bed every night freed her in some way to embrace a less conflicted future. This wasn't the right time for her to have this baby, I reassured myself. She wanted Flora to have opportunities she couldn't give her.

Intercountry adoption enjoys a reputation for being a win-win solution that solves America's fertility problem and saves the world's babies in one ecstatic rainbow-colored swoop. But what about the women who grow these children inside them and then can care for them only in their hearts? I don't know if every woman who places her son or daughter for adoption suffers from the pain of losing that child. But I know that Beatriz does. And being witness to that despair—not to mention experiencing firsthand how the system in Guatemala can take advantage of foster mothers like Maria—has changed how I view intercountry adoption.

If I'm purposefully sketchy about the details surrounding Beatriz's decision, it's not because they are somehow sordid or shameful. Rather, it's because I'm still not sure how much—if any—of this story is mine to tell. Adoption stories—rooted as they are in the dark corners of crisis and loss—are naturally compelling. On the one hand, I believe that speaking openly about Flora's life before us honors both her and Beatriz. We keep nothing from Flora, and a photograph of Beatriz, her eyes glancing shyly away from the camera, commands center stage on Flora's bureau. But I also worry that it's not fair for other people to know the particulars of Flora's and Beatriz's stories before Flora is old enough to understand them and share them herself. So the fact that I'm not explaining whether Beatriz is married or unmarried or the mother of one or three or five children is simply because I'm trying to be a good mother and decent adoptive parent. What I will say is that girls as young as twelve place their babies for adoption. So do 40-year-old mothers who can't afford a fourth or fifth child. Some women have sent more than one child to the United States. Poverty leaves one with no options. So does a culture where abortion is illegal but giving birth out of wedlock literally ruins a woman and her child's lives.

I realize that the stories I'm spilling are in many ways far more intimate and revealing than the facts of my daughter's Guatemalan life. My perhaps naive hope is that I'm sharing a few facets of intercountry adoption not commonly discussed—outside the adoptive community, that is—to paint a more complete picture of its gains and losses. Like most parents of children adopted from other countries, Jonathan and I often find ourselves being praised for our decision to adopt. We've learned to deflect well-meaning strangers who tell us our daughter "has no idea how lucky she is," by earnestly explaining that *we* are the lucky ones. People usually nod condescendingly, as if we're merely spouting an empty platitude. Their smugness speaks volumes about how most Americans think about adoption. The way these people see it, Jonathan and I are saints because we're doing something—loving a child who is of a different race and gene pool—they could never do themselves.

What they don't understand is that in those first weeks after we brought Flora back to our house, I was so nuts about her that I felt—and still do—that in many ways adoption is a more powerful experience than giving birth. You expect to love a child who comes out of your body and shares your strong eyebrows and slate-blue eyes. But to give yourself over so completely to a baby who has no genetic link to you puts you face-to-face with the glorious fact that human beings are just plain hardwired to love a child who is theirs to raise. For the first two months that Flora was with us, I was swept away by the same giddy infatuation that I associate with the all-consuming early days of a romantic relationship. I held her all day, only relenting to hand her to Jonathan or my sons. I told our families that this hovering was necessary for Flora to develop a secure attachment to me. And while that's true, it's also undeniable that I didn't want to share her.

Many adoptive parents describe their connection with their children as something that was destined by a larger force. "God brought us to each other," they'll say. "We were meant to be a family." While my love for Flora makes me understand why people would believe that an attachment so powerful can only be explained spiritually, I feel that Flora is my child because something went terribly wrong. To believe otherwise would, in my opinion, dishonor Beatriz.

For many Americans, it's unimaginable that a life of poverty might be a life worth living. For them, Flora's adoption is measured completely by what she gains: private schools, soccer camps, piano lessons, college. They don't factor in the trauma of being taken not only from the arms of both her first mother and her foster mother, but also the tastes and smells and sounds of her culture. To gain a family, Flora had to lose a family. And to

background become an American child, she had to stop being a Guatemalan child.

* * *

A month after Flora turned two, Jonathan, Mimi, and I sat on the floor of Flora's bedroom, punching numbers into the phone. Flora was tucked into the curve of Jonathan's arm as he turned the cardboard pages of *The Very Hungry Caterpillar.* He was too nervous to read the story, so he pointed to the illustrations and ticked off the plot's highlights: caterpillar, leaf, apple, salami, butterfly. Outside, the bare branches of our neighbor's oak tree scratched the gray November sky. I imagined it was just the opposite in Guatemala City. There, the dry season had begun; even the tiniest raindrops had dissolved into the thin mountain air.

"We're calling your Guatemalan mommy," I said to her. My voice was so overly calm and falsely upbeat that I was sure even Flora could tell I was stressed. "We're calling Beatriz."

Beatriz had told the searcher that it would comfort her to hear our voices, so we'd agreed on a time to talk. But I was still uneasy that in my desire to do something caring toward Beatriz, I was taking away Flora's right to make her own decisions. After what felt like forty rings, Beatriz was on the phone.

"Elizabeth?" she said, after hearing my accent.

"Beatriz?"

As with all the other phone calls to and from Guatemala, I was too jangled to be able to pick out actual words from the lightning streak of Spanish. After a few minutes, Jonathan held the phone up to Flora's ear. Because Mimi only speaks Spanish with her, the song of the language was familiar, comforting. She smiled.

"Say *hola* to Beatriz," I said.

Flora turned her head from the receiver and arched her back. I knew that Flora was only a toddler, and the possibility that she would remember this moment was slim.

"Say *hola*," I whispered.

After a few more tries, Flora grabbed the receiver and listened.

"Hi," she said and passed the phone to Mimi.   → English, not Spanish

I didn't have to be on the line to hear the muffled agony of Beatriz → short exchange, sobbing. And once again I was confronted by the fact that Jonathan and I not daughter were—and still are—too new to adoptive parenting to be making such to mother. important decisions based on what our hearts tell us is right. Unlike our open domestic-adoption counterparts, we don't have the benefit of university-sponsored longitudinal studies and books detailing best practices. We don't have the directors of adoption-research institutes evangelizing across the country for the benefits of openness. We don't even really have an open adoption. Yes, we are in contact with Beatriz, but the arrangement is jerryrigged, a slipshod improvisation. Beatriz did not get to choose us to parent her child. Nor does she get to decide the terms of future contact. There is no legally binding document that sets the terms, only a tendril of trust woven from the fact that Jonathan, Beatriz, and I all love the same precious child.

Mimi tried to sooth Beatriz by telling her how well Flora was doing. "She's the princess of the house," she said. "She's very bright and loves school. She's very, very happy." Suddenly Mimi was crying, too.

"Beatriz wants to talk to you again," she said.

I picked up the receiver and explained that I was sorry I couldn't speak to her very well in Spanish and that I would practice so that we could talk more. Beatriz paused. I wondered if I had said something to offend her.

"Thank you," she said in English. It was the most heartbreaking gratitude I've ever received.

"*Muchos besos*," I said. Many kisses. I wanted to tell Beatriz that I was sorry we had changed Flora's name, but I was too overwhelmed to know where to start. I also wanted to tell Beatriz that I loved her, but we still hadn't met face-to-face and I worried that she would think it was inappropriate. With Mimi whispering the correct words, I instead said that we loved Guatemala and were raising Flora to love her country and her Guatemalan family.

"Thank you," she said again. "Thank you."

"*Muchos abrazos, Beatriz*," I said. Many hugs. I reached for Jonathan and Flora. We huddled together as I held out the receiver.

"*Hasta luego, Beatriz*," we said. That we didn't know what direction this relationship would take made saying goodbye that much more painful, so we waited just a bit longer. Flora darted across the room to find another book.

Finally Beatriz broke the silence.

"*Hasta luego*," she said. "*Hasta luego mi amor*."

Many of the names in this essay and a few identifying characteristics have been changed to protect people's privacy.

WOMAN OF HEART AND MIND

by Denise Gess

SAM KNEW WHERE TO SIT when he came into my house. That night he knew not to snuggle up to me on the sofa where until now we'd mixed foreplay with conversations about law school, Orwell, and Reagan, naturally intertwining the political and sexual. And that is probably why, although I was wearing the shorts Sam liked and the white shirt he loved, he chose to sit in the blue-velvet club chair. In June 1984, nine months after our first date, everything between us had changed as certainly as a tornado lifts sturdy oaks and hurls them hundreds of yards, trailing their roots in the dark wind like wild strands of hair.

He was holding a manila bank envelope and he moved it from one hand to the other as if he might transform it into a white dove, or a long, blue silk scarf, or a riot of purple irises. But when, after thirty seconds, nothing happened, when it remained merely a sleeve filled with crisp new bills, Sam laid it on the coffee table. "Here's the catastrophe money," he said. Then he leaned forward, dropping his clasped hands in the space between his legs. Hunkered, sheepish.

I'd noted his worn-out sandals, noted that he was more tan than he was the week before, which told me he'd headed out to the beach those two days he did not have classes, and I'd noted that his mop-ish brown hair—streaked through with blond, and wiry, surprising grays—had grown shaggier. He nudged the envelope with the tips of his fingers, making it glide like a small paper boat on the freshly polished cherrywood tabletop.

"You need a haircut again." It was all I could think to say; anything more would have been—in Sam's lawyer-speak—"begging the question." We'd had the weighty, difficult conversation already:

Do you love me?

I can't say that I don't love you, but… I'm not in love with you.

I had asked the important question far too late.

We began dating in late September of 1983. I was in my last year of graduate school at Rutgers University in Camden, New Jersey, divorced after ten years of marriage, working on the rewrites of my first novel, raising my daughter, attending night classes, and teaching freshman composition as a graduate assistant. Sam was finishing up his last year of law school there. He came to law late, having spent several years working and traveling before relocating to Philadelphia and investing money in real estate—"BR&R" he called it, shorthand for buy, renovate, and rent—which yielded an income large enough to put him through law school.

A mutual friend decided we should meet and although I wasn't even thinking about dating, I agreed. Secretly, I hoped that we'd take one look at each other, say a few words, and decide "no go." I was straddling the line that year between two selves: one public and one private.

The public self was a 30-year-old woman people assumed had, as they had, gone away to college, lived dorm life, indulged in the requisite partying, anarchy, and musical beds. And they assumed, because I'd had the ridiculously good fortune of having my novel accepted before I finished graduate school, that I was worldly.

But my private self was a different person altogether, a woman who had been raised Catholic and had been slavishly, if goofily, devoted to emulating one of my religion's most luminous icons: the Blessed Virgin Mary. I was the firstborn in a home of Italian descent where my father played a Perry Como rendition of the classic "Ave Maria" on the upstairs hi-fi while I sequestered myself in the basement and listened to Mitch Ryder's *Devil with a Blue Dress* on a portable record player. I had taken my grandfather's advice, "*una regazza per bene non lascia il petto paterno prima che si sposi*—a good girl does not leave her father's house before she's married—to heart. In the Italian-Catholic paradigm a good girl was a virgin when she married (I was), became a mother (I had), and embraced that motherhood zealously (I still do). Even my part-time jobs revolved around caring for children who were yoked under the then politically incorrect labels of profoundly retarded and emotionally disturbed.

In 1983, although I was a mother and a writer, I was still an apprentice to academia, and was unschooled, or more accurately, doltish, when it came to dating. I masked the inexperienced self who'd never gone to concerts in a van or dropped acid at a party, who'd spent the better part of her early twenties learning to make french onion soup from scratch, reading *Madame Bovary*, and teaching myself to write while my husband taught high school math.

According to my friend, Sam was witty, charming, and very tall; he had graduated from the University of Connecticut. In fact, I was told, his former love, a woman I later came to refer to as the Great Diane, whose genius I felt dwarfed by, was awarded a full professorship fresh out of graduate school. All reports (including a few unsolicited reports from Sam) indicated she was destined for unprecedented fame.

It's only now that I've come up with a word to describe men like Sam. I call them "piners"—men who walk away from the woman they claim to love the most and then spend the rest of their lives pining for her, finding all others deficient in silly ways—feet too big, snores, cooks too well, doesn't cook well enough, likes the wrong music—flaws that render others less suitable than the goddess of their invention. (A goddess, by the way, who barely remembers him, and in most cases, in addition to succeeding in her chosen career, has married and had children while he is still coddling her ghost.) To be fair, women are guilty of this kind of sabotage, too.

Anyway, despite my initial reservations, Sam and I met for a drink on a rainy September evening. I can't say that I remember a single thing we talked about, but what I do remember is that at one point I made Sam laugh so forcefully he spilled his scotch in his lap, which made him laugh more, and as he pulled the bills from his wallet, I noticed he had lovely hands, strong yet elegant, the fingers good for playing a musical instrument or dentistry. In the car, he kissed me and, once again, neither one of us could stop laughing. "Come home with me," he said. "Tonight. Just come with me."

Of course I didn't. I had a sitter at home with my 3½-year-old daughter and, well, going home with a man on a first meeting was something I would not do.

The following day Sam called and we made plans for an official date the coming weekend. Dinner in Chinatown followed by a Spaulding Gray performance. We dated for several weeks before sleeping together and by then I'd been fitted for a diaphragm and had invested in the strongest spermicide. I wasn't taking any chances; I was, in fact, obsessed about preventing pregnancy.

Our beginning was by all standards promising—beginnings often are—but my now 26-year-old daughter recently observed, if one looks back to the first visceral discomfort or dustup, it's the preview, the trailer of how a shaky relationship will end. Smart girl.

My first dissatisfaction came one night in March 1984.

"Where are you going?" I asked Sam who was standing next to my bed, pulling on his clothes. It was after midnight. Outside it was 20 degrees. He was layering one sweater, a thick cabled wool, over a thinner gray v-neck.

"You know I don't sleep well here," he said. The scarf was next, a simple black cashmere.

Sam had been by my side at the glorious pub party my publisher had thrown in January; he'd remembered Valentine's Day; he'd met my family; we'd fallen into the routine of seeing each other for dinner one night a week and we spent the weekends when my daughter was with her dad together either at his home in Philadelphia, or at my house in New Jersey. My house was on the market and as soon as it sold, I hoped to move to Philadelphia, where I'd always wanted to live.

"Since when?"

He was up to the parka. He zipped and he never zipped all the way up. "You know how I am."

This was beginning to become his answer for everything, as if knowing the how of him explained the what of him.

"Don't forget your gloves." I pointed to the thick leather gloves on the dresser. They were still molded in the shape of his hands, like soft Rodin casts, the fingers curled into claws. As he walked to the dresser, he glanced at himself in the mirror when he didn't think I was looking, but I saw it, that fleeting expression of mastery and self-satisfaction in his green eyes before he returned to me, wrapped in his scarves, ready to brave ridiculously cold weather for no good reason I could think of.

He bent over, his breath blowing across my face, a tiny pungent breeze smelling of coffee and sex. Sensing him about to lunge for another kiss, sensing his desire to place a leathered hand upon my breast, I pushed his face away.

"Be careful driving home."

"You're not going to walk me to the door?"

"I don't go to the door after midnight."

He felt around in his pockets, pulling out his car keys from one, my house key from the other. He still hadn't given me a key to his place, but he assured me he was "working on it."

"Okay. I'll lock up."

In the time scooped out of his departure, I'd created an indelible moment from nothing, so that when he left I focused on this: the sound of his shoes against the hardwood floor, the weight of him stirring the air as he crossed the living room, the false intimacy achieved because he had a key with which to let himself in and out as if we were a genuine part of each other's lives, when, really, we were moving across the interstices like ions. I began to understand that I'd tracked the gestures of his departure as a way of steeling myself, of acknowledging that his departures were all I could count on.

Things shifted after that night, slowly unraveled. We continued dating, but my dissatisfaction began to harden like rock candy, especially whenever he begged off any invitation that might include an activity with my daughter. When I wasn't with my daughter or teaching, I was busy traveling around giving readings and talks to promote the novel which he'd read. He said he liked me more than the book. After Easter in April, my mother began asking whether or not we were serious, because if we were then why hadn't he taken me away with him on his little four-day jaunt to Mexico? I thought she was being ridiculous. I couldn't have gone away even if he had asked, not with so many responsibilities, my daughter only one of them, at home. "But he didn't even ask, did he?" my mother countered. Ten years later I would recall that conversation with her while

I was writing my third novel in which the heroine, besotted and blinded by her ambivalent love interest finally realizes that *there are all sorts of reasons for a man to avoid a woman and none of them are good.*

My mother's question fueled a few of my own, though, and by May I finally mustered the courage to ask the question I should have known the answer to months earlier. Ironically, the day I asked if he loved me—Sam had left, then returned a half-hour later, claiming he had missed me by the time he got to the bridge—was also most likely the day I became pregnant. The diaphragm was still in place, we used more spermicide, he loved me, but wasn't "in love with" me. He saved the biggest shock for last: he would be moving to D.C. by September.

I've always had a deep connection to the inner workings of my body, an eerily strong sense of its thrums, its aches, its processes. I swear sometimes I can feel my spleen shift when I am angry, feel my heart knock down on my stomach when I am frightened. And didn't I instantly sense I was pregnant the night I conceived my daughter?

That was the story I told, because it was emblematic of everything it meant to me to be a mother, to choose to be a mother. I'd say my daughter and I have always been closer than a mother and daughter have a right to be. Sharing a radar of such high-pitched frequency we've always joked that maybe we'd been dolphins in a former life, our gurgle-ly language lucidly vibrating oceans away. It was always her contention that she picked me and I've never tried to convince her otherwise because the circumstances by which she came into being were as purposeful and intentional as putting on my shoes each day.

My husband and I had been married seven years; we'd decided that we wouldn't have a child before we could buy a house. In January of 1980 we found a modest twin home we could afford, one that needed tons of work. I stopped taking the pill. On Valentine's Day that same year we had dinner at our favorite, inexpensive beef 'n' beer restaurant, then made love later that night. Afterwards, giddy, Wayne said, "Den, I think we made a baby. I'm not kidding. I know it." We fell into a pleasant, exhausted sleep, and later that night I had a dream so vivid it woke me. I dreamt of a bald-headed baby girl, her head gleaming like a doll's, with eyebrows so clearly defined and mature they seemed comical. I believed I'd seen my daughter's face in that dream.

As the pregnancy developed we started thinking about names, as all couples do. Justin Taylor for a boy. My daughter's name was arrived at by accident one afternoon at my mother's house where my sister and I were visiting.

"Maybe the child of a writer should have a literary name," I joked.

"Leo Tolstoy Gess?" my sister said.

"Elizabeth Barrett Browning Gess," I countered.

"Jane Austen," she said.

"Leigh Hunt Gess."

The last moniker stopped us cold. My sister grabbed a notebook and pen. I wrote the name, Austen Leigh. Wayne was already fond of the name Leigh; he liked the way it looked on the page. Naming a boy was easier somehow, but a girl? I wanted a first name that didn't immediately announce gender, one that suggested strength, talent, and erudition. And several weeks later, although we'd had no ultrasound to confirm the sex of our child, during an evening walk in the park, Wayne surprised me when he said, "I want it to be a girl."

She was late by two weeks—what the doctor called "post-mature"— a difficult and harrowing labor during which she experienced fetal distress, nixing our plans for natural childbirth (she was a forceps delivery with a spinal block administered in the final hours of labor). I wasn't surprised when I saw her. I gave birth to a bald-headed baby who became the talk of the newborn wing, known to all the nurses as "the baby with the amazing eyebrows."

My daughter and I are still suckers for our own folklore of each other. How we came to be mother and daughter is the loveliest story we share, certainly more glamorous and more romantic than simple DNA. Whenever she has asked, "Do you love me?" I've always sensed she asks because she likes my response: "I loved you before you were born."

Cynics, skeptics, and perhaps scientists might say that I've played tricks with my own memory, that I've supplanted the dream after the fact of my daughter's birth, but even if that were so—and I'm sure beyond a shadow of a doubt it isn't; I have Wayne's corroboration to this day—they would be missing the most salient point: the unmitigated willingness, pre-paredness, forethought, desire, and sincerity with which we decided to become parents, the clear knowledge we possessed that, even in the best of circumstances, having a child would open our lives to more risk even as it expanded our love. We could not know beyond the solid Apgar scores one iota of what was in store for her beyond her safe entry into the perilous world. In having her we'd flayed ourselves, made both ourselves and her vulnerable not only to the possibility of joy, but also to that inscrutable team Loss and Sorrow.

I had no dreams or nightmares, no psychic warnings or rumblings, no prescient visitations from an unborn child in 1984. Over breakfast with Sam one Sunday in late May, most of our talk focused on the future we wouldn't be sharing. I nearly swooned when the waiter placed my eggs, smelling as repellent as dead lizards, before me on the table.

"What's wrong?" Sam asked.

"I'm pregnant." Naming gave the idea a sound, a dissonant, unsynco-pated riff in my heart, a burp in the valve, blood stalling its natural leap.

Inappropriately, Sam laughed. "Mizz Gess, you're one funny lady, but that's a bad joke. Are you seeing another guy?"

I know why he asked; it was because we'd never *not* been vigilant about birth control. It would be another year before I learned through friends that his question about cheating was his subconscious way of telling on himself, but that morning his deflection sailed by me. Then, "How late is your period? Maybe it's just a few days late," he said, trying to sound upbeat, but I saw he'd lost interest in his omelette and pushed his plate away.

"I'm not late. Believe me, Sam. I feel it. All over." I realized I was about to vomit, so I hurried away from the table to the ladies' room where I endured five minutes of dry heaves and tears.

That day I bought a pregnancy test, and the morning after I followed the directions to the letter, then sat in my kitchen waiting for the results.

At 7:00 a.m. I heard my daughter calling me from the upstairs hall, "Mom? I'm up."

The donut ring, signaling positive had formed. I dropped my head onto my folded arms, squeezing my eyes shut until pinpoints of white light blinked behind my eyelids like miniature stars. I couldn't hear a thing, not even my daughter's footsteps on the stairs.

"Mom?" she said, standing in the doorway of the kitchen.

I told my sister, my ex-husband with whom I was on good terms, and my friend, Linda. No one judged or tried to advise me, but when I said I was thinking that perhaps I should proceed with the pregnancy, Wayne said, "How? Why? If you're thinking he'll be around after, don't. Do it knowing it'll be you alone."

I was at most four and a half weeks pregnant. My salary as a graduate assistant was $6,478.00, and although I had some money from my book advance I had yet to embark on the arduous task of securing a teaching position with my new degree. Thus began the one-week war I waged between reason and faith. A part of me still loved my faith, with its dramatic overdrive and all the martyred saints with their seismographic powers of belief who'd been speared, burned, and tortured and who, for the love of God, had offered up their own plucked eyeballs and severed breasts on silver platters. I recalled those sketches of angels from my Baltimore catechism and Sister Renata telling us, "The human mind knows things only by study and experience. Human power is very limited." Oh, but those angels, they were spirit without body. "They have brilliant intelligence and do not have to study," she'd said. "Angelic power is far greater." Clearly, I was neither a saint nor an angel. My religion would cast me as wanton, one of the bad women like Salome or Lilith. I was raised in the faith that forbade not only abortion, but also birth control.

Sam had no patience with talk of angels or saints. A lapsed Irish-Catholic himself, he bristled when I mentioned Sister Renata. He also made it clear that children—my daughter and his potential child—were not in his plans. He would, however, *of course, of course,* pay for the abortion, *no question,* and be there to take care of me when it was done.

My Irish-Catholic gynecologist didn't perform abortions, but he supplied me with the name of a reputable doctor who did, and he supplied me with the reason it had happened in the first place. "You've lost weight," he told me, "more than five pounds." I suppose I'd been so busy with the readings and teaching I hadn't noticed. My doctor explained that had been enough to alter the fit of my diaphragm. After seeing him, I drove around, unaware that I was driving to my mother's house, the house I'd grown up in, until I pulled into our cul de sac, Catalina Court. No one was home and I was relieved. I don't think I went there to confess my situation or ask for advice. I didn't go inside although I had a key. Instead I sat on the front step, looking at the McHughs' split-level next door. The McHughs had moved away years before and no one had heard of them since, but the memory of them lingered.

They were the waif-like progeny of Pat and Lydia McHugh. Lydia was a former Miss Sarasota, a woman with disarmingly long legs and strawberry blond hair. Despite the ravages of age and continuous childbirth, she wore bright blue and red shorts and midriff tops.

We called her Mad Dog because of the way she attacked her clothesline on hot summer mornings, yanking with the fierceness of a rabid animal, her mouth filled with clothespins. My sister and I could read what kind of day it was going to be for the McHugh children in how violently she snapped the wet clothes before clipping them to the line. Usually, if Mad Dog seemed particularly vexed in the early morning, she would forget to give her children lunch, so Mary and I would make a picnic in our backyard, snitching peanut butter and jelly from our own kitchen to prepare the sandwiches outside on the redwood picnic table. We would lure the McHughs, seven girls and one boy, Patrick, with food. I wrote plays to amuse us and to keep the McHughs occupied, out of the line of fire.

But there were too many summer nights of Mad Dog's revenge. She saved her most exotic, cruel punishment for Patrick Jr., which made sense considering that Patrick Sr. was a volatile, alcoholic car salesman who thought nothing of yelling so the whole cul de sac could hear him through the screened windows. In the wake of his drinking or shouting, he usually banged out of the house, stirring up the gray gravel in the court and drove off leaving them without money for even a quart of milk. Was this how she paid him back? By taking her sorrow and fury out on the only one of her children who bore his name?

"Go, go, go!" we'd hear her screech. "Walk ten times around."

We were equally lured and repelled whenever we saw Patrick, with his awful eyeglasses held together with masking tape over the bridge of his nose and his hair shorn close to his knotty skull, forced to wear one of his sister's dresses as he marched around and around while Mad Dog sat on the front step, a sorry excuse for a mother. Counting his laps. I always broke down, dissolved at my own helplessness.

I don't doubt that Lydia, a Catholic of the times who did not use birth control and procreated as the Church commanded, loved her children. Even Patrick. But as I sat there sweating in the intense light of early afternoon, I didn't recognize Lydia's style of loving—filled with so much anger—as anything I wanted to risk. I had no way of knowing whether she would have been any less hurtful if she'd had one, instead of eight children. Did I fear I'd become like Lydia McHugh? I didn't *think* I would, but I wasn't entirely sure either.

Recalling those summer nights made me consider every option even more carefully.

Adoption? No. Giving a child up for adoption was unthinkable. And Linda had told me about a woman who, in a situation similar to mine, chose to carry the fetus to term because the man had promised to marry her, but when she was six months pregnant, he left her, then married someone with three children. I admired the woman's fortitude for keeping her child and bearing up under the weight of such a betrayal. Sam had not even offered the *illusion* that if I chose to stay pregnant he would take at least minimal responsibility for a child. Hadn't the betrayed woman proceeded because of the promise of love and marriage, not out of a desire for another child? Before I got into my car, I looked once more at the McHughs house. If nothing else, I knew my limitations.

Driving home that day, one by one the influences of Lydia McHugh, the Blessed Virgin, the angels and saints, and the betrayed woman began to fall away. I was more willing to shoulder the decision to abort, and whatever consequences that decision might bring, than proceed with the pregnancy. I could not, and did not want, and had never intended to be, the *single* mother of two children.

I made the arrangements. My daughter would stay overnight with her dad and he would return her to me late in the afternoon the following day. There would be two prescriptions the nurse explained over the phone, one to control bleeding and the other to prevent infection. She was cordial; she called me "hon" before hanging up. My friend Linda agreed to drive me to the procedure, wait there for me, then drive me home when it was finished. And Sam? Well, Sam.

The night before the abortion, as he sat there in the blue chair the envelope between us on the coffee table, I had a sudden urge to show him the drawing my daughter had made that day at nursery school. "Look at this," I said.

He took the drawing from me, raising one eyebrow. Now, twenty-three years later, I wonder whether perhaps I needed to show it to Sam to gauge his reaction in a last attempt to confirm his limits—as a boyfriend, as a potential father—and confirm my own as the possible mother of his child. Or to confirm in those long hours before morning, the rightness of my decision? It was a drawing of a beach; in the sky there was water and the sea was pink. Sam smiled for the first time since he'd entered the house, his dimples showing; they seemed preposterous on a 40-year-old face. He handed the drawing back to me. "Very nice," he said.

"Did you look at it?" My voice veered on shrill.

"Yeah. It's cute."

But he hadn't looked, not really. He had not seen what she'd drawn, what had struck me as inventive and startling. When I first looked at it, I immediately turned it around. "No, no," she'd said, "*this* way," turning it back again.

"But the sky is on the bottom."

"It's an upside-down beach, Mom. See?"

I put the drawing on the table. Sam titled his head toward the television, noticing, I suppose, that the screen was streaked with my daughter's fingerprints. He pulled a handkerchief from his pocket, then rose to wipe the screen clean before turning the set on. It was eleven o'clock, time for the nightly news. It was a terrible television, unreliable and quirky, with a picture that alternated between fuzzy and clear, and a horizontal hold that sometimes refused to hold.

"You need a new set. I wanted to buy you a new one," he said, looking at the screen instead of at me.

"I don't watch it much anyway."

Where I'd been I knew well; where I was going was trickier—the gauzy tumble of it, like being caught in a net of crinolines, hands in the air, vision obscured, made me dizzy: Would there be paralyzing sorrow? Would I be haunted later by the face of the unborn? Hate myself? I couldn't have known that a month after it was over Sam would write me a letter, admitting for the first time that he'd never felt "bonded" (yes, he would actually use that word) to me, that all along he'd known he wouldn't be taking our relationship further. "You are far more grown up in these matters than I," he would write. Nor could I have known that in the year that followed I would feel mostly relief, some days a free-floating sadness, but mostly relief, or that my future would hold more love, the death of my best friend, more books, the death of my grandparents and father, literary failures and successes, even cancer—but not regret.

That night, I knew only that I was ready.

I stared at the envelope.

"Two-fifty, right?" Sam asked.

"Yep. Right. Two-fifty."

MATTERS OF THE HEART:
To Be a Dragon Slayer

by Velina Hasu Houston

I AM AWAKENED, not by the sound of an alarm, but by the sound of my son gurgling and cooing. It is a happy sound from a charmed baby. I hear a knock at the door. Babe in arms, I open it. A celestial light nearly blinds me as I am greeted by an elegant Japanese woman in the kind of kimono one might wear to a special family celebration. I know instinctively that it is my maternal grandmother, Fusae Takechi. To the side of her is my long-dead father and behind her are hundreds of other people: Japanese, Africans, Native American Indians, and African Americans. It is clear to me that they are all members of my family come to commemorate the birth and homecoming of my firstborn.

That was the dream that I had when my son was born, and I brought him home to begin the long and fulfilling journey of a single parent.

I am no stranger to controversy. Perhaps it can be said that I thrive on it. Born of an immigrant Japanese mother from the southern province of Matsuyama and a Blackfoot Indian and African American father from southern Alabama, I arrived on the planet as a woman of multiple ethnicities, cultures, and nations; someone who possessed an immigrant-of-color's view of the United States that was imbued with a healthy curiosity and skepticism about the accessibility and nobility of the American Dream. As a child growing up in the 1960s, the training of my Japanese culture taught me to aim high, achieve beyond the horizon, and follow the standard path.

When I was five, I began to be curious about the phenotypical difference between my mother, who was alabaster-pale, and my father, who was of a deep brown hue. There were other differences, too, such as the fact that my father could speak very little of our code language (Japanese). I decided to get to the bottom of this mystery and, in so doing, learned how alike my parents were and that they shared a unified dream for the survival of their children in the U.S.

"Mama, why are you vanilla and why is Papa chocolate?" I asked at the breakfast table. Even the breakfast offerings underlined difference to me: my father was eating bacon and fried eggs while the rest of us were eating raw egg, minced green onions, roasted fish, and *shoyu* over steaming white rice with hot green tea. He liked most Japanese foods, but nothing with raw egg.

Later that day, my father came home with a carton of Neapolitan ice cream. He set the carton on the kitchen table and opened it up. I stared at the three stripes of flavors looking like a flag.

"You see this vanilla stripe?" my father asked. "That's like your mother. She's from Japan. See these strawberry and chocolate stripes? They're like me. Red and brown. Because I'm Blackfoot Indian and Negro." Then my father scooped ice cream from each stripe and mixed it up in a bowl. He blended it until the stripes had turned into a cinnamon brown, smooth mixture. He held it up for me to see. "You see this? This is like you: a mixture of three things." He set the bowl in front of me, as if challenging me. "Now, can you take this brown mixture and separate it back into the three stripes?"

I shook my head. What a ridiculous notion.

"That's right. Because three things have become one new thing. You can no more separate this mixture into three things than you can separate yourself into the three things that you are. Be all that you are. And, because you're something new, be ready for people to be suspicious, curious, maybe even downright hateful. But don't let them stop you. You rise above it and give your 200 percent and show them what you're made of."

My mother added the practical elements to this call to battle. "Always take good care of yourself. Brush your hair, take care of your teeth, wear nice clothes. Let people know who you really are. You wear raggedy old clothes and nobody will respect you. You must dress nice, carry yourself well, and get a good college education—and then you will be better than them because you never doubted yourself in the first place."

And so I tried and it took me all the way to California to a master's degree and eventually a doctorate. Along the way, it also gave me the strength and courage to listen to an instinct bigger than me that said my child was meant to be born. It was not exactly the standard path that my mother may have wanted for me, but then the notion of following a standard path has always invited my skepticism.

The first truly critical choice that I made about my body and my life was to have a child on my own. I was twenty-seven years old and about five years into a promising literary career. I made my living using my writing skills as a playwright, a journalist, and in film and television. But in my personal life, I was in a three-year relationship that had spiraled into something insalubrious.

We were in Vancouver, British Columbia. But forget about the autumnal splendor of Stanley Park or my red roses that were probably a gift a woman had given to him (a frequent occurrence). Reality hit when I decided that I'd had enough of Vancouver and wanted to return to Santa Monica. It was a little more complicated than that. The boyfriend had "borrowed" my cash and my credit card was missing, leaving me no choice but to telephone a friend and ask him to wire me funds to come home, which he did. Enraged by this "betrayal of our faith," the boyfriend began to drink in excess. Once smashed, the boyfriend became like an *oni* (demon) from the Japanese fairy tales of my childhood. He became shatteringly loud and energetic in a destructive way, looming too large like the *oni*: hideous, threatening, and painfully pathetic. I was tired of that *oni*. I was done.

Or so I thought. Once back in Santa Monica, I discovered that the trip to Vancouver, in its sweeter, pre-"abandonment" times, had given me a surprise, a secret that was going to lead to one of the most significant, transformative choices of my life.

On the first day of what was supposed to be my next period, a drop of ruby red blood descended from me and I wondered at its *mizutama* (as perfect as a polka dot) look. I did not know at the time that it was not a menstrual cycle at all. I experienced no period to speak of and, twenty-eight days later, the next one did not arrive either. I told my now stark-sober boyfriend. (He had returned from Vancouver by this time and spent a few days banging on my door imploring me to reconsider.) He said, "Well, you can't be pregnant because there was blood. Nobody's ever pregnant when there's blood, even a single drop." So, when my doctor confirmed a pregnancy, the boyfriend (whose sobriety was quickly becoming history) said that it must have happened after Vancouver and that, because we had not had post-Canadian relations, it must not be his child. This statement just confirmed that my departure had been the right choice. An electrical, magical sort of feeling was keeping me awake now, hurtling me toward a door that I had not intended to open for several years. My gynecologist and I thrashed out the realities of my situation: single, young, an artist. Before I made a decision, she asked me to meet one of her patients, a white Jewish paralegal single parent.

I knocked on the door of the woman's apartment with a sense of trepidation.

The woman was attractive, but her beauty had an infrastructure of steel.

"This is it," she said, her chestnut eyes not landing on me for more than a moment at a time, her fatigue evident in the dark circles under those eyes. "No glitz, no glamour, but a whole lot of love." The woman—let's call her Jane—stared at my shoeless feet and then at my shoes by the door. "You might want to put your shoes back on; when there's an infant around, your lovely socks could get slimed." The Japanese in me cringed inwardly, but, on the outside, I smiled and said it was fine. "It'd better be or you don't want to have a baby." Her toughness abraded me briefly, but it was a good thing—there was truth to what she was saying.

It was an evening without fanfare that focused on the infant: playing with her, changing her, bathing her. I could see the aspects of genuinely caring for one's baby, beyond clichés ("sleep like a baby"). I saw the drool, the spit-up, the crying, the fussing, and the messy diapers along with the cooing, the infant smile, the marvelous scent of freshly washed baby skin, and the love. At the evening's end, I was exhausted, too, but it was a good exhaustion, like at the end of a day of writing: I felt tired but fulfilled.

Once the baby was asleep—eight o'clock on the dot—Jane and I put away toys in the living room. We talked about other realities: the difficulty of dating as single parents, the economic sacrifices, how to balance work and family life, and—a big matter for us both—family members' reactions. "It is one thing to be a divorced woman who is co-parenting children on some odd custody plan," she said. "But if you are unmarried with a child, people treat you as if you're inferior, as if having a baby wasn't your choice but something you got stuck with because you couldn't hold on to your man. They never consider that maybe having the father involved didn't make sense, that it was a choice between eliminating a child or raising that child on your own." I realized that Jane had made a true choice. She could have had an abortion or put up her child for adoption. She could have stayed with the child's father and created a nuclear family that would have been miserable. Instead, Jane had chosen to accept the responsibility of raising a child on her own. "The hard part about being a single parent is that you have to make all the decisions on your own," Jane said and then quickly, with a smile, added, "and the best part about being a single parent is that you *get* to make all the decisions on your own."

As I drove away from her apartment, I felt good. I was not choosing to become an "unwed mother." I was choosing to become a single parent.

"Do me a favor," my older sister said. "When you tell Mom, give me a day's notice so that I can be in another country."

She had a point. One of the hardest things about my pregnancy was the prospect of telling my mother. I thought she would be angry at me, and disappointed; however, she surprised me.

"You can have an operation and be done with the problem," she said. I was stunned, but why should I have been? She was having a Japanese reaction to "the problem." Japanese society is not politically opposed to abortion like some of its Western counterparts. It is considered a clinical procedure akin, say, to extraction of a tooth or cyst. Despite the surprisingly open-minded nature of this view (since, in most other areas related to women, Japan is perceived as being woefully behind Western standards), Japanese society closes its doors on the idea of a woman having a child outside of matrimony. In the U.S., abortion is made into political event: demonized by the right and upheld by the left as a woman's right to choose. Given the puritanical tensions, it is no surprise that U.S. society still opposes the idea of single parenting. I am talking about *true* single parenthood: a single person who makes the choice to have and rear a child on her own.

Studying the look of astonishment on my face, my mother appeared exasperated. "This happened to me once. I was already married to your father. We had adopted your brother, you and your sister were born, and then another pregnancy." As my amazement grew, the pace of her recollection hastened. "We could not afford to have another child. I also knew that I could not raise another child; I did not have the energy or patience. My peace of mind would have been lost forever. Because of the way things are in the States, I could not just go to the doctor and take care of the problem. I had to get an illegal abortion." I pictured my mother going to some backstreet doctor's kitchen, or a hotel room where a shady physician took her cash and her dignity in one fell swoop. "There was no choice. It was a girl. You would have had another sister. But that did not matter. It was not meant to be and I took care of it. All of our lives would have been different if I had not done so." Clearly, she meant that our lives would have turned out for the worse. Of course, neither of us would ever know. As she told me about the nice Japanese American doctor who met her at a hotel room and helped her—and later asked her to run away with him— I struggled with how to tell my mother that I had a choice that was not merely a matter of scheduling an appointment to eliminate a problem: I could choose to be a single parent and never even consider marriage. My mother was pro-choice without any consciousness of the U.S. feminist movement; but, to her, pro-choice meant choosing abortion, not single parenthood.

"You don't understand, Mom," I said. "I just have a feeling that this baby is meant to be born. And I don't want to have an abortion."

She grew quiet, even a little bit angry.

"We have our own way of doing things," my mother said, referring to our Japanese cultural perspectives. "You do not want to marry the father, you do not even want to be with him anymore, so why the fuss?"

"It isn't about the father. It's about the child. It's about my instincts. Haven't you ever felt that, despite everything that may say something is not the best choice for whatever reasons, something was meant to be? Like your marriage to Papa?"

"That was different."

But was it so different?

"If you have this child, I do not want to have anything to do with this project."

I nodded, but cringed at the word "project."

"This is not like a new play," my mother warned, "some dream you have that you have to put on paper. This is forever."

Art was forever, too. And I had poured myself into important dreams and this seemed the most important. To run from it because I lived in a society that frowned upon single parents seemed like cowardice and self-ishness. I focused on summoning the courage to carry through with my pregnancy.

I had long known that, despite my mother's encouragement and call to adventure with full vigor, there were some enterprises that she believed should not be pursued, such as the arts. When I told her (at the age of six) that I was going to be a writer when I grew up, she was discouraging.

"The daughter of a Japanese immigrant cannot become an artist," she said. "Being an artist is a luxury. You have to wait at least one generation."

Surprised, I wondered why my mother—who always had urged me to dream big—was telling me to exclude certain dreams.

"We are immigrants," she said. "We have to focus on the basic neces-sities of life, on survival. Art is a luxury."

But hadn't my mother's personal choice to marry my father signified a break from convention, a break that caused her family and society to reprimand and ostracize her unflinchingly? Hadn't she, because of per-sonal nuptial and reproductive choices, had her character and reputation attacked in the name of preserving what was supposedly proper and good in Japanese society?

When I moved to Los Angeles at the age of twenty-two, my mother related to me what had happened when she had told her family that she was going to marry an American and, later on, how Japanese society had reacted to her first Amerasian child.

My mother had attended dressmaking school in Kobe, chaperoned by her older cousin. During that time, my mother met my father, a military policeman, when his helmet fell off while he was driving his jeep. Despite her cousin's protestations, my mother picked it up and gave it back to him. Had she stayed in Matsuyama, it is unlikely that she would have met any Americans because there were no bases on the southern island of Shikoku. But, bored in the countryside and desiring the company of her vivacious cousin, my mother had convinced my grandmother to allow her to live temporarily in Kobe. That decision—and my mother's decision to return a fallen helmet to a Yankee—changed her life.

Five years later, after a friendship and then a postal courtship, my father returned to Japan and asked for my mother's hand in marriage. She explained to him that her mother was ill and that she could not leave Japan. Shortly thereafter, my grandmother died. When she announced to my grandfather that she was going to marry an American, he was already in a state of deep depression over the loss of his wife and the loss of the war. While he did not disown my mother, he rebuked her with severity.

"How could you do this to our family?" he asked her. "How could you do this to me?"

My mother moved to Tokyo, where she found a job with a tailor (her expert dressmaking skills were paying off). For the next few years, she dated my father until they were finally married. All in all, they had known each other an uncommonly long time for a war-era marriage—nine years. But this long investment in their relationship did not matter. All except one of my aunts quietly found it difficult to make time to visit my mother in Tokyo; once she married, they found it even more difficult.

So there was a time when my mother made unconventional choices that to many seemed rich with futility—just as she perceived my desire to become a literary artist. Maybe it was this very experience that made her not want such notoriety for her daughter. I knew, however, that my very existence depended on unconventional choices having been made. If my mother had not been courageous enough to marry my father and selfless enough to leave behind her family and her country, I would never have come to be.

My sister was wary when I first told her about my pregnancy, but she never tried to influence my choice. When she observed that I had made up my mind, she had very little response. On the other hand, my friends, who were mostly the daughters of Japanese immigrant mothers with a few second-generation ones thrown in, were much more vocal.

"Are you crazy?" one asked. The calls started coming in.

"You're choosing the hard path," the husband of a friend said as he tried to set me up with an older male friend of his.

The most challenging response, however, came from a fellow artist, a writer who had always chided me for saying that writer's block did not exist. "You'll never write again," she said.

"Never is a long time," I replied.

I thought about all the ignorant remarks that had been directed at me due to misperceptions of my ethnicity. Now, I was learning about the ignorance directed at single parents.

"You were such an interesting person before," one of my friends said to me. "But now you're always going to be like this unwed mother with a kid. And just wait, you won't have any time for writing and no time for us to hang out anymore. We won't be able to go shopping without a screaming kid. We won't be able to go get our nails done. And what about going out dancing or going to parties?"

I was willing to sacrifice the mall, the nail salons, the smoky dance clubs full of aggressive and uninteresting men in order to raise my son. I also knew that my writing would be richer because of my choice.

Shortly thereafter, I interviewed a female pediatrician as a prospective doctor for my son. When she told me that she had become a single parent through divorce, I shared with her my friend's remarks. She smiled with the wisdom of a woman who had been raising two children mostly on her own for a year.

"Don't let her brainwash you," she said. "The reality is that most of the men out there make a night at home with the kids look like nirvana. You'll date again. If you want to. Just make the right choice."

My reproductive choice meant preparing properly for the life transition ahead, the first big event being my child's birth. Planning my child's birth, like rearing him, was going to be a solo flight that I must and would manage. But everybody from the hospital admitting clerk to the nurse who brought the paperwork to process my son's birth certificate had an opinion. My sister came with me for the birth. My mother, however reluctantly, agreed to come after I was released from the hospital to help me for two weeks. I was alone when the nurse arrived with the birth certificate papers. He watched as I filled out each section. I stopped at the blank for father's name.

"Just place your husband's name there," he said, looking around for someone to fit that designation.

"I don't wish to state the father's name," I said. "There is a biological father, but not a father as in parent."

The nurse's sunny professionalism quickly disintegrated.

"There's always a father," he declared, "whether you like it or not. Please place his name in that space."

"Perhaps you didn't hear me," I said, the staples and stitches from my emergency cesarean beginning to burn in my abdomen. "What does one write when one does not wish to include the male donor on the birth certificate? For example, what would one write if one went to a sperm bank?"

"Undeclared or unknown," he spat out. Without hesitation, I wrote "undeclared."

I returned to my quiet Santa Monica home with my son, who, from the moment he opened his eyes and looked at me, exuded a sense of joy and grace about living that was to enrich my life from that point on. Any fears I had were replaced with the courage and wherewithal needed to protect him and help him thrive. Two days later, my mother arrived. When I extended my son to her, she looked nervous.

"What's the matter, Mom?"

"Nothing."

But she still did not reach out her arms to hold my son. At first I took it as a political comment, then I saw that it was pure fear.

"I do not remember how to hold a baby," she mumbled. "After all, it has been many years."

Positioning her arms to hold an infant properly, I sat her down in my rocking chair and then placed my son in her arms. She was stiff, even more anxious, and at a loss. She had always been a splendid mother and I had just assumed that included a natural affinity for infant care. I was wrong. Over the next two weeks, my adeptness at taking care of my son on my own impressed her. In addition, she fell in love with her first grandson to the point of finding it difficult to return home.

"You sure you will be all right?" she asked.

I assured her that I would be more than all right. And then came the healing apology.

"When you were dating his father, I said please do not marry him. Then, when you were pregnant, I said to myself, now she has to marry him. But you do not have to marry anyone. You are doing just fine. In America, many artists have children on their own and the fathers are absent."

When my son was four, my mother and I took him to Japan. The four Takechi sisters—my mother was the youngest—had not been in the same room together in forty-five years. The eldest was Misao Obasan, the one known as the classic Japanese beauty. After having married well, she moved with her husband to Manchuria (then a Japanese settlement). The next oldest, Sumiko Obasan, had moved to Manchuria to assist Misao Obasan when her first child was born. In the colony, she met and married Tohta Tomizawa, a tailor. As WWII ground to a close, both families were forced to flee Manchuria with nothing but the clothes on their backs. Both went from upper to middle class in the blink of an eye, and had spent their lifetimes rebuilding their fortunes and recovering from the shame of the war. They had succeeded admirably, but the result was that their need to protect and preserve their lives had become even more acute.

Before we all sat down to our first meal together at the home of Haruko Obasan, my mother's closest sister, my son sang Japanese children songs with Haruko Obasan's husband while I hovered in the kitchen, helping my aunt in any way that I could. My mother slipped into the room looking nervous. She beckoned me to her side.

"If any of your aunts ask," she whispered in English, too certain that my aunts would not understand, "tell them that you are divorced. And do not tell them that you are a playwright; that is not respected here. Only tell them about being a professor." There it was, my mother's fear about unconventional choices challenging my life. While she had learned to live with my choice, she was still bothered by it. She seemed to be saying that it would have been so much easier to have chosen abortion.

"You're like Murphy Brown," a white male editor on one of my free-lance jobs once said to me. He laughed for a moment and then stopped suddenly. "But seriously, Velina, when are you going to get married? Don't you like men?"

This was indeed a significant issue in my decision to become a single parent. I remember a young advertising executive from Florida whom I had dated briefly. After he gave up on the rigors of Californian life, he returned to Florida and wrote me a letter. "Thanks for babysitting me," he said. "I think all my problems stem from the fact that my mother never circumcised me." Then there was the Filipina-obsessed architect, the "dark Asian"-obsessed orthopedic surgeon, the entrepreneur whose life decisions focused on his Lutheran minister father's approval (Jesus loved all the differently colored children, but His disciples apparently did not need to), and the journalist who invited me to a Halloween party and picked me up dressed as a member of the Ku Klux Klan. Not much room for choice in such a field. Unfortunately, I only had encountered men who seemed to have been reared in forests without mothers. Uninspired by such associations, I deeply valued my independence. I did date, but not with nuptial objectives. A contraceptive accident in late 1995 placed another reproductive choice in my lap. I did not consider abortion. I wanted a second child and since the first one was—in nearly everybody's view including mine—a gem, I answered the call to adventure a second time.

In the delivery room, as my daughter was born, a blond nurse beamed hugely at the sight of my daughter's golden skin and auburn curls; an African American nurse looked displeased.

"Are you Polynesian?" the white nurse asked. I told her my ethnicities. The black nurse's displeasure increased at the mention of mixed races. As the blond carried my daughter over to the scales to weigh her, she was so happy that she hummed.

"Another ABC baby!" she exclaimed. "The more I see of them, the more I want to see of them. They're so beautiful. They're the future."

"ABC?" I asked.

"Asian black caucasian!" she said.

The gnashing and grinding of the black nurse's teeth made my own teeth hurt. When the blond nurse left to clean my daughter and wrap her in bunting, the black nurse cleaned me.

"Excuse me, but how are you going to raise that child?" she asked. I was startled by the intrusion. "I see you're not married so it's just you and that baby. What's she going to be?"

"She's going to be herself."

"Is she going to be black?"

"She's going to be Japanese, English, Blackfoot Indian, *and* black," I said.

"If people think she's black, she's black," the woman said.

I wondered if she might slip a few staphylococcus germs into my incision if she was enraged enough. Why was she so angry? "Thank you very much for sharing, but I am not about to have others define me—and the same goes for my children."

"You can do what you like, but one thing you share with a lot of black women: you're a single parent and white people are going to stereotype you for that. They'll think you're on drugs, on welfare, and going nowhere." For the first time, her eyes softened and she looked directly at me.

"Are you a single parent?" I asked. She nodded. "Divorced?" I asked. She shook her head. "Do you want to be married?"

"Hell no," she said quickly. "One thing to raise a baby, another thing to have to raise a man. No thank you." We smiled at each other with new understanding.

"I wish you luck," I said.

"ABC," she said quietly.

We both knew that, being dark-skinned women in America, it would never be as easy as A-B-C or 1-2-3; the steps in the dance toward success would be much, much more complicated.

I had never been one to resign myself to the easy life. Neither of my parents had succumbed to the conventional life nor could I. With the birth of each of my children came increasing peace and prosperity. By the time my son was three, I had become a professor and also been hired to write several projects for film and television. I bought a three-bedroom townhouse in Santa Monica and was able to place my son in a private school. Of course, the mothers of my son's schoolmates always asked me, "What does your husband do?" and office personnel referred to me as "Mrs. Houston." Politically, I was pro-choice, but my personal position with regard to my own pregnancy was to forego abortion and have a child on my own. To some, this seemed like a choice against abortion. To others, it seemed like a choice for life. The decision, however, was not political at all. It was personal. Purely. And nobody's business.

When I returned to Kansas for a high school reunion, a former friend pulled me aside and said, "Now tell me what it was really like! You just went out and found yourself someone like you choose something at the grocery store? You always liked to do things differently!" I was rural legend. This is how myths are created, rumors are fueled, and ignorance is propagated.

Parenting my children was, of course, not constantly effortless. My son had the energy of a bullet train (not unlike mine, but in the muscles of a toddler and small boy, it was funneled into mischief, mayhem, and love). But there were never any huge challenges between us. Mischief translated into climbing out of his crib at eighteen months and pouring a large canister of baby powder all over himself and his bedding, then crying from the stinging in his eyes. His tear streaks made him look like a sad snowman. I could not help smiling before I cleaned him up. When he was four he climbed on the sofa and pretended to glide through the air like the Silver Surfer, finally resulting in a cut on the head; twelve internal stitches and ten external—and only a plastic surgeon would do the work because of the hairline location. All through the surgery, he watched the surgeon at work and did not flinch or cry. Before my daughter could crawl, her determination to be by my side made her invent a new transportation mode: she lay on her side and rolled to me. When she was four, she asked, "Mama, when you lived in Kansas, was it in black-and-white? Do we live over the rainbow?" It taught me that, to her, life was colorful and good. My children were full of love—for me, my immediate family, animals, and friends. To this day, we remain extremely close and talk about subjects that other mothers complain their children would never even think of broaching with them. Of course, parenting always includes frustrations. Ours stemmed mostly from my children learning that immigrant-kindred people of color must work harder and truly strive for excellence to realize the American Dream. Timeliness, tidiness, manners, and pure ambition had to be a mantra. Such lessons are challenging for children—even gifted ones—to learn as I knew from my own upbringing. It is the constant vigilance that can create frustration in both *sensei* and student. But learn you do, and must.

In the early years of being a single parent, the day-to-day challenges were managed by instinct. I had never babysat or spent much time around infants and toddlers. While I did read a few parenting books, I primarily followed my instincts about how to care for human beings and make them feel self-confident, necessary, and loved. Our mornings were breakfast and then drop-off at school. Most days, I picked them up at three and went home to cook dinner. I supervised homework and we had D.E.A.R. (Drop Everything And Read) time. My son had daily math enrichment exercises; he had started writing his numbers and doing minor equations at age three, so I had enrolled him in a program to stimulate his mathematical gifts as the age-level school math was uninspiring and mind numbing. After that, it was bath time, a time when they would share the most about their school day. My son reported that an older boy had peed on him in the bathroom, his teacher had told him that no one under the age of twenty-five knew what love was really about, someone stole his *makizushi* from his lunch box, a girl gave him a pencil box, a new boy came to school whom he thought might become a good friend. My daughter wanted us to care for the class bunny over holiday break, the blond kid hit her in the back again and then took the best part of her lunch, her white teacher said she couldn't be Japanese if she was mixed race. The weekdays amounted to approximately seven waking, non-school hours each day to parent my children with as much strength as I could.

The hard times of single parenting were when my children or I became ill. When they were sick, I had to shift my work schedule around and forego sleep to catch up with the projects. Two years before my daughter was born, I had a life-threatening experience that reinforced my resolve to put my children before anybody else in my life. I was baking cookies with my son on Christmas Eve 1994. I began having extreme abdominal pain and vomited bile. I called my sister; she was busy with a dinner at her mother-in-law's and suggested an antacid. My mother was busy with the same dinner and afraid to renege. I called four friends, all busy with parties. "We should call 911, Mommy," my son, eight at the time, said. We went to the hospital via ambulance. My son never left my side. I underwent emergency surgery to untangle ovarian adhesions that had tied a knot around my lower intestines. When I awoke, my son was there. In the room's shadows, my mother stood pale as a ghost. In such moments, it becomes crystal clear who truly values your existence. I genuinely matter to my children and that is not a given for parents. We have to earn that.

It would be years—twenty in fact—before I would take the time to lounge in a nail salon again; I would go with my son, his girlfriend, and my daughter, and we would have a group mani-pedi. What was girl-time before became family time.

The best thing about being a single parent is the deep, marvelous, special bond that I have built with my son and daughter. For the first sixteen years of my son's life and the first six years of my daughter's life, I raised them as a single parent. Their fathers had vanished into the ether so successfully that it would be an exaggeration to hail them as deadbeat. Because of my one-on-one parenting of my children, we developed ways of communicating and relating that are without subterfuge. The few people who have stayed my friends on this journey marvel at the depth and strength of my bonds with my children. I feel brilliantly blessed by them.

While art and life in the academy have shown me a few splendid stars, much of the starlight in my life is created by my children. What it means to be a single parent is to be courageous and valiant, to let society's slurs and vilifications roll off your back like water off a duck even though some-times it is damn hard, and to believe in your power to create and cultivate meaningful lives rich with unconditional love for your children.

Most of all, being a single parent means that one must be a slayer of dragons, many dragons. And so I raise my sword—my pen—in the name of choice.

TREES IN THE DESERT

by Sarah Messer

IN 1985 THE MOUNTAINS around Salt Lake City looked like the knees of giants pulled up under blankets. That winter, in one of the mountains' most popular ski areas, the Gold Miner's Daughter Lodge waited to explode. In the center of the Mormon Temple, in the center of the city, a couple dressed in white clasped hands in the room of Endowments, re-enacting the Garden. The Temple was the center, the whole city expanding outward in the four directions, a grid that stretched on until it reached the tundra of the salt flats. Here the Donner party had stopped before their deadly winter in the Sierra Nevadas and walked over the hard surface, which crunched beneath their boots like snow. One hundred years later, the Enola Gay dropped bombs on the same spot; later still, motorcycles, cars, rockets, flew past each other here, faster than any on earth. In 1985, it was the place where a Swedish sculptor listened to Beethoven's 9th and continued building, with tons of concrete and 2,000 ceramic tiles, an 87-foot-tall "Tree of Life" in the middle of the desert.

We were trying to get the abortion over with by the time my parents came to visit. The Indian doctor at the Women's Clinic said, "You are too skinny—see, I can feel all your organs," pushing on me with her hands. On my back on the papered examining table, my belly sloped concave between hipbones. A white hospital sheet dangled from my neck like a mammoth paper towel. The doctor's hands were warm and soft. My parents and three sisters would be arriving in a week for a spring-break skiing vacation. They didn't know I was getting an abortion. The doctor was a large woman, wearing aqua-blue eyeliner. "Go home," she sighed, "you aren't pregnant."

But I was pregnant. In our second-floor, shag-carpeted treehouse of an apartment, my boyfriend, Thomas, and I did another test. I had become an expert at not hitting my hand when I peed into the cup, which was the same size as the top of the discount mouthwash bottle, the only thing we kept in our mirrored medicine cabinet above the sink. Thomas sat on the bathtub across from the toilet—we had no shower—his feet rubbing back and forth on the carpet, making ski-tracks. He took the warm cup from me and placed it on the back of the toilet like a small china lamb.

We decided to smoke a joint on the balcony. You could hardly call it a balcony—the floor slanted so violently toward the street that we had to wad up paper and shove it under the front legs of our chairs so we wouldn't slide out of the seats. Bored, we picked at the rotting porch columns with long barbeque forks and tried to remember not to put any-thing—like a beer bottle or a glass one-hitter—down at our side because it would roll off the edge and fall to the cracked brick steps and sidewalk below.

The first story I'd heard when I moved to Utah three months earlier had been about the mother who talked seven of her children into jumping from a hotel balcony; those who wouldn't jump she pushed, before jumping herself. She was a member of a Jack-Mormon cult centered around her husband, Immanuel David, who declared himself God. Everyone in the cult changed their last name to David. Matthais David, Jonathan David, Jericho David, and Rachel David, the wife and mother to Immanuel's children. The entire group was a family, and God was the father. Several of the members, men who had owned karate studios, were made into "archangels" and sent to Washington D.C. to wait for the end of the world. He gave them each $100. Waiting, they became homeless and slept in the streets. They called God collect from payphones. They waited for further instruction. Eventually God told them to return to Salt Lake City, because he had found a set of holy tablets. When the archangels returned to Salt Lake City they said, "Let's see the tablets."

"You're looking at them," Immanuel David replied. And when they asked where, he said, "Right here," putting his hands on his chest, "I am the tablets."

The guy who told me the story did the same thing to demonstrate: put his hands on his chest, sitting in Dee's Family Restaurant, where two weeks later I would begin working the graveyard shift. He was a dish-washer at the Mexican restaurant where Thomas also worked. His name was Geraldo. From Geraldo we also learned about the Mormons' sacred undergarments, "which look like normal undershirts," that Mormons had sex in a white room after they were married, and that the city streets were wide enough to contain the length of an entire wagon train. "The whole city is a grid," Geraldo said, "the center is the Temple," he said.

But what about the woman, I asked, all her kids.

"They all died except one," Geraldo said, "a 15-year-old girl."

I was eighteen, and I also had six sisters and one brother. I tried to fit the surviving girl into my own family order; to imagine myself falling 100 feet from a balcony. I saw my siblings' bodies as if from a great distance, tiny and crumpled eleven stories below, and I wondered if the girl's brothers and sisters had broken her fall.

Geraldo kept staring at Thomas, as if he were speaking only to him. He told us that not long after Immanuel David declared himself the holy tablets, they indicted him for mail fraud. He drove up the canyon and sucked on the van's tail pipe. Three days later Rachel David and the children all went off the balcony. The surviving girl had also been named Rachel David. But after the accident, the cult members called her Eve.

"Where's Eve now?" I asked.

"Somewhere," Geraldo said. "I dunno. She's kind of brain-damaged."

Beyond the plate-glass windows, the shadows came down from the mountain, each a long wagon train turning itself around in the street. Dee's served breakfast twenty-four hours a day, and every meal cost around $1.99; people were eating waffles and drinking Postam grain beverage. The dining area was decorated like a seventies deluxe mobile home—browns and oranges, tan naugahyde booths.

"All those baby nagas slaughtered for their baby naga-hides," Thomas had said when we walked out, running his hands over the tops of booths. I think he might have been quoting Frank Zappa. He was always quoting Frank Zappa. "Them poor lil' nagas!"

He sang it like a heart-sick cowboy. And Geraldo laughed so hard that no sound came out of his mouth.

We hadn't really talked about whether to have a baby or not. When I did the first test, after it showed positive, Thomas made me do it again. When that one, too, was positive, we called and made an appointment at the clinic. Thomas had the ability to make anything seem like no big deal. "Yeah, Jenny and Suzanne both had abortions," he said, speaking of his former girlfriends, "it's a real easy procedure." Thomas had shown me pictures of Jenny and Suzanne, women he had been with. He was eight years older than me, and the women in the picture were older still. The pictures were arty, black-and-white, with dramatic shadows lengthening from their arms. It all seemed very adult. "Of course," I said.

I had dropped out of my freshman year of college to move to Salt Lake City and live with him. I had danced ballet my whole life, and I told everyone I was trying to become a dancer in Ballet West, but really I had moved to be with Thomas.

Thomas was this kind of guy: every two years he rode his bike across the country. Sometimes one girlfriend or another would go with him, but none of them ever made it the whole way. When he wasn't riding across the country he lived on one or the other coast, or somewhere in between where he could still bike a lot, tending bar or waiting tables until he saved up enough money to do it all again. He was a very good artist but never seemed to finish anything. He would start a lot of drawings and they would hang unfinished taped to the wall; he would write up elaborate to-do lists and plans for the future. Together we spent a lot of time reading underground commix like R. Crumb and *The Fabulous Furry Freak Brothers*, and talking about eastern mysticism, which was summed up for us in the Kama Sutra.

When I first moved in, Thomas bought a waterbed and we filled it up with a hose pulled in over the balcony, in through the busted french doors. Every night, Thomas lit a bunch of Santaria candles and put on Bob Marley or the Moody Blues. Whenever he asked me to put on sexy music, I would suggest The Police, or Godspell, or Cat Stevens or Boston or Beethoven's 9th—it was the only music I really knew. "Those aren't sexy," Thomas would laugh and then he'd add, "you are very eclectic, I like that," in case he'd hurt my feelings. And we'd put Bob Marley back on.

We looked at pictures in the Kama Sutra book and tried everything. Together we bought lacy lingerie that snapped at the crotch, hot massage oils, and pairs of edible panties. Most of the time, I thought it was incredibly romantic. But in truth, we were extremely poor; the light of day would reveal the smoked candles, the beer cans, Thomas's tube socks and tin-foil pipes. No matter how hard I tried, the sheets always slipped off the waterbed during night, and I wound up sleeping butt-naked on warm plastic. We never had anything for dinner but potatoes and Coke. My parents, upset that I had dropped out of a prestigious liberal arts college, decided not to support me financially or to speak to me really at all. Thus, their upcoming visit was the peace pipe—a beginning of the end of months of wintry distance. Or so we all had hoped.

And now I was pregnant. The test on the back of the toilet seat proved it. "Do you think we should wait longer?" Thomas asked, as if maybe the act of waiting itself could change the color. Stoned, we sat side by side on the edge of the bathtub and stared.

"I gotta go to work, Baby," Thomas said finally.

"Yeah," I said.

"You should go back to the clinic."

"Without you?"

"To make another appointment."

Then he grabbed his black pants and shoes and "How Bout that Jazz" T-shirt for his other job as a bartender at the Utah Jazz-themed sports bar at the Marriott Hotel. "Have a great night!" he yelled as he left.

"I'll do some laundry!" I yelled back, which made no sense. I was still sitting in the bathroom on the edge of the tub, holding the test. Then I was walking down the dark carpeted hallway and three flights of stairs to the laundry room in the basement. Except I didn't quite. I stopped at the landing right across from the outside door, and sat down again. I couldn't really bring myself to go into the laundry room. Plus, I had forgotten the laundry, and was too tired to climb back up three flights. At some point, Katie, my neighbor, came in the door.

"Oh!" she said.

"Oh hi," I said. "I am on my way to the store," I said and stood up, as if I had been waiting for this moment, waiting for her to allow me to leave.

Even though it was almost March, each night the snow came down in giant fat flakes, covered the ground like movie-set snow. Then by noon the next day, the sun would have burnt it off, leaving only cold wet patches beneath trees and parked cars.

I made it to the Safeway with its barrels of bulk food—candy and yogurt-covered raisins and sesame sticks. Thomas had read somewhere that if you ate the bulk food while you were in the store, no one could charge you. So this is what we would often do, wander in, fill up plastic bags and then walk slowly up and down the bright-lit aisles looking at all the things we could not afford.

I had three bags—I walked through the frozen meat section, and then into the dairy section. I thought again about Geraldo's story, about the couple in the white room. In my mind they were naked, the room was completely white, and even though it had no windows, it glowed as if lit from the inside, lit from their bodies, which were entwined and also filled with light. There was no bed, they were alone, their universe made of light. So fused with each other, they seemed to be made of many limbs. What about the girl who had fallen and lived? If she truly believed her mother, that they were going to heaven to be reunited with God, their father, wouldn't her survival be seen as some kind of tragedy? Would it have been better not to be born at all? To merely stay safe in a room of white light? I had not been raised with Christian ideas of heaven and hell, or of the soul as a concrete, unchanging entity. I believed that something, a consciousness, continued after death, but not in the way Christians believed. I didn't think about sin or sinners, rather, why people acted the way that they did, the ways that their actions hurt others, whether they meant them to or not.

"You'd better be planning to pay for that," a man in a red apron said.

"Oh yeah," I said.

"Great," he said, "Come on, I'll check you out." I followed him down the aisles, still eating out of my bag.

When I got to his register and put the bag down, it had six Hot Tamales in it. And at that moment I realized that I didn't have any money,

I had walked out of the apartment empty-handed. Seeing the look on my face, he said, "Forget it. Get out of here."

I walked further out on the grid. Voices rang out from a house in the hills, singing "Happy birthday, dear Moroni, happy birthday to you!" Moroni was the angel on top of the Temple, the angel who heralded the second coming and who came one night to Joseph Smith's room in the first of Smith's many visions. The angel appeared dressed in a white robe and standing in the air. The room was filled with light as bright as the noon-day sun, Smith had written in his journal. The singing coming from the house was beautiful. Was it the angel's birthday? Or the birthday of someone named after the angel?

Eventually I made it to the clinic. When I walked in, the receptionist treated me like a family member. "Oh, hey there," she said. It was unusually quiet at the clinic that day, no protesters, no one crying in the waiting area.

I asked to make another appointment, and the receptionist said, "Do another test," handing me a plastic cup.

"I did one at home," I said.

"Yes, I know, but we have to keep our own records."

I went into the bathroom with its pink and lavender women's health posters and did the test, pushed it through the tiny door in the wall marked samples, and returned to the waiting area. Fifteen minutes later, a nurse in Raggedy Ann scrubs called my name and motioned for me to follow her into a back room.

I had convinced myself that the clinic would say I wasn't pregnant— some strange belief that the condition only existed while I was in my apartment. But I was pregnant. When she suggested the following Wednesday, I said okay, even though I knew it would be right in the middle of my parent's visit.

That night at work, the usual: brown-and-tan striped polyester waitress uniform, thick nylons and clumpy black Reeboks. Mormon families ordered chicken-fried steak and Postam until 8:30 p.m., then a lull until 9:30 p.m. when we were hit with the mall employees, the men's choir group, and girls with claw bangs giggling their way to the bar. Another lull. I cleaned glass coffee pots with ice, lemon slices, and salt, shaking them like giant maracas; I rolled the silverware into tiny napkin burritos. Slowly the wait-staff and the assistant cooks grabbed their coats and left out the back walk-in area with the greasy floors and employee bathrooms. Soon it was just the manager, the dishwasher, me, and Adam, the cook.

Most people wanted the breakfast special, with pancakes or toast, with bacon or country ham, their eggs scrambled or over easy. Occasionally some wise guy or lady on a diet would want something special, and I'd wait to try and catch Adam's eye as he stormed back and forth behind the chrome order-counter and the wheel of green tickets. He wore a walkman and turned up loud heavy metal that blared muffled through his shaggy lion hair and long walrus mustache. Adam was calm as a wound spring; any moment he might throw a spatula at the wall.

The restaurant was completely dead by 4:00 a.m., so Adam and I hung out in the walk-in—Adam getting high, sitting on the lettuce crates, me watching him. The floor was slick with congealed grease, and I moved my feet back and forth making tracks, our knees close together. I had a tiny hole in my nylons, right at my knee, I tried to hide it with my hand. I asked Adam about the white room in the temple where people had sex after they were married.

"Not true," he said. He was an ex-Mormon. "No sex goes on in the Temple. That's a goddamned lie. People do wear white," he said. "A weird sheet thing, and then they get the garments, a new name, and an apron with green leaves on it."

"No way."

Adam started giggling, "No, I am serious, man. Serious." We both laughed out our noses and Adam coughed up some smoke.

"And after all that," he said, "you stand before the veil and God touches you through the veil, through the tiny holes in your undergarment. I mean, there's a guy pretending to be God, and he reaches his hand through and he touches you with his finger like this." He untied his apron and held it between us, then he reached his hand underneath and touched the tip of his finger to the hole in my tights.

"Hey!" I said.

"Now you can go into the room. You are immortal."

"So what about the couple in the white room?" I asked.

"You mean, getting married in the Temple?"

"Yes."

"They are anointed through the garment, they kneel, there are some hand signals, but they'd disembowel me if I showed you."

"Shut up," I said. And Adam lit the pipe again. "Sure you don't want any?"

"Nah. I'm pregnant," I said.

"For real?"

"Yeah," I said.

"Your guy know about it?"

"Yeah he knows. I'm going to get an abortion." Adam didn't say anything, just nodded his head.

"I got a little girl," he said, "lives down in St. George. I never get to see her enough. Her mother's a crazy bitch."

"Oh," I said. He could have been twenty or fifty-five. "How old are you?" I asked.

"Just turned twenty-five, man," he said, "A Capricorn."

"My boyfriend is older than you," I said.

"Guess so."

"Yeah, don't ever have a kid with someone you don't love," Adam said. And I was about to say, *I love Thomas*—but then we heard the night manager calling our names.

My parents arrived on a Monday. When I told Thomas that the abortion would now take place during their visit, he said, "I think we can tell them."

"Are you crazy?" I said.

"I mean, they will be more supportive than you think."

He might have been right. I just couldn't bear to tell them. I had flipped a switch in my mind, a switch of not-telling. Even to consider anything else seemed impossible. "Please don't say anything," I said.

And he didn't say anything, even at the airport when my mother burst into tears. Even when, standing silently around our apartment, my sisters asked if I had seen this or that movie, or when I blurted out that I was anemic, that I'd had strep throat and the flu all at once, and my father, a doctor, looked at me and sighed.

It was determined that my parents and sisters would go to Park City, to the time-share condo, and Thomas and I would join them at Snowbird and Alta on the weekend. We had lied, saying we couldn't get off work.

"I think you could tell them," Thomas said, as soon as they left.

That night I played the game again. I'd lie further and further away from Thomas. I called it "The Edge." I wanted him to reach for me and ask what was wrong. But he never did. So I'd move closer and closer to the side of the bed until I was lying on the vinyl waterbed bumper. Then I'd roll off and lie on the floor. Sometimes I'd fall asleep there. Sometimes I'd crawl to the living room and lie on the couch. Then I'd move to the edge of the couch. Then roll off again. I liked the feeling of tipping off the edge, the way gravity held my body, pulled it down—even a foot or so—off the bed or sofa.

That night I lay for a long time on the carpet between the sofa and the glass coffee table. This was furthest edge I'd reached. I could look up through the glass surface, as if trapped beneath ice. I couldn't stand this feeling. I couldn't stand for anyone to know. Yet I desperately wanted someone to know. In the next room, Thomas began to snore.

So I walked out of the apartment. It was 3:00 a.m., and I wore only a pair of Hawaiian shorts, a large T-shirt, and a pair of canvas slip-on shoes. I carried nothing in my hands. The cement sidewalk held me up. As long as I kept moving I didn't feel cold. I moved between the pools of street-lights, block after block.

I'm not sure how long I walked past dark porches, chain-link store-fronts, and men sleeping on bus station benches. I saw gold light from a restaurant pouring out into the street. I realized it was Dee's, and that I'd found my way back here, coming from a direction I'd never been before.

I walked in the front door like a regular customer. It felt thrilling. It felt like a relief.

The night manager barely looked up from her calculator, just a slight nod. Perhaps she thought I was coming to work. The waitresses were happy to see me. No one thought anything was strange. No one, that is, except Adam.

"What are you doing here?" he asked, pulling one earphone aside from his blaring headset. I was sitting in the back of the kitchen on a giant plastic tub of napkins.

"Just walking," I said, standing up again. "You know, around the city." I twisted the corner of the T-shirt. It pulled down my chest, and I let it go again. I realized I wasn't wearing a bra.

"You have no jacket." Adam said.

My nose had started to run, and I realized suddenly that I was shivering—my skin covered in droplets of cold water, my hands red. The thrill I had felt walking the city, walking into Dee's as a customer, was gone now.

"Fuckin' looney," Adam said shaking his head and grabbing a box of frozen chicken-fried steak from the walk-in. I leaned my head against the wall. "I mean, whatever," he said, softer now, brushing past me. The light in the room was plain and gray. I looked down at my Hawaiian shorts, my red legs, and my thin shoes. I remembered I was pregnant.

I left through the back door, stepping into the parking lot by the dumpsters. I ran now, across the asphalt, across median strips planted with saplings. I tried to find the quickest way home. What would Thomas think, would he be worried? Maybe he'd even called the police.

But when I reached our block, I saw no police cars in the driveway. The door was still unlocked as I had left it. The apartment door too. When I stepped into the living room, the air was still. And when I got into the waterbed, Thomas rolled over and sighed. "Your feet are cold!" was all he said. He never knew I'd been gone.

Thomas came with me to the clinic the next day, but he wasn't allowed into the room. I was given the same poncho-like white paper gown. Then my feet were placed in stirrups, and I was asked to scoot down the paper on the table. Various nurses and the Indian doctor touched me beneath the sheet. She said "This will all be over soon." The ceiling tiles were made of coffee-stained clouds; everyone wore pink or white or blueish gray. "You will feel a pinch," someone said and then the nurse patted my arm. "Bite down on these wings," she said, placing two triangles of cotton in my mouth. She held my hand in hers.

A suction. Flutter, vibration, a butterfly trapped in a jar. My knees were two snow mountains. I couldn't look beyond the sheet that stretched between them. I knew only that the doctor's hand was occasionally there, reaching through the barrier to touch my leg or my belly, moving me slightly. Behind her, loud equipment hummed and was rolled this way and that.

And then I was in another room with a thin blanket pulled over me. Thomas sat beside me. I am not sure how much time passed until a nurse came in and gave me maxi-pads and ripped a prescription from a clip-board. And then Thomas held my arm as I got out of bed and was given my clothes.

That weekend Thomas and I stayed with my parents and sisters. We slept on the living room floor in front of the couch. At night, the shadow of the mountain blocked the sky, but the moon shone in the condo window, distant and blueish, and I could look up at the room's vaulted ceiling beams, imagining cathedrals.

The last day of the visit, I skied with Thomas and my sisters, although it quickly became apparent that I couldn't keep up, so the group split. My youngest sister skied with me. We were a run behind; riding in the chair lift back up the mountain, sometimes we'd glimpse our family skiing by below. Eventually we spent the entire ride trying to spot them—their tiny bodies zooming over the white trails through the trees below us, distant specks. Then everyone looked like them.

At the end of the day, they all left, and I didn't tell them anything and neither did Thomas.

Two days after that, a propane leak caused the Gold Miner's Daughter Lodge to explode, trapping a 12-year-old girl in the wreckage. News reports said that the girl's hand was crushed by tons of fallen concrete, and that's what kept her there, the building's refusal to let go of her hand. We had been at that lodge just days before, eaten lunch out on one of the decks. My father took pictures, which would fill up part of the family photo album for 1985. "Visiting Sarah in Utah," the caption would say. But it could have said, "Visiting Sarah after her abortion," or, "This lodge will blow up in two days," or, "After this, only a ruin."

Which was true. Because I didn't get away with it, ultimately. Everything that had seemed bad before, only got worse until it hit bottom, the very worst, and I stopped lying, I couldn't lie any more.

My parents had given us $50 for groceries, but instead we borrowed Geraldo's giant Cadillac and drove through the salt flats to the Wendover gambling casino, to try and increase our bounty. We lost it all. "Bend over in Wendover," Thomas said as we drove back home through miles of whiteness. I saw then, for the first and only time, the Tree of Life sculpture. It was still unfinished, just steel framing and empty cylindrical shapes, half the trunk, a mass of concrete and steel rods. We could see it for miles away, a crooked launchpad. Up close it didn't look like a tree; it was modernist with giant round leaves like planets, and broken crescent moons "fallen" to the ground. It would never look like a real tree. And there would never be an exit ramp, there would never be a way to stop and see it up close.

"That thing is never going to be finished," Thomas said.

After that, the blood clots began. It had been a week and a half since the abortion, and I was suddenly passing dark clots. I called the clinic and they put the Indian doctor on the phone. She said, "What color, what size?" When I said maroon, she said "Good. Now the size. In money, what size?"

"What?"

"What size coin. If the clots are coins, what size are they. You know, dime, nickel, quarter."

"Oh," I said, "dimes, they are dimes."

"If the clots become like quarters, then you call me." she said, and hung up.

I got ready for work. I put extra maxi-pads in my bag, I brushed my hair and pinned it up. Then someone stuck a knitting needle in my gut.

Then a kitchen knife. This was what it felt like—a knife plunged in to the handle and hari-kari to the right. I couldn't think straight.

The doorbell rang. It was my neighbor, Katie.

"He's gone," she said, "I didn't think he could get out. I was in the laundry room."

"Who?" I asked.

"Petey," she said, "my bird, Petey." A button-eyed white cockatiel. Gone now, out the window.

"I'm going out," I said, "I'll look for him." And then I was locking the apartment door, my bag slung over my shoulder. The cramps had disappeared.

After I'd walked a block toward Dee's, they returned. I had to stop and bend over, lean against a tree. They came in cycles, like an off-balance washer, banging louder and louder until some hand righted it. I made it to the restaurant when another round came. Adam looked up as I ran by the kitchen. I hadn't seen him in weeks.

The clots were now the size of quarters. But the hostess kept giving me tables, and I kept not saying no. I don't know how long it was before I felt it. Something slipped inside of me. I felt a warmth between my legs and then when I walked into the waitress station next to the pie case, a wetness in my shoes. I looked beneath my skirt, and two red stripes painted themselves down the insides of my legs. For a moment, they looked like someone else's legs. Blood running over my ankles. And my body jackknifing. I hobbled, bent like an ironing board, through the fake-wood swinging doors into the kitchen, past the grill, the line-up, through the second set of swinging stainless steel doors into the back room with the walk-ins, the storage shelves, the bathrooms. Each door I passed through slammed behind me, each had a round window like a port-hole eye. Four eyes fluttering.

I was lying on the bathroom floor near the toilet, trying to get my tights off, unlace my shoes, but I couldn't make my body straighten.

"Are you OK?" Adam asked, his head in the doorway. I put my hand up to tell him to go away. There must have been blood on it, because he said, "Oh man, oh fuck."

"You didn't get the abortion," he said.

"I did get it," I said.

"Then what. Then what—oh shit," he said. "I'll be right back." And he closed the door quietly, but I heard him running away.

I want to say it was beautiful, to find some beauty in it. Because beauty is never completely absent from any horrible thing. But in that moment I didn't know the faces of any one who came and went. I hardly remember what I owned, what was mine. The color of the blood was beautiful, I can say that. This incredible red. I sat at the edge of the toilet, my nylons like wet sea ropes around my ankles and I couldn't believe the redness I had in my hands. I'd never seen anything like it. So many shades of red, so deep and bright. All coming from inside.

The mass came next. I held it in my hands. Blueish, not made of blood, something else. I put it in the toilet. There was blood everywhere. And voices. The voice of the night manager, a calm woman's voice, calling my name. Adam had told her. Adam was telling her. And Adam's voice calling my name. A door opened and someone wrapped a blue coat around my waist. And my nylons, my underwear, the pad all thrown in the trash. Everything I touched left a blood-smear. Who was going to clean it up? "Don't worry about that," Adam said. And someone led me to a car. Then up the wide cement sidewalk, beneath the portico of the hospital, the green EMERGENCY sign.

Inside the examining room I was in the white robe again, sitting on the white table, my feet hanging naked in the air. The doctor made me lie down and touched me gently beneath the sheet.

"Did you save it?" the doctor asked. It was not the Indian doctor. It was an older white man. He looked very concerned.

"Did I save it?" How could I save it?

"If you had saved it, we could tell how far along you were," he said.

"I put it in the toilet," I said. And now that seemed wrong, too.

He asked what size it was, and all I could think of was the Nerf football we had in our apartment, a small one that Thomas tossed into a thin wire hoop he'd fastened above the kitchen door.

"A Nerf football," I said, "a small Nerf football. Not a big one."

"Try something else," he said.

"An orange?" I said.

"OK," he said.

He told me I had lost a lot of blood. He used the word "hemorrhage." He said "incomplete abortion," and "spontaneous miscarriage." The nurses were moving very quickly, there was no waiting.

An operation. A bag of blood hung by my side on a pole. I was put in a recovery room all my own. The abortion, it was explained to me, had failed. It had left the fetus alive but damaged enough that it quickly died. My body expelled it. The knife pains I had felt were contractions. It was a birth.

This made me cry. Hot wet tears that sprung from my eyes. Not birth. Not that word. I imagined it hiding in some corner, under my ribs, a wounded animal.

Thomas wasn't there. Katie and Geraldo were there, but Thomas wasn't there. Adam had called the Mexican restaurant, but Thomas had already left; Geraldo had gone to the apartment looking for him and found Katie looking for her bird.

"We came as soon as we heard," Katie said.

"Does Thomas know?" I asked. They had told him. He was stuck at the Marriott trying to get someone to cover his shift. I don't know any of these people, I thought.

"We're here to drive you home," Geraldo said.

"Did you find Petey?" I asked.

"Not yet, baby, but we will." It was weird to hear her call me that.

Then I was home. Katie put a glass of water and some Kleenex next to the waterbed. Geraldo stood near the doorway, fidgeting.

"Thomas will be here soon," he said. Katie said she was going to walk around the block again and look for Petey. "People think I'm crazy," she said, "walking around looking at the sky like something's gonna fall out of it." Then they left.

It got dark. It got late. Thomas didn't come home. The doorbell rang, and Adam came in. It was 11:30 p.m. He was carrying a bouquet of daisies.

"I just came to check on you," he said. "They let me off early to check on you." He stood there, looking around the apartment, looking for someone. He was completely un-stoned. I had never seen him like this. He looked both kind and serious. His face was clear.

"Thomas isn't back yet." I said. "I guess he didn't get anyone to cover his shift."

"OK," Adam said. "Well, I can wait with you, if you want. If you don't want to be alone." I told him I wanted him to.

He sat in a chair next to the bed. At one point I woke up and most of the lights in the apartment had been turned off, but Adam was still there, under the one lamp left on. The clock's red letters said 1:30 a.m. Then 2:00 a.m. Then I heard loud voices near the doorway. I heard Thomas sobbing. I smelled bar mats, spilled beer, and cigarettes. "Come out in the hallway," Adam said, "I have to talk to you." I heard raised voices, the door slamming again and again. Adam didn't come back.

Eventually Thomas stumbled in. He was crying, blind drunk. "I felt so bad, Baby, I felt so bad, I couldn't bear to see you. I. Just. Couldn't. Stand. It." Then more sobbing, his body thrown across me, making the waterbed wave.

"Did he hit you?" I asked.

"Huh?"

"Did he punch you? Adam. Did Adam punch you?"

"No, why would he punch me?"

"Never mind," I said.

A few days later, they found Katie's bird. He was sitting on top of a very tall spruce tree at the back of the driveway, a white flag fluttering. The fire department arrived, and firemen unfurled a long hose and dragged it halfway down the block to the hydrant. Water ran in streams down the driveway. The entire apartment came outside to watch. Thomas was at work. I was feeling better—I could stand and walk around—so I went outside for the first time in a while.

"What are they going to do?" I asked Katie.

"They're gonna shoot him down with a hose," she said. And that's when Adam walked up.

"That's a big fuckin' tree," Adam said, after we had told him the story. "It must be 70 feet up there at the top." It was true, the bird did seem very far away. The top of the tree was not as high as the balcony the family had fallen from, I thought. Rachel David, or Eve as they called her, would live a long time into the future, would never walk but would still think about her family and her father returning to earth as God. Stuck here without them, she would enjoy coffee, listening to Neil Diamond, paint-by-numbers, and going outside, if anyone would take her. She had fallen farther than the bird would fall with its feathers wet and stuck together, and she would not remember what it was like to fall that far, to land on top of her family.

The firemen lobbed long streams into the air, raining down on the garage, the parked cars, rippling the lower branches. The next arc hit the tree top and we watched as the small white bird hovered in the air for a moment, then fell into the tree, dropping like a sock with a rock in it.

But they never found Petey. They never knew if he died or flew away with wet wings. The force of water caused him to disappear. And after that, after looking everywhere in the wet pine boughs, the leaves, beneath parked cars, in the limbs of other trees, Adam took me for a drive.

We drove up into the canyons toward the ski areas, and off the winding road of a development, parallel to the hills. He took me to his mother's house, but I didn't get to meet her. We parked down the road and walked back across the yard and into the woods where a small stream ran over rocks. Everything was green beneath the water and quiet among the trees. Adam told me that with the warm days there'd been a thaw, and now you could hear the frogs wake up. If I sat still enough, the frogs would start singing. He thought I might like to just sit and listen.

The girl trapped in the wreckage of Gold Miner's Daughter Lodge was eventually rescued; out in the desert, the sculptor would finish the tree and offer it to the state of Utah as a gift, but the state wouldn't accept it until ten years later; birds flew into it, confused by the light reflecting off the tiles, littering the ground with their bodies; I would call my parents and tell them everything, and I would leave Thomas, but not until later. I think of the white room, the couple making love in my mind, the couple that becomes me and Thomas with our bad music and strange positions, and I think of a bird, a girl, or an angel standing on the edge, at the doorway, trying to come in. But the door is closed. One of the disciples of Immanuel David would tell a newspaper that even though he wasted years in the cult, he did have spiritual experiences, he felt great things he could not explain. The world is filled equally with suffering and beauty. The Swedish sculptor looked at the vast white desert and saw something uplifting in the emptiness, he carved the words to the "Ode to Joy" in the base of the tree.

After that day in the trees by the stream, I never saw Adam again. There is no other way to say it. He left me there for a while, sitting by the water listening for frogs. Awake early, he had said. Brand new to this world. And I loved him for it. After a while, I thought I heard them. Yes, I heard them.

PORTRAIT OF A MOTHER

by Stephanie Andersen

"It's still snowing out there," she said.

Mom and I were tucked under her blue comforter on her bed late one afternoon, staring out the window into the backyard. The snow had settled on the pine branches, and the windows shook a little in the November wind. I pushed my head into the space between her arm and breast, tracing the hardness of the catheter buried under her skin. She was holding a tiny portrait of a young Victorian woman with big brown eyes, soft curly hair, and pursed lips.

"This is how I imagine you'll look when you grow up," she told me.

I stared at the face of the woman and tried to imagine myself as her. She seemed gentle, her hands folded neatly in her lap, her eyes shy and hopeful, her breasts round and high.

There was an intensity about my mother's stare I couldn't yet understand. I wondered what it was about the woman in the picture that made Mom stare the way she did. It was the same way she looked at me while I climbed under my covers at night and asked her to stay a little longer, just until I fell asleep. I watched as my mother smiled, shifting her head from the right to the left, squinting at the picture. Then I decided there was something my mother knew I didn't. I certainly didn't look like the woman in the picture. I was smaller. And my hair was shorter. And my nose was thinner. I was only nine years old, and it was the first time in my life I ever seriously considered the possibility of becoming something else, other than the child I was.

I had grown to need those few hours alone with Mom in the afternoon. I watched the snow land on the foggy glass and transform into water drops that dripped away or disappeared into the push of the wind.

Mom found the lump in her breast five years earlier, and the doctors had told her she had only three months to live. But she did not give up. She told the doctors to go to hell then started her treatment. She changed her diet, exercised, meditated, repeated positive affirmations, lost her hair, burnt her skin with radiation, and begged God to save her life. She had a little girl to take care of.

She lived much longer than the doctors had expected. Six years longer. But when they told her they would have to remove her breast, my mother refused. She told my father that she was sure losing a breast would take something from her, something she wasn't prepared to lose.

At nine, I had not yet developed my breasts. All I knew of womanhood was the shape of my mother's body, the way she fit around me in her bed, the way she smelled of St. Ives lotion, of baby powder, and of ginger. I had no interest in attaining any of this for myself. I did not desire to be shaped like her, to have roundness, softness, to smell sweet. I loved the simplicity of my own body, my ability to run barefoot and shirtless in my own backyard. I was thankful that I did not bleed from my private parts and have to leave diapers drenched with blood in the bathroom garbage. My father and I were free of this, untangled by the chains of what kept my mother from throwing off her shirt and jumping into the lake at the park with us. While she set up the picnic table, I chased my father through the woods. And while my mother slowly died from a sickness I could only identify as womanhood, I grew to see her as a martyr who took the heaviness of life upon herself and away from my father and me. At night, I heard her crying through the walls. "I don't want to die," she screamed, over and over, until her voice was raw. And in the morning, my father would take me on a bike ride, remind me how capable I was as he pedaled ahead of me. Then he'd teach me how to calculate the exact number of bricks under the pavement on which we rode. "See, Stephanie," he said. "Math empowers women." Then he would smile. "Women can do anything a man can do."

But I didn't want to be a woman. I didn't want my mother's body. Strength was freedom, and a woman's body was weak and stifling.

At night, when I woke up with a stomachache or a sore throat, I would cry for my parents. But my father would never come. It was always my mother. It didn't matter that she was constantly undergoing some sort of treatment, in and out of the hospital, and most often sick to her stomach. She always came, patted my forehead with a wet cloth, and waited for me to go back to sleep. I would rest my head between her breast and her arm, wrapping my arms around her chest, smelling her, praying that there would never be a day that I couldn't call for her. Her selflessness and dedication fascinated me in a way my father's energy and freedom never could. I wanted to be her child forever, breastless, free and in her arms. But I never wanted to be her.

One morning, I woke up with a sharp pain in my chest. I ran to my mother.

"I have a bump on my chest," I told her. "And it hurts."

She smiled. "You're getting your breasts," she said, rubbing her fingers gently over the tiny bump. "You're becoming a woman."

I backed away from her. Never. I would never become a woman. "It's breast cancer, isn't it?" I asked. "It must be."

For several weeks, my mother argued with me, explaining that I was not dying, just growing up. But I could not be convinced until she took me to a doctor for a thorough examination.

"I don't want breasts," I told my mother. "My life is over."

"No, Stephanie. Your life is just beginning. You're going to be a woman. And that is a magical, wonderful thing. You'll see."

"Breasts stink," I told my mother after school a week later. "And so does womanhood." Then I stomped into my bedroom and slammed the door.

Two months before my twelfth birthday, I stood over her, studying her lifeless body. She lay stiffly on a hospital bed in our den. I raised her cold hand and tried to memorize how her fingers felt between mine. Above her, on the wall, hung a picture of us, me as an infant in her lap, her hands wrapped tightly around my waist. It was only then that I realized why my mother stared so intently at the picture of that Victorian woman. It was the only image of me as a woman that she would ever see. And as this realization crept through my thoughts, I suddenly felt a new desire that I had never known before. I wanted to find out what it was about a woman's body that my mother had sacrificed her life for. I wanted to understand what I had been missing.

I was finishing my junior year of high school when I made it happen. I stood in front of the bathroom mirror one afternoon. I was supposed to be studying for a history final. My boyfriend was still in my bedroom as I watched his white ejaculate drop from my abdomen. I imagined what the sperm looked like under a microscope as I studied how it appeared against my tan, summer skin. It wasn't that I didn't know it was wrong. I was too young. I was certainly not considering the other party involved. Of course. But I was curious. I wondered if I was capable, if I could grow and swell like other girls I had seen at school. In the late nineties, in upstate New York, teenage pregnancy was no longer a surprise. My hometown, a small suburb just outside of Binghamton, was home to at least five pregnant adolescents in 1997, and they were not the first of their kind. These girls came late to school, flaunting growing bellies and exciting plans for their very own apartments. Two-bedroom, two-bath. They let us all touch their stretching skin with circular strokes. They said things like, "Only two more months," "We think it's a boy," and, "I don't have to take gym anymore." They were separate from the rest of us, more grown up, more in touch with the future, more interesting, and far more sexual. I watched them as they waddled down our high school hallways with heavy book bags, heavy bodies, and severe looks of bewildering determination. And as their eyes veered away from my gaze, I found myself eager to know what it felt like to be watched and touched, to be mysterious, and to have such unavoidable purpose. These girls were anomalies. They were all at once scorned and cherished. They were our future and our failure. They were not ready but going ahead with it. They were dismal and exciting statistics. They were pregnant.

The longer I stood in front of the mirror, the more honest it all seemed. I was built for it. I needed it. I told myself that in the end nothing I did would matter to anyone else. It was my body, my choice, my wish. Naked and horribly immature, I lifted the hair off my neck with both hands and looked at my eyes, imagining the big brown Victorian eyes of that portrait.

Ten years and six hundred miles later, I hold a cell phone to my ear and listen to a little girl tell her sixth knock-knock joke in three minutes.

"Knock knock," she says.

"Who's there?" I ask.

She giggles. "Egg."

"Egg who?" I say.

"Egg knock's my favorite drink too." Then she laughs uncontrollably, squealing and hiccupping into the phone.

It's difficult to fake a laugh. But I do. I giggle nervously, tell her it was "a good one," knowing that she had made it up on her own and is proud.

"What did the picture say to the wall?" she says, not ready to quit yet.

I pause for a moment as if to think about it. Then I admit, "I don't know."

"I've got you covered." She squeals again with delight, hiccups twice, sighs, and continues laughing.

Elianna will be ten years old this year. She lives six hundred miles away, in upstate New York, just outside my hometown. She hiccups if she laughs too hard. She likes to read; she loves to draw. She takes gymnastics but accidentally kicked her instructor last week at practice. She's tall for her age, almost five foot now, and embarrassed by it. She's good in school, always has a good report card, likes to impress her teachers. She enjoys jumping on the trampoline in her backyard, swimming at the YMCA, shopping for clothes at the Limited and Old Navy, listening to music— mostly Hillary Duff; she loves going to yard sales and has been begging her parents to let her start taking piano lessons. When she heard there were people in the world without hair, she grew hers out, cut it off, and donated it. Her favorite color is blue. She watches *Survivor* every Thursday night at eight o'clock. She loves having her nails done, being an older sister, and staying up past her bedtime. She doesn't like bras or mean people. When she grows up, she wants to be an artist. This is the first time we have ever spoken directly to one another on the phone, but she has a picture of me in her bedroom she stares at, brings to school for show-and-tell, and sleeps with. She has never met me, but Elianna, the girl on the other end of the phone, is my daughter.

What I want to say to her: *None of this is your fault. It was never you. I want to smell you, your head, your hands, your toes. I want to know what your hair feels like between my fingers. I want to see the way your thighs turn into your calves and your calves into your ankles. I want to find out, for myself, if your big toe is shorter than your second toe. I want to know the direction in which your arm hair grows. I dream about you, wake up in the middle of the night worried that you are sick, sad, angry, afraid. I want to crawl in bed next to you, wrap myself around you, finally feeling the shape our bodies make together. I want to feed you, cook the food myself, make you strong and healthy. I want to help you learn how to read, write, paint. I want to read you my favorite stories, the ones my mother read me. I want to walk through a mall with you, help you try on clothes, tell you how beautiful you look in blue. I want to know the people you know. When I hear your voice, see your picture, I want the pain in my breasts and abdomen to go away. Forgive me. Let me kiss your face, your arms, your ears, your fingers. Your jokes, as much as I love you, are really not that funny.*

What comes out: "Very clever, Eli. Very clever."

Before we hang up, she tells me "Good night" and that she loves me. I tell her, "Sweet dreams."

And I am back in my apartment, in North Carolina, on this bed, under this blue comforter. And I cannot complain about much here. I have just finished with school, earned a master's degree. I work at a community college, teach freshman English. I rent a nice little apartment outside the city on the third floor of a brand new building, behind an almost-finished Walmart. I have a large friendly group I am lucky to call my friends. There is no boyfriend, but this doesn't seem to bother me. I run through the routine, wake up early every morning, walk my dog. Life is normal enough. I am free and strong, a product of my father's firm encouragement to be an independent woman. "Women are no different than men," he always said. "Women can do everything a man can do. Don't ever sell yourself short."

The only signs of weakness are the colorful stretch marks on my breasts, the grip I still have on the phone long after she's hung up, and the picture of my daughter hung on the wall over my bed.

A baby. I would make it work.

"No," my father said. "It will ruin your life."

"I can do it," I begged.

"Not in my house." He ran his fingers through his beard, flipped through his mail, sipping his hot tea. "I won't be a part of it. If you have this child, you will never know what it means to be independent, to be successful, to accomplish all that you're capable of. If you choose this path, you choose a life I can't support. Find another place to live."

No problem. I would find a place to live. A charity organization. A family who would give me a home, tell me it was okay to be a mother. At first, inventing myself as a pregnant teenager, a mother-to-be, was fun, exciting, simple. I collected baby clothes, pacifiers, bottles, and tiny bonnets. My charity family gave me a tiny room in their basement. And at night, as I lay alone in the dark, staring up through the windows into the flower bed outside, I had no doubt that I was where I wanted to be, becoming who I was meant to become. As my breasts and abdomen grew, I became thrilled with the changes, finally feeling like I was being given the opportunity to be a real woman. School no longer seemed important. Homework seemed petty. College seemed like a fantasy. In the waking hours of the morning, I would get up out of bed, my bladder full again, tiptoe up the stairs, and stare in the mirror. In my reflection I searched for a change in my face, something familiar, any sign of the mother I planned to become. But my face never seemed to change. My growing breasts and the bulge in my abdomen always seemed alien, growing on their own, without my permission, separate from my eyes. I'd crawl back into bed, running my fingers over my stomach, feeling my daughter kick my hands through my skin. I'd ask her to have patience with me.

I wanted to keep that baby just as naturally and vehemently as I wanted my mother to live. And I tried for seven long months to find a way to do it. But 1997 was a difficult year. Clinton reformed welfare, making it impossible for anyone under the age of eighteen to receive aid, and I couldn't find a way to keep a stable job, finish high school, and care for a job all at once without at least a little help from the father, who was unwilling to even admit to his parents that he had a girlfriend. At seven months pregnant, it became clear. There was no hope. I couldn't do it. It had all been a fantasy I couldn't live up to. I was no mother. In fact, I was little more than an irresponsible teenager with a penchant for the dramatic, no job, and no future.

Worse, I found myself desperate for reprieve. I wanted out of the martyrdom. I didn't want to wake up in the middle of the night for anyone, much less in a basement room for a child I had nothing to offer.

And one night, as I collapsed in the corner of my borrowed basement room, I dug my fingernails into the skin of my chest, knowing, with the most horrible sincerity, that I was unwilling to give up my freedom and security for my womanhood, for the natural inclination which drove my body to such change in shape. I didn't want it bad enough. And when the realization came, I wanted to empty myself of my miracle as quickly as possible, renewing myself to the state of freedom, loneliness, and asexuality I had become so accustomed to.

I would do what my father had told me would win me strength. I would be everything my mother wasn't. I would graduate high school, something she never did. I would go to college, pay my own bills, travel, and live a long, successful life.

"I'm so proud of you," Dad said, his eyes red with weepy gratitude. "This was a hard decision to make but a very strong one."

"I want to be strong," I told him. "And successful."

"I know you will be," he said.

And I believed him.

* * *

I met Angel and her husband, Matt, just over ten years ago, in late January 1997. They had been trying to have a baby for eleven years. Every month, for all of those years, she had hoped she was pregnant, picked out a name, constructed themes for the nursery, imagined the baby's face. And every month, when the blood came, another imaginary child died. She had long since lost count of all the faces that might have been.

"I can't do this," I told her over the phone. "I've decided to go to college. I just can't do this alone." I listened to her cry, for several moments, in what I would later find out was relief, wondering if she would ever speak. Part of me hoped she would tell me she would adopt both of us, the baby and me. I wanted to tell her how desperately I wanted to keep my baby, but I just needed her to help me. I wanted to explain what it felt like to feel a human being growing inside me for so many months, to learn what sounds made her sleep, to learn exactly the way I needed to walk in order to lull her. I wanted her to know that a part of me knew what I was saying was dangerous for me, that my body would never forgive me.

"Can I meet you somewhere?" she finally asked.

"Okay."

We chose McDonald's on Main Street.

Angel became a mother then, when I nodded my head across the table from her, licking the ice cream cone she and her husband had bought for me when I said they could have my baby.

It would be Angel who held Elianna minutes after she was born. It was Angel who held her when she first cried, learning the motions of her tiny body, the difference between hungry and wet. It was Angel who brought the tiny baby home for the first time, who lay her down in a bassinet, who waited for her to cry in the middle of the night, who woke up to calm her with warm milk from a bottle. It was Angel, whom I met by accident when I doubted my ability to be faithful to my own feminine instincts, who watched my child grow from a seven-pound, eight-ounce infant into this 9-year-old girl who tells knock-knock jokes and giggles until she hiccups. It was never me.

It is because of this that I cannot now complain if Angel, this other mother, chooses to explain the adoption in such simple terms as "You grew in Stephanie's belly but in Mommy's heart." I cannot blame this woman for waiting so long to let my daughter communicate with me. I cannot tell my daughter that her jokes are not funny or that it is the hope of one day meeting her that keeps me waking up in the morning and trying to be successful, impressive, and strong.

Friends ask, "How do you talk to your daughter on the phone so casually?"

And I respond, "How do I not?"

Since they brought my daughter to their home for the first time, this couple has repeated my name in her ear like a mantra, wanting to "do the right thing," to make her aware of her heritage, to be proud to be adopted. My daughter's only questions have been whether or not I love her, why I gave her away. "Of course she loves you," her parents tell her. "Stephanie was just so young." But Eli repeats the same questions, seemingly waiting for a truth she's sure she has not yet heard.

When her parents first told her she could speak with me, she hesitated, decided it wasn't time. Instead, she listened over the speakerphone while her mother spoke to me. When she did this, I tried to adjust my voice, attempted to comfort her with my words, even if I was only telling Angel about the weather in North Carolina. Sometimes I would hear her giggle in the background, whisper something to her mother. But she wasn't going to talk directly to me, not for six more months.

"Eli's doing really well in school," Angel would say.

"Oh, wow," I responded, trying to express a pride my daughter will recognize in my voice. "That is so wonderful."

I heard a tiny giggle in the background.

"Stephanie's proud of me," she told her mother later.

"Yes," Angel said. "She'd be proud of you no matter what you did."

Angel always calls and tells me the whole conversation later, tells me all the questions Eli asks about me, about the glazed plate my daughter, her daughter, is making me for Christmas with my name and my dog's name printed across the front in child's handwriting and swirls of purple and blue along the edges.

It was my sister's idea to create a website for Elianna. It may be against the rules for a 9-year-old to have her own MySpace profile, but it isn't against the rules for a birthfamily to create a profile entitled, "We Love Elianna." With a few keystrokes by my sister, the profile displayed several pictures of all of us, even my mother. There were pictures of me as a baby, of my sister and me carving a pumpkin when we were children, of my father, of Elianna on her first day of fourth grade, of Elianna when she was a baby, of Elianna when she was still inside me. I emailed Angel the password, and we waited.

Three months later, I received a message from Elianna over MySpace.
DEAR STEPHANIE
I AM JUST STARTING TO TYPING. WRITE ME BACK PLEASE! I WOULD LIKE TO MEET YOU VERY MUCH. WELL I HAVE TO GO. BY LOVE. ELIANNA

"At Olive Garden," Angel told me later. Apparently Eli imagined a girls' lunch, the three of us, at the same restaurant I had celebrated her first birthday, one candle stuck in a scoop of ice cream, my father and I wondering how to celebrate without the birthday girl.

"Does she mean it?" I asked Angel.

"I don't know," she said. "I guess we'll see."

"Why now?" I asked.

"I don't know," Angel said. "I asked her, and she said she wanted to know what your favorite color was. And she really wants to meet Daisy."

Daisy is my Jack Russell Terrier. Eli refers to her as the "birth dog." I paused. "Will she ask me why I did it? Why I gave her..."

"I don't think so."

"What will I say to her?"

"I don't know," she said. "Tell her what your favorite color is."

"When?" I asked.

"Are you coming home for the holidays?"

I haven't been home for Christmas in three years. In fact, I rarely go back to New York for any reason. I opt instead for distraction, grad school, affairs with married men, menial social melodrama, heavy drinking, various jobs I latch onto and pour myself into, my writing. And last year, my father left New York for a two-year stay in Africa. He wasn't there to visit. I never have a problem finding reasons to stay away. Now I dial my sister's number, tell her I'll be home in a month for the holiday.

She says, "Okay," but I can tell she doesn't believe me. She'll wait for me to change my mind.

"Elianna said she wants to meet me," I say.

She's silent for a minute. "Are you ready for that?" she asks.

"I don't know," I say. I think about the last time I went home, what we did, but I can't remember whose idea it was to spy on my daughter. We had never driven by Elianna's house before, and whether it was my sister's idea or mine, we decided to try it. We hadn't expected her to be climbing out of a minivan in her driveway, her face so much like mine, with moving legs, with a real mouth, a living, breathing little girl. I slammed on my brakes, fumbled for my sunglasses. My sister slid down in her seat, thinking, like me, that Eli would look up, somehow recognize our car, see the North Carolina plates. We'd be caught. But she never did, and we pulled our car behind the tree across the street, stared out the windshield, watched her for a minute while she waited for her mother to unload the van. I held my sister's hand, surprised at how much we were shaking.

"That's your baby," my sister said, shaking her head. "That's her."

I knew she was waiting for me to do something remarkable, become the lioness confronted with her stolen cub. She stared at me, watching the way my face trembled, hoping these long years had been enough to awaken the mother inside me. But after Eli disappeared into her house and the door closed behind her, I shifted the car into reverse and drove up the hill, away.

My sister has often tried to stir my maternal instincts. There have been days I cry in her arms, tell her how much I regret it all. And she'll call an attorney, tell me to get creative, get angry, claim duress, anything. Just get my daughter back. But I have never tried. And I know I never will.

Now, she repeats her question. "Are you ready for this?"

"You're not ready for this," my boyfriend, Elianna's father, told me, ten years ago, the night before I would promise my child to another couple. And then I was hitting him. I punched him for all the decisions in the world I felt I had no control over. I clawed at his chest for my dead mother and the baby I couldn't find the will to keep. I spit in his face for the picture of that Victorian woman, for the mystery of my own identity, and I screamed because I couldn't remember my mother's face, I would never see my daughter's, and I couldn't find my own. He let me go on like that for several minutes as the snow fell against the windshield and melted into water. And by the time it was over, I had found a silence again. I curled into a ball, wrapped my arms around my legs, and closed my eyes.

There wasn't anybody who wanted to help me be a mother. But there was a world of people who wanted to help me go to college. And slowly, this became my answer. I constructed a new truth, a new face out of what I decided the rest of the world expected of me. I learned that most everyone would respond delightfully to my change of heart. Teachers gave me extra time on my assignments, my father bragged about me in church, my boyfriend thanked me with wet eyes, told me he loved me, that he would marry me one day. Over and over, for years to come, all I had to do was say I gave a daughter up for adoption, and people would do everything but bow at my feet, chanting the popular "what a selfless, brave decision to make." This gave me identity. I was the teenager who gave her daughter up for adoption. But the only image I had of the life I was choosing was the word my father repeated to me over and over throughout my childhood. College, I kept thinking. "I'm going to college." And now that I had no choice, it sounded so good.

I waited, but no matter how many times I recited my mantra, "I'm going to college. I can't be a mother," my hand still found its way to her, and I still spoke to her, cried over her when she kicked at my fingers. I knew then that I could not make the baby go away.

It has been three days since Eli wrote me to tell me she wants to meet me. And as I make plans to go home, whether she means it or not, I tell myself that nothing, no lunch at Olive Garden, no knock-knock jokes, will ever make me her mother.

In the small box in the corner of my bedroom, I keep two ultrasound photos secretly tucked away, the two I once hid from myself, just in case one day I needed to remind myself the pregnancy actually happened, that Eli was not a dream. I take them out occasionally, stare at them. I keep her second-grade picture sitting on the antique end table my mother left me in her will.

A year ago, Eli sent me a box for my birthday, a collection of her things she thought I needed to have. Inside, there are leopard print pillows, blue sandals, necklaces, pictures she drew in school, photographs of her swimming, lotions, beanie babies, and a letter that she wrote, explaining the little details of her life. I keep the box in another corner, sit next to it sometimes, smell the little pillows, hold the earrings in my hands, study the letter. Once, for a reason I'm not sure of, I took out the sandals, tried them on. They fit perfectly.

Eli's need to show me who she is does not surprise me. These years without my mother and daughter have brought me no happy endings or clear answers, but I have realized that the real tragedy has not been my inability to become the Victorian woman in the portrait. My mother did not show me that picture to assign me an identity to live up to. That picture was for her. She would never know how my face would evolve as I grew older. This woman I have become, nothing like that portrait—with all of my regrets, with my two diplomas hung on my wall, with an absent daughter—is a woman my mother will never know.

My daughter and are I left to struggle through this strange distance from each other, memorizing pictures of each other, unable to put the pictures away. When asked whether or not I regret my decision to give my daughter up for adoption, I answer honestly. Yes. Going to college has never made up for the nagging regret. I can still smell the rotten milk that leaked from my breasts for a week after she was born. The smell of those leopard pillows is still more comforting than any freedom I have earned, than any success. But what I am left with is not a gift I take for granted. I have my daughter's face, changing in every new photo, her eyes like my mother's, like mine, next to me as I sleep, in the box in the corner, its own nuances, unexpected, miraculous.

Elianna was born on March 7, 1997 at seven o'clock. She was seven pounds, eight ounces. Lucky seven baby. As I pushed her out, I begged the doctor not to let anyone take her from me, but my words were ignored, dismissed as nothing more than the emotional roller coaster of a 17-year-old girl in labor. My father stood over me, covered my eyes as she slipped from between my legs. I heard her gurgle for a second, and then she was gone.

I saw her only once before I left the hospital for good. Angel's husband was holding her behind a glass window in the nursery. He passed her off to Angel who brought her into the hall for me.

"Do you want to hold her?" she asked.

I looked down at the baby. I waited for something in my mind to click, come alive. I waited for whatever it was inside me that might have become a mother in the last nine months to react, but nothing happened as I clung to the IV stand I had wheeled along with me. It was over.

"No," I whispered.

"Is there anything you want to say to her?" Angel asked.

I thought about it for a second. But only one thing came to mind.

"Yeah," I said, "I guess there is." I reached into the blanket and found Eli's hand. She wrapped her fingers around one of mine as I cleared my throat. "Go to college," I said. Then I pulled my finger from her grip, turned around, and walked away.

* * *

I will not meet my daughter this Christmas. She'll change her mind, lose the courage, send her mother in her place. I will have lunch with her mother alone, offer Angel a picture of Daisy and me along with a wrapped gift to take home with her and give to Elianna. It will be a necklace that splits into two halves. Angel will sit across the table from me, run her fingers over my hand, tell me Eli has my fingers.

"Are you okay?" I'll ask her, watching the way her eyes well up at the sight of me. I understand that I am a reminder that Eli will never have her eyes, her fingers, or her lips. She will never be able to know what it felt like to carry her daughter to term in her own uterus. And she will watch me remove the necklace from the box myself. I will keep one half and Eli will keep the other. I'll never take my half off my neck, running my fingers over the charm while I am at work, driving, grocery shopping, or staring out my apartment window into the Walmart parking lot.

"I'm dealing with it," she'll say. And she will return home to my daughter, maybe brush the hair off her forehead, feed her dinner, and tell her what it was like to have lunch with Stephanie, the birthmother.

Back in North Carolina, I will continue to occasionally stand in front of the mirror naked, staring at the scars on my breasts, at the ever-changing slope of my abdomen, which has never shrunk back to its original size, swelling in cycles, its own terrain of hills and valleys that retells my story repeatedly, reminding me that there is still a part of me I am missing.

And then one night, to my surprise, my 9-year-old daughter will call with an unusual question. "Do you have big boobs?" she'll ask.

"Elianna's getting her breasts," Angel will say in the background. "And she's not happy. She has to wear a bra."

I'll laugh and tell Eli that mine aren't so big, that there's nothing to worry about.

"Okay," she'll say, sighing.

"I know how you feel," I'll tell her, picturing her standing there, staring hopelessly down at her swelling chest. "I didn't want to get boobs either."

And after a small silence, she'll clear her throat. "Well," she'll say. "Your boobs look big in your picture."

We'll laugh, and she'll hiccup, both of us remaining somewhat damaged and slightly delighted.

"I don't think she'll ever take this necklace off," Angel giggles in the background.

And I'll be thankful, with the phone held tight to my ear, for my own breasts, for the shape of my body, and even for this regret.

WATER CHILDREN

by Nina de Gramont

EVERY YEAR IN WILMINGTON, North Carolina, pro-life activists stage a silent protest. For a single day they stand on either side of Oleander, one of the city's main thoroughfares, holding up neatly lettered placards. It's a harbinger of autumn, and I know that the long, southern months of Indian summer have arrived when the quiet chain appears. It goes on for miles—solemn and plaintive faces of all ages. Last year there were nearly two thousand of them, their lips sealed in self-restraint as passing motorists hurled eggs from car windows. The eggs didn't hit anyone, just splattered *disagreement* angrily at their feet, slowly cooking on the still-hot pavement.

Oleander is a road I drive down often, and in the three years I've lived here I've always managed to stumble upon the so-called Life Chain. The first time, in the moment I recognized the nature of the demonstration (words steadily hanging in the air: "Abortion Kills Children"), I started to make a reflexive gesture at the protesters, who stared—insistent and inquisitive—through every windshield. It wouldn't have been a hostile gesture, nothing obscene. Just an exaggerated frown, a dramatic shake of my head, perhaps accompanied by a raised and wagging finger, to let them know how vehemently I disagreed.

But somehow, returning the protesters' unspeaking gaze, I couldn't manage an expression of disapproval. As a teenager, I had been deeply involved in protesting nuclear weapons, and took intensive courses in civil disobedience and non-violent protest. That long river of silence struck an admiring chord. It impressed me and it moved me. If I didn't agree with their politics, I could still appreciate the poetry of the gesture, and the undeniable power of silent numbers.

I have a friend who's opposed to abortion. Recently, she asked me if I'd ever had one.

"No," I answered truthfully.

"Would you have?" she asked. "When you were single?"

"I guess so," I said. "It was always my contingency plan."

As a single woman—from my teens and into my twenties—I was assiduously careful about birth control. The closest I ever came to an unplanned pregnancy was one drunken night on Nantucket, with a good-looking and cocky boy who'd never read *The Catcher in the Rye*.

"I don't really like to read," he'd told me, back at the Chicken Box, the only bar that would accept our fake IDs. I remember sipping my sea breeze and feeling sad for the boy, who didn't realize he'd just blown his chances.

Several hours and several sea breezes later, literary credentials didn't seem so important. As we made out on a deserted beach with no birth control in sight, I remember having a very specific, very drunken thought: that if I got pregnant, the subsequent abortion would be another life experience, like getting lost on the London tube or drinking wine with homeless sailors on the docks at Key West. Perfectly in tune with my youth, the trauma would make me a deeper, more fully realized person. These ideas, or something close to them, actually formed in my foggy head.

Luckily, a weeping friend interrupted our embrace, distraught over an altercation with her boyfriend. The boy who didn't like to read disappeared into the night—as surely as he would have had the evening proceeded to its inevitable drunken conclusion.

I used to know a girl who became pregnant during a similar encounter. Describing her subsequent abortion, she'd said, "I wanted it out of my body as fast as possible."

If I'd become pregnant on Nantucket, by a boy I barely knew and didn't even like, never mind my conscious decision—in the supposed heat of passion—to take my chances; I would have felt precisely the same way.

At the southern university where I teach English, students are not so cavalier about premarital sex, let alone abortion. Many of them come from deeply Christian backgrounds, and I regularly receive passionate and well-written papers about love for Jesus, the importance of chastity, the evils of

abortion. During classroom discussions on the topic of abortion, the pro-
life students speak fervently, their spines straight and certain, while the
pro-choice students slump apologetically in their chairs. Once, when I
asked students to separate into groups and discuss the issue of abortion,
a group of young men—athletes, mostly—came back with the conclusion
that they had no opinion either way. "It's none of our business," they
explained. "It's something for women to decide."

A student who had already identified herself as pro-life turned around
in her chair with an assertive snap of her ponytail. "That's pro-choice," she
informed them, and then turned back toward me, her chin raised in self-
assured defiance. When I was not much older than she, I volunteered for
NARAL's phone banks and escorted women across picket lines into abortion clinics. I would never have associated with someone who felt the way
she did.

But the passage of time has made it hard for me to see the world in
absolutes. I liked seeing a teenaged woman confident enough to challenge
a group of handsome men. When she looked at me for approval, I couldn't
help but smile at her.

time & context

My first pregnancy was accidental but certainly not catastrophic. I was
thirty-five and married. After I took the test, my husband David and I
stared at that faint, pink line—leaning over the bathroom sink, our heads
moving closer to the stick in a comic, disbelieving double take. Our astonishment soon gave way to an odd kind of euphoria. I've always been slow
to make life-changing decisions. An accidental pregnancy was probably
the only way I'd ever have a child.

And the chances of getting pregnant at that particular juncture
seemed slim, not just because of my indecision, or ambivalence. I was past
my most fertile years. My husband had undergone an orchiectomy as
treatment for testicular cancer. I'd been using birth control.

pregnant against the odds

All of which convinced me: the child I carried was uniquely devoted
to her own existence.

Still, I did feel that pregnancy had been sprung on me. On the phone with my friend Danae—the mother of two—I admitted that I hadn't stopped taking my daily runs.

"You have to change your thinking right now," she cautioned. "Your body doesn't belong to you anymore."

"This baby's going to adapt to our lifestyle," I told her. "Not the other way around."

selfish? naive?

We lived on Cape Cod at the time, and in the growing heat of New England spring, I stuck to my minimum twenty miles a week. The needle on my scale barely rose, a fact that secretly pleased me.

None of this meant I wasn't excited about the baby. Every day the surprise joy of expectation mounted. While I ran, I would think about my child. The dogwoods had started to bloom, and the countryside blurred in fragrant pixels of pink and white. Certain I carried a girl, I would list names in my head. I liked Genevieve. Suddenly, my future seemed rolled out before me in a more serious, more permanent way. I would be somebody's mother. I might even be a grandmother one day.

Meanwhile, Danae signed me up for newsletters from a website called babycenter.com. Once a week, I received an email updating me on what was taking place inside my body. The first one came when I was five weeks pregnant. "Deep in your uterus," it told me, "your embryo is growing at a furious pace. At this point he's about the size of a sesame seed, and he looks more like a tiny tadpole than a human." I disliked this description, conflicting as it did with the image I'd already constructed of a fat and pink-cheeked baby, gurgling inside me contentedly, already aware—somehow—of my love and good wishes. I longed for the nine-week mark, when my baby would graduate from embryo to fetus.

At my eight-week checkup, the nurse warned me that we might not pick up a heartbeat. "A lot of people don't this early," she said, pressing the fetal Doppler to my still-flat stomach. In an instant, the room filled with pounding, rapid drumbeats. The nurse and I burst out laughing.

The percussion of my own child's heartbeat: I carried it everywhere. According to contemporary etiquette, it was too early to announce my pregnancy. But I couldn't help boasting about that heartbeat's strength, its *[handwritten: proud/happy abt baby]* resonance, its insistence on being heard. I told everyone I knew.

The week after that doctor's appointment, I went to New Jersey to visit my parents. As I lay alone in my childhood bed, I felt acutely aware of the other being in the room with me. Inside my body. The strangest feeling, being two people: a definite and welcome haunting. When I touched my stomach now, it was with the protecting and attentive hands of a mother. The energy between my fingertips and my belly—what lay within my belly—felt sacred and palpable.

It was hot that June in New Jersey. Never one to mind the midday heat, I did a favorite old run—up Next Day Hill, one of the steepest in Englewood. I ran past the playground at Flatrock Brook, imagining the day when I'd push Genevieve on the swings there. When I came home sweating, my mother scolded me. For running in the heat. For not eating enough. For not slowing down.

I ignored her, smiling to myself as I chugged a glass of water. I was six days past the awaited nine-week mark. According to babycenter.com, Genevieve's vital organs—lungs, kidneys, intestines, and brain—had all begun to function. She had spinal nerves, fingernails. Her elbows bent. Her legs kicked.

My pregnancy had announced itself against the odds. It had broken down my maternal ambivalence with the force and spirit of a Hun. The life I carried seemed so insistent, I didn't believe anything could halt its arc.

The first blood appeared two days later, back on Cape Cod. It started as light brown spotting. "Nothing to worry about," my OB assured me, over the phone. "Just try to take it easy." I knew such spotting was common-place during pregnancy, so I wasn't particularly worried. I even went to a barbecue at a friend's house, my version of taking it easy, sitting rather than standing while I told people about our impending parenthood.

What happened over the next twenty-four hours occurred in a sequence of indelible moments. First my cat, bringing a sparrow through our open window and releasing it in our bedroom. My eyes fluttered open in concert with the bird's frantic wings and a sharp, stabbing pain in my abdomen. While David chased down the bird, I limped to the bathroom and felt a brief moment of gratitude over the clean pantyliner before a thick stream of blood released itself into the toilet.

Standing at the admit desk at Cape Cod Hospital while David parked the car, I was too wracked with sobs to tell the nurse what had happened. The security guard—probably thinking I'd been attacked—came over to help her make heads or tails out of what I was trying to say. "Miscarriage," he finally interpreted, from my unintelligible gurgling and frantic gestures toward my belly. I could see both pairs of shoulders relax, in sympathetic relief that nothing more terrible had happened to me.

banked too much on "miracle child"

My blood pressure was through the roof, a dangerous situation for a pregnant woman, regardless of the viability of the pregnancy itself. They couldn't perform an ultrasound before the radiology department opened in the morning, so the primary medical business became getting me through the night in an non-hysterical state while—still hoping for the life of the fetus—I refused any sort of sedative.

"This doesn't necessarily mean you're miscarrying," the ER doctor promised, his latex gloves bright red with blood from my examination.

"What about the cramps?" I asked.

After a long pause, he admitted, "The cramps are worrisome."

Still, I was willing to cling to the line of hope they offered me. I wasn't able to sleep, but I remember a deep and calming fondness at the sight of David napping on the gynecological exam table, his long legs draped over the stirrups. By morning, my main concern became the overwhelming need to urinate, which they wouldn't let me do before the ultrasound. Although I was only at ten weeks and had gained barely three pounds, recalling this scene I envision myself as hugely pregnant. I know this image is flatly incorrect and yet it persists. I see myself waddling from the bathroom after the radiation technician allowed me to pee just a little bit, and joking with her about the inhumane practice of making a pregnant woman hold her bladder. I picture my stomach making a tent of the thin hospital gown, as if I were just about to deliver.

mental image

But the most pivotal image was the one I never saw. The ultrasound screen discretely and pointedly faced the technician, but I could read everything I needed in her blank expression as she clicked away at the screen. I knew that if the fetus were alive, she would have turned that screen toward me.

"Just tell me," I said.

And in a harrowing experience marked by the compassion of my caretakers, she did the most compassionate thing yet. She told me the truth.

"There's no heartbeat," she said.

After my D&C, David brought me back to his mother's house to rest. She was standing by her garden in the bright sunlight, a tangle of weeds in one hand. Before David had a chance to come around to open my car door, I got out myself, and stumbled up the hill toward her. It was a terrible moment, the pending admission that would make my grief real, and the knowledge of how the news would disappoint her—the lost grandchild.

"It's gone," I said. And fell into her arms. She held me tight. Having lost two pregnancies herself—one in the fifth month—she knew the road I'd just traveled all too well.

"Poor baby," she said, thumping my back. "Poor baby." For a split, dizzy second, I wasn't sure if she meant me or the child I'd miscarried.

With the notion of Genevieve lost, I felt awash in grief and contradictions. Everyone—doctors, friends, even the condolence email from babycenter.com in response to my plea for a stop to the fetus updates—assured me that the miscarriage was not my fault. But I had left my first prenatal checkup laden with pamphlets, telling me what a pregnant woman must do and not do. She must not drink or smoke, obviously. Less obvious, and harder to keep track: she must not eat soft or unpasteurized cheese. She must not eat deli meat or tuna or swordfish, or clams or oysters or sushi. She must avoid nearly all medication except for Tylenol—and even that only when necessary. She must not change kitty litter, or go to the dry cleaner's, or sit in a hot tub.

I remember, during that first pregnancy, unthinkingly popping a slice of brie into my mouth. And then suddenly remembering that proscription with certain and self-incriminating dread.

Despite all the rules and cautions, it's never a woman's fault when she miscarries. From every direction came assurances that nothing in the world could have prevented it. It didn't matter that I'd eaten that slice of brie, or had green tea, or gone for long runs in the blazing sun.

"I've had patients who were crack addicts," the doctor who performed my D&C told me, when I told him about the green tea and excessive exercise. "And they've delivered perfectly healthy babies. It's all a matter of luck."

A few weeks later, at a checkup with my OB, I confessed again—like an obsessive—to the five-mile run I'd taken three days before my miscarriage.

"The heartbeat had probably already stopped," she promised, giving me that same smile—that practiced and careful sympathy.

"But next time," she added, before I left the office. "Try to keep it to two."

In her first trimester, my friend Katie Hogan placed third in a triathalon. She climbed Long's Peak when she was five months pregnant. Her daughter Melanie was now a healthy toddler.

Take crack. Run marathons. Eat brie. Drink one pint of Guiness a day, as my friend Trudy's Dublin OB recommended. The doctors had no idea what had or had not ended my pregnancy. They only knew that in the absence of any explanation, there was no reason not to assure me of complete inculpability.

In her essay about miscarrying while traveling in Japan, Peggy Orenstein explores these medical contradictions and other, more political dilemmas. "My own pro-abortion-rights politics defy me," she writes in her book *Waiting for Daisy*. "Social personhood may be distinct from biological and legal personhood, yet the zing of connection between me and my embryo felt startlingly real, and at direct odds with everything I believe about when life begins…I tell myself that this wasn't a person. It wasn't a child. At the same time, I can't deny that it was something. How can I mourn what I don't believe existed?"

Orenstein goes on to say, "…there is no word in English for a miscarried or aborted fetus. In Japanese it is *mizuko*, which is typically translated as 'water child.' Historically, Japanese Buddhists believed that existence flowed into a being slowly, like liquid. Children solidified only gradually over time and weren't considered to be fully in our world until they reached the age of seven." In Japan, where the legality of abortion is not so passionately in dispute, women make offerings to their miscarried and aborted fetuses. They leave toys and baby clothes at altars of Jizo—the bodhisattva who is the Budhist version of a patron saint of lost pregnancies.

The Sunday after my miscarriage, David constructed our own version of a Jizo shrine. He walked through dunes and spartina to a secluded spot, a few yards back from the beach, and built a small memorial out of stones and sea glass.

The body is an amazing thing. Everything in mine—hormones, uterus, psyche—obliterated my previous ambivalence about children and conspired with passionate single-mindedness toward one ultimate goal: getting pregnant again. Δ from before – big decision

First, though, I wanted to be sure that my body had not caused the miscarriage. At the ultrasound, fibroids had been detected. David's mother had told me that her own miscarriages had been the result of a hormonal imbalance, and I wondered if my situation were the same.

"It doesn't make sense," my OB told me, when I insisted on further testing. "Miscarriages are extremely common. A woman isn't considered infertile until she's had three or four."

I blanched at the word "infertile," a horrific notion when my entire body screamed to resume its spinning of new cells and fetal tissue. At home, I called my friend Danae and told her what the doctor had said. "She wants me to try again and see if I miscarry," I said. "But I can't risk losing another pregnancy. Not just because I don't want to go through that again. But because..." I let my voice trail off, not certain how to put it into words.

"Of course," Danae said, understanding as always. "These are your children."

And that was the thing. Three days after my miscarriage, I sat naked in an empty bathtub, my knees pulled up to my chest. I sobbed and rocked and keened, my greatest display of emotion in the course of a highly emotional life. *No, no, no*, I sobbed, again and again.

No. I had not just lost a pregnancy. I had lost a child.

It was difficult to reconcile this reaction, this gut belief in the loss of an actual person, with what I'd always considered our ambiguous beginnings. Suddenly it didn't seem outrageous to believe life began at conception. Conception is, after all, when the DNA, the chromosomes, the molecules that form our bodies meet and merge. It's when we start brewing. Each of us can trace our present, physical existence back to a single, precise moment: of father's sperm joining mother's egg.

the science

My brief attempt at pregnancy had made me an expert. A week after conception occurs we exist as a tiny blastocyst—a ball of furiously multiplying cells. Our organs don't begin to develop for another week, when we reach embryonic status. Still not attached to the uterus, the placenta under construction, one more week to go before heart chambers form and start pumping: this is when most women discover their pregnancy.

It's a vulnerable state. One in three pregnancies results in miscarriage. Include the pregnancies that end before we get around to taking that pregnancy test and more than 40 percent of all conceptions may be lost.

prev pro-choice
↓
slow change in feeling
ble emotional attachment to lost baby, but not change in stance

Considered in these terms, abortion seems a simple and almost obvious act. What harm to dispose of a collection of cells the size of a sesame seed—a sweeping act that nature performs on a random and routine basis?

Still, I found my opinions changing in subtle ways. Although loath to ever agree with President Bush, I found myself approving of the Unborn Victims of Violence Act, which—when a pregnant woman is a victim of violence—counts a fetus that is injured or killed as an additional victim. Imagining myself murdered any time before my miscarriage, I couldn't help but consider the perpetrator liable for two deaths.

My students often compare embryos to full-term babies—in defense of both pro-life and pro-choice positions. I regularly assign my students a short story by T.C. Boyle. "The Love of My Life" is about a teenage couple who conceal a pregnancy and then throw their newborn infant—wrapped in plastic but still breathing—into a dumpster. My pro-life students invariably equate these actions with abortion, a comparison that rankles me no end.

Amazingly, some pro-choice students make that same comparison. In an argument paper defending abortion rights, one student cited the ancient practice of exposure—leaving infants with cleft palates, or twins (considered bad luck) out on a hillside to die. He discussed the Roman laws permitting infanticide. "Nobody judges the Romans for what they did," he wrote. "Why judge American women who want to abort?"

I stared at the paper with my brow furrowed, at a loss for comments to write in the margins.

An old friend from college was diagnosed with breast cancer during her first pregnancy. In order to have the mastectomy and chemotherapy that might have cured her, she would have had to abort. She chose to go through with the pregnancy, and died not long after giving birth to a healthy girl.

The best mother I know aborted her first pregnancy, in her early twenties, because she didn't want to marry her boyfriend and wasn't ready to have a child.

Another college friend—also a great mother—aborted a fetus when the amnio showed Down syndrome.

An old friend's sister had an abortion so she would fit into her wedding dress; she became pregnant again, with her first child, a few weeks after the wedding.

One of my dearest friends gave a child up for adoption. In her early forties now, she hasn't had another child. It was an open adoption, and she sees her son—now a teenager—once or twice a year. She worries daily about his well-being. His loss—his distance—is a constant, unending sorrow.

My OB agreed to a series of fertility tests, and declared me fit to try again. The August after my June miscarriage, I was pregnant. Six weeks along, on a trip to Colorado, I contracted an intestinal bacteria. At the hospital in Boulder, we waited behind the ER curtain for the doctor's diagnosis. I barely remember anything he said about my own physical health. But I remember these words exactly:

"Don't worry for a second about your pregnancy."

Despite the persistent and frightening symptoms of my wrecked gut, all fears dissipated into the filtered, Pine-sol air. That doctor could have told me anything. He could have told me I had leukemia, and as long as the pregnancy was safe I would have breathed a sigh of relief.

My concern was primal, focused, and absolute. As long as I knew the baby would be all right, I didn't care what happened to me. I remember the same feeling, eight months later, signing a consent form for a cesarean. My OB listed all the possible complications—from uterine tearing to uncontrollable hemorrhage to deep vein thrombosis. The only moment I balked—actually saying "Don't do that" out loud—was when she told me she might accidentally cut the baby while making the incision.

About fifteen weeks into my second pregnancy, I dreamed that I'd discovered a window in my belly button that allowed me to look inside and see the baby. Through that filmy glass, she waved back at me madly, smiling, then swam away to do the most gleeful rolls and somersaults, like a sea otter.

One week later, at the 3-D ultrasound I'd chosen over an amniocentesis, the baby moved so wildly the radiologist couldn't get a clear picture. He called in the OB, who frowned at the screen, then couldn't help but laugh—the fetus would sit still for a split second, then turn around the other direction, then somersault. Every shot was blurry, but not so much that he couldn't tell with fair certainty that I was carrying a girl.

fetus has personality

I asked him about spina bifida.

"We can rule it out with this test," he said, trying to point out the healthy spine on my galloping fetus.

"What about Down syndrome?" I said.

He looked at my chart to check my age, and frowned when he saw it. "You're not getting an amnio?" he said.

"No," I told him. After the miscarriage, we'd decided we wouldn't terminate a pregnancy, regardless of test results. So there was no point in risking another miscarriage just to comfort ourselves.

The doctor watched the baby, jumping and leaping and waving her arms. He shrugged. "Unlikely," he said.

I asked him to give me the likelihood in the sort of statistics that his profession so revered.

"One in five hundred?" he said. "But you need an amnio to be sure."

If I'd had an amniocentesis, I would have waited another two weeks for the results: the genetic makeup of my child. In the unlucky event that makeup was faulty, a decision would be needed—at nearly five months pregnant—whether to carry her to term.

I'd received my weekly email update that morning. At eighteen weeks, a female fetus already possesses a developed uterus and fallopian tubes. Judging from the picture on the ultrasound screen, she also possesses a personality.

The doctor left the room, on to his next appointment. My OB performed an AFP test, and reported the fetus's likelihood of Down syndrome was one in 6,700. Within a few weeks we had named our daughter, and her movement became a constant matter of my existence. At night, I'd lie with my belly against David's back so he could feel her World Cup kicks against his spine. He often managed to sleep through the kicks. I seldom did. I would lie awake, staring at the ceiling, feeling the never-ending and jubilant movement. And I would think, "Is this kid *ever* going to sleep?"

In fact, the fetus's insistence on movement was a salient trait of the child. She didn't sleep through the night until her second birthday.

About aborting two of her triplets, pro-choice activist Amy Richards writes, "Even in my moments of thinking about having three, I don't think that deep down I was ever considering it." Richards's multiple pregnancy was natural—the consecutive conception of a stand-alone and a pair of identical twins. She decided to terminate two of the fetuses by selective reduction; a specialist administered a shot of potassium chloride to the heart of each of her twins.

When I read about the sort of events that inspired "The Love of My Life"—oddly, perversely frequent—I am aware of a sympathy that has shifted since my pregnancies. Not that my strongest sympathy wouldn't have been with the baby in the past; but I would have allowed flickers of excuse, surges of empathy with that teenage girl—her terror, her confusion, her embattled hormones. But now, when I reach for that empathy—wanting, quite strongly, for it to exist—I find myself coming up empty. Grading a response paper by a student who stated that China and Jeremy, the teenage couple, should be wrapped in plastic and tossed in a dumpster, I horrified myself by nodding in agreement.

feels more fl baby than mom- motherly instinct

I have a similar reaction when reading Amy Richards's story—of anger, and moral judgment. I don't want to have that reaction. I don't like it. But there it is.

A baby is considered full term at thirty-seven weeks. By then she's a complex, if not independent, life form. Once delivered, her lungs will function, meconium will be passed, eyes will focus about eight inches—the approximate distance from a mother's arms to a mother's face.

So different from an embryo, a life form simple enough to be frozen for later implantation.

I assigned Amy Richards's essay to my English 101 class. In response, one of my favorite students—an 18-year-old boy from rural North Carolina—wrote about his Fundamentalist Christian upbringing. He had always been pro-life as a matter of course, until in a typical freshman night of debauchery, he got drunk and had sex with a young woman he barely knew. When she became pregnant, there was a question of paternity. While waiting for the test results, my student agonized over the few moments that might have inexorably changed his life, and the responsibility for which he felt nowhere near ready.

This boy had huge dark eyes and pale freckles across the bridge of his nose. In late August, he had shown up in my classroom wearing a backwards baseball cap and Carharts. By late November he sported a pierced ear and dyed-black hair. This was a smart and sensitive boy, a witty and good-natured smart aleck. He had only begun experimenting with his identity, figuring out who he wanted to be. I couldn't imagine demanding a halt to this evolution, forcing him into the responsibility of fatherhood—to say nothing of the terrified girl, carrying a stranger's child.

My student turned out not to be the father. Despite his relief, his heart went out to the girl he'd known a scant few minutes. Knowing how he had felt, and imagining how she still felt, how, he wrote, could he ever again insist on someone else's course of action?

Defending Amy Richards, he cited her legitimate reasons for not wanting multiples: possible medical complications, inevitable bed rest, financial difficulties, irreversible interruption of career.

"I can't say what Amy Richards should do," he wrote. "It's her life. It's not mine. I don't see any reason I should have anything to say about it."

Sometimes, life experience fosters compassion. Sometimes, it fosters the reverse.

"You can't feel that way if you're pro-choice," a woman told me, when I admitted my discomfort with selective reduction.

But I did feel that way. And I understood that what I felt had nothing to do with Amy Richards's right to do exactly what she'd done. It wasn't my choice—it was hers. The fact that I disagreed with her choice, that it made me uncomfortable, wasn't relevant. Furthermore, I had no way of knowing how my ideas about selective reduction might change if I became pregnant with triplets. Daunting enough, after all, to carry one child to term.

It is worth noting here that my daughter—the child of the second pregnancy I so dearly wanted—was conceived on Nantucket. I greeted the news of that pregnancy with a joy tantamount to the horror I would have felt, nearly fifteen years earlier, had I been impregnated by that boy on the beach. The fact that I now understand my old friend's decision to risk dying from cancer to safely deliver her child doesn't mean I've forgotten what it feels like to be a young and impetuous woman, with my self and life existing mostly as a question mark.

It is also worth noting the ease of my decision to forego an amniocentesis when my odds of a child with Down syndrome were one in 6,700, my odds of spina bifida nonexistent. If the results had been different, my thoughts about risking miscarriage might have drastically shifted—never mind how my feelings could have changed, had amnio results been dire.

How easy to pass favorable judgment upon your own actions when luck is on your side. The truth is, my new reverence for the process of incubating a human life had not undermined my pro-choice beliefs. It had solidified them. → variety of
                              experiences

I believe that life begins at conception. I also believe that every woman has the right to terminate a pregnancy without explaining herself. Without ever telling a living soul, if she so chooses. Or if she prefers, to tell her story—as loudly as she needs and without apology.

I believe both these things because life is contradiction, and opposing facts stand side by side as a matter of course. For example there is my daughter, who—in all her specific, frenetic, defiant, and quirky splendor—is the central joy of my life. There is my daughter, who never could have existed if that first pregnancy had gone full term. And shouldn't that very fact—the impossibility of someone I love so immeasurably—eradicate any grief over the original loss?

The small memorial David built after my miscarriage still stands. Hidden in a thicket of scrub pine, beach grass, and poison ivy, nobody but us and white-tailed deer ever go there. It's a simple shrine—a ring of stones and seashells, with one thick, cradle-shaped rock in the middle. We visited the place often in the months after the miscarriage and during my second pregnancy. Less often after our daughter was born, and we moved to North Carolina. But it's still a place we go when we visit Cape Cod, to leave sea glass and pretty stones. To rearrange whatever offerings we brought last—scattered after months of wind and rain, the best pieces of sea glass buried, sometimes irretrievably, beneath the sand.

I will go there again, and again, and again. I will never stop going there. To sit beside the little Jizo shrine that David built without knowing Buddhist tradition, but on the grieving impulses of his own heart. To offer my lost child pieces of the beach, and to think about her, and to let her know I haven't forgotten.

All this while knowing that the child I grieve—the personal pronoun I assign, the thought of her as an existing consciousness—is a construct of my imagination, having little to do with the failed assemblance of DNA that my body carried for a while, and then rejected. If for some reason I had chosen to end the same pregnancy—not knowing my actions were jumping nature's gun—I don't expect I would have this lifelong intention toward quiet mourning. Although surely I would have wondered, from time to time, what might have been if I'd acted differently.

chosen end
v.
accidental
↓
diff. emotions

There is no Genevieve. There was only, for some brief weeks, her spectral possibility, replaced in time by an actual child—corporeal and spectacular.

Still. I'll tell you this. If by some macabre stroke of magic, I found out that my original child had not died. If through some inexplicable twist—the stuff of soap opera, science fiction, and daydreams—I discovered she had not died but lived, and now existed: somewhere out there, away from me.

I would go anywhere, I would do anything. To find her.

ACCIDENTS:
A Family History of Choice
by Karen E. Bender

MY FATHER WAS CONCEIVED by accident, the sixth child—four living—in his family, in Eureka, South Dakota in 1931. At the time, his siblings were seventeen, fifteen, ten, and four years old; his parents had been living in Eureka for about sixteen years, his father immigrating, in a peculiar route, to the midwestern United States from Odessa, Russia. They were the only Jews in the town of Eureka, drawn there by the Homestead Act by cousins who had settled in North Dakota a few years before. It was a bad time to get pregnant. My father now tells me about the world that existed before he was in it: His father's mother, who was living with them, had just become ill. His oldest sister, Frances, would be going off to college out of state, which was another expense. The stock market had plummeted almost 75 percent since 1929. There was a drought in the Midwest and many people in Eureka were on welfare. Customers would come into my grandfather's store and put a little money down toward their long bills for canned goods and clothes.

When my grandmother discovered that she was pregnant with my father, she, in a fit of panic, jumped down some stairs.

I heard this story growing up, both from my father and in passing: "Daddy's mommy jumped off a stair when she found out that she was pregnant and then always said how much she loved her darling boy!" It was a story that was dropped, casually, by relatives, at odd moments; it had the strange quality of gossip. The story was always startling whenever I heard it. These were midwestern Jews, not prone to impulsive behavior in general, be it jumping off stairs or passing around stories about a relative trying to end a pregnancy.

I always hated the fact that my father knew this story. Perhaps my relatives were thoughtless in passing it around, or perhaps they were awed by this piece of information; I personally found it thrilling, at first, to hear this action, this behavior by a grandmother who had died when I was very young, who was described otherwise as "very nice." What was going through her mind? Did anyone see? Did she get hurt? And what did this action have to do with my father, sitting by me at the kitchen table, help-fully pouring me a glass of soy milk, eating his unique concoction of oat-meal mixed with avocado and orange juice for breakfast—the man who was my father, here?

It was the most complex thing I ever heard about her. It is also the only action that made my grandmother seem human to me.

What had happened? I asked him.

"They had thought the family was complete," my father said. "They were worried about money."

After she jumped down the stairs, my grandmother had gone to the family doctor, a Dr. Gerdes. Had she been taken there? Had she gone there, secretly, herself? I tried to imagine my grandmother, hurrying, in January, across the small, frozen town that called itself, optimistically, Eureka. Was she weeping or hopeful? What was she afraid of as she sat down to talk to the town doctor, what were her fears?

I don't know if she actually had options, if her only strategy for ending a pregnancy was to try to give her body a little jolt. I don't know if her action was a frantic attempt to get reassurance, or if she intended to try again, with more determination.

We must all have these peculiar moments in our ancestries—either our parents or grandparents or beyond—in which a woman knew that life was flickering inside of her and thought: no. My grandmother told him that she was unhappy. The doctor, said my father, "spoke kindly to her. He said that this is going to work out. She would have a great kid. She said she felt much better. And she decided to go ahead."

Thus, my father was born, and then, thirty-two years later, me.

We are all spectacular accidents. Our existence depends on so many fac-tors colliding at once. Our parents have to meet, one way or another. We are the unique combinations of a particular sperm and egg. The cells have to evolve from zygote to tadpole to frog-like creature to a human. The pregnancy has to come to term. And then we are born.

At that moment, my grandmother decided to go ahead and have my father. If I had been my grandmother's friend then, seen her with four children, about thirty-nine years old, anxious about money, an ill mother-in-law, I would have told her—forget it. Stop the pregnancy.

"You don't need to have another," I would have told her. "You have four children."

My grandparents had four children—in fact, at one point they had had five. Twenty years before my father was conceived, there was another child, their first child: Rose. The story of her life is this: she was sickly and died. That was all anyone knew about her.

"How old was she when she died?" I asked my father.

"I don't know," he said. "Weeks? A few months? No one talked about it."

No one even knows where Rose is buried. She wasn't buried in the cemetery in Eureka, where the family lived, or in Ashley, North Dakota, where other relatives were buried. Her brief life would have happened around 1912. Were my grandparents unable to save her? Was she born unhealthy? Was the pain of losing their first child so profound they could never talk about it? How did it affect them, newly married, trying to create a life in this prairie, to lose their baby girl? Did they just want to forget about her? How did it lead them to their other children, and what fears did it create?

"You have enough to do," I, as a family planning advisor, would have told my newly pregnant grandmother. "Give your other children your attention. It's okay."

And then my father—and, of course, I—would not have been born.

The idea makes my head spin. It is an accident that I am here—that I, myself, would have stopped. I have the brash confidence of the living. I am me. Who else could I have been? Or could I have been nothing?

Sometimes, right before my period, I have dreams of babies being washed away; I wake up strangely, deeply sad; that, too, is, in a sense, a loss—one that is part of life, of the cycle of being a woman. Trillions of people exist, half-formed, in women's bodies; most are never completed, made; millions are conceived and, by miscarriage, abortion, do not arrive at their lives on earth.

It is an accident, of one form or another, that we are all here.

Then I think—am I rationalizing? If my grandmother had decided to have an abortion, my father would be gone. And what would it have been to have lost out on the chance of being myself?

She had my father and loved him, fully, so that he always spoke of her with great tenderness, loved him so that he listened when she told him this story.

She was lucky.

Many times as a child and then as an adult, I took a journey with my mother and grandmother to visit my Aunt Joan in one of the assisted living homes where she lived. The homes themselves were places that collected people who could not care for themselves. We wove through the assortment of screamers, the people who had lost their minds from age or disease, communicating with language both alien and animal. The aides were young and assumed plastic, blank expressions when they were not ducking out to smoke or flirt with each other. There was the smell of air freshener and rot. Joan was usually the youngest one there. My aunt was often drugged with high doses of anti-psychotics, such as Halidol, and she was often dazed, staring into space.

What did she do all day? I wondered. What did she think of our visits? My mother and grandmother huddled around her as though she were a holy figure.

"We brought you something," my mother would say, with their offerings: stuffed animals, candy. We sat outside for a few minutes, pretending that the parking lot was a good view. She might introduce us to her roommates, when they were nice, or we might hear her complaints about the ones who stole her candy or cigarettes. My mother or grandmother would track down some authority figure whom they hoped would solve the disaster of the week—the doctor who had improperly prescribed medication, sending Joan into a coma, the aides who were supposed to keep an eye on Joan but left her by an open door when they went out for a smoke.

Sometimes we went out for lunch, the four of us sitting in the orange booth at Denny's. My mother carefully cut Joan's pancakes into tiny pieces; Joan's teeth had rotted because she always forgot to brush them. My grandmother's radar was up for whatever Joan needed; could she get extra napkins, more syrup for her pancakes? She tried to figure out what Joan needed before Joan knew; it was what she was used to doing for forty, fifty, sixty years.

We never stayed more than an hour or two. My mother and grandmother gripped Joan hard when they hugged her, a sweet and desperate gesture; it was as though they were trying to press part of themselves into her. "We'll see you next week," they said.

It always seemed a crime to leave her, and we always did.

I remember sitting in the car with my mother and grandmother as we drove from the visits with my aunt. My mother and grandmother sat in the front seat, eyeing the freeway, talking in the fast, monotone way they did when they left, as though their voices were speaking without them, trying to figure out ways to solve that week's disasters, trying to beat back the carelessness of the world that contained Joan. My aunt was uprooted from various assisted living facilities because of her difficulty or their own negligence; in one place, located in a private home, she was walking around at night and fell into a pool.

They could not solve all the problems. Joan could not be solved. Once, I asked my mother if Aunt Joan was the child whom my grandmother may have wished had never been born.

"No," my mother said, "your grandmother never said this." She paused. "But if they had amnios when I was pregnant, and it had been abnormal, I would have ended the pregnancy. Seeing what happened to Joan."

My mother was six years younger than Joan, who had an abnormally large head; she suffered a head injury during the forceps birth. She suffered significant brain damage—it was never clear whether this was an accident from the birth itself or a genetic accident that occurred in the womb. Besides her mental retardation, she had numerous, complicated emotional problems and psychotic episodes—my mother calls her retardation and severe mental issues a "triple whammy."

When my mother talks about Joan, her voice becomes flat, as though she cannot allow herself the feeling that must arise when she describes her sister's life. She describes the trauma of public school in the 1950s, with no special education classes for someone like Joan; she was afraid to go to school as a child, often wetting her pants because she was afraid of the noises in the bathroom. After she was shuffled through high school, there was no place for her to go; she got depressed and tried to cut her wrists. She had sixty shock treatments and once reacted strangely, falling off the table and getting a concussion.

My mother understood, as the sibling of a handicapped child, that a cute baby would not simply remain a baby. The baby would grow up, and her problems would not fall away; they would expand. And it was not just the baby to be concerned about, she said, it was the lives that surrounded the child. Who would care for Joan after my grandmother died? Her other sister and brother seemed to want to forget about her. They rarely called or visited her; it was easier to pretend she wasn't there. They had their own reasons—Aunt Joan had sucked most of the attention from their mother—my aunt's cavernous needs had left her other siblings lonely, wanting. They ran from Joan into their own jobs, their own families, the lives they had made. One older sibling did not call or talk to Joan for months. My aunt's presence had proved so painful that her sibling's strategy was to just pretend she did not exist. My aunt was born into the human world of limits.

And yet.

At times, Aunt Joan was relatively okay—when her medicine was prescribed properly, when she was in possession of herself. She seemed glad for our visits, clasped my hand with a bone-cracking grip and told me she wanted to get me a birthday present, even when it wasn't my birthday. She laughed, a raucous, toothless laugh.

How can I say that my aunt was too much of a burden when, in her rare, clear moments, she could be astoundingly kind and even strangely smart? My mother remembers my aunt coming to her cabin during summer camp, when my mother was having trouble going to sleep. "She said goodnight to me," my mother said. "She made me feel loved and special. She made me into a better person."

Once, when Joan had acute double pneumonia and was recovering in the hospital right before my wedding, my husband-to-be Robert and I visited her. I sat beside her head and she stared at me as I nattered on ridiculously about the flowers and the cake, as I tried, somehow, to be entertaining.

A nurse came in to give her a shot of penicillin. In an attempt to seem helpful, I asked her if she wanted me to hold her hand.

"No, you hold Robert's hand," she said.

She was very ill, in her hospital bed, and she was not thinking of herself. She was not trying, in any false, sentimental way, to buddy up to me. She was just thinking of me.

These rare moments could be tortuous for my mother and grandmother, because they seemed like accidents of hope. Once, when Joan was relatively calm, my grandmother talked about taking a trip with her to Hawaii. She had never been on a vacation before. For a short time, my grandmother Ardie talked about what island they would visit, how they would drink piña coladas and sit on the beach. It was a touching fantasy, and bewildering, as though my grandmother's dream life for Joan, dormant for years, was suddenly unleashed.

Then Joan fell apart again and there was no trip.

Driving home from the visits with Joan at the homes where she lived, my mother and grandmother would fall into silence, a silence with a particular weight to it that I knew well from my childhood. It was a silence born of guilt and sorrow and hopelessness bumping up against stubborn hope; it was a silence that bore down on my grandmother and my mother; it deformed them. How had Joan's care, in some ways, aborted their own lives? How would their lives have been lighter if they had not had the sentences of this sadness?

You think: whose life do you choose? I cannot imagine a world without my aunt; it is impossible to imagine her erased. A child is born. She brings herself into the world, in all of her fortune and ruin; she is here. But if my grandmother had known, before Joan was born, the burdens that Joan would have, over and over and over again, what would she have chosen? For herself? For the other children? Would she have thought Joan was an accident, a mistake?

I believe my mother said she wanted an amniocentesis because she did not want another sentence.

I was thirty-eight years old when I was pregnant with my second child. My family moved to North Carolina when I was four months pregnant—I had marked the calendar for the first possible date for my amniocentesis. At my first appointment at a new OB practice the secretary sent me to a ten-minute appointment with a nurse's aide who looked to be sixteen years old, said brightly that I should keep "eatin'" and briskly signed me out. At the checkout desk, I felt panic take over me.

"I want to see a doctor to schedule my amnio," I said.

The secretary looked at me. "The doctor's free in two weeks," she said.

"But I'm sixteen weeks. I need to schedule an amnio. Now," I said.

With painstaking, terrible deliberation, the secretary flipped through the schedule. "Two weeks," she said. "You need to see the doctor first."

I could not wait two weeks. I wanted to find out now. I could feel the being inside me beginning to move, and I wanted my pregnancy to stop, to stop this process, if the test result was positive. I did not want to be given this same sentence of sadness.

I began to weep. The secretary stared at me, puzzled, then handed me a Kleenex. I must have seemed overwrought, bratty, but I knew what I needed. I knew, from being a child and then a parent, of the wild uncontrollability of parenthood, the difficulty inherent in every day, even with children considered "easy."

I had watched my mother and grandmother live the other.

I wanted to be able to control this much.

My own path to having children was slow, and at first, nonexistent. I wanted to find someone whom I could love, and who would love me. This was not, sadly, a linear process; it was characterized by its own accidents, idiocies, failures of judgment, misplaced hopes. I was obsessive about birth control, watching the calendar warily as my cycle ended each month.

When I was in graduate school in Iowa, I was rather shy and mostly dated men because of the mere, startling fact that they liked me. The truth was that I did not really know what I wanted in a partner; I wanted the men I met to tell me. In this sadly passive state, I began to date a man I'll call Dan. One night, we had a birth control accident. His condom fell off.

"Oops," Dan said. It was a simple word, but uttered with such coolness, I was suddenly awake to his strangeness. I was ashamed, fully, for him and also for myself.

I didn't think there was an actual danger that I was pregnant, but I had heard of Plan B, the morning-after pill, and I wanted to be sure that I was not. I was in my mid-twenties; I was not married; I pieced together an "income" as an absurdly low-paid adjunct instructor so I could try to write a novel; I could barely support myself; I was not fit to be a mother to any child. So that morning, I set off with a friend of mine to the local women's clinic.

It was a small, dingy office, with dim fluorescent lights overhead and dark wood paneling. I sat on a plastic chair and waited. I was the first client of the day; it was just 9:00 a.m. I sat politely on my chair, waiting to be saved.

When the doctor finally walked in, I was frantic, not only over the mistake, but over the certainty of my impending loneliness. I was sure that seeing this man was an accident, a mistake. I felt the slow, deflating sensation of knowing that I was alone again. How long would this loneliness last? How long would it take to find the person I could love, who would love me back?

The doctor invited me to sit in the hallway of the clinic. She was an older woman, with short gray hair, clad in a white doctor's coat. I smiled at her, a maternal figure. I was far away from my family and wanted someone to take care of me. I hoped she would smile back.

I explained that I had had a birth control accident and I wanted to get the morning-after pill to make sure I did not get pregnant.

"What kind of birth control did you use?" she asked.

"A condom," I told her.

"You should be using more than one method," she said. "Is that all you've been using?"

Yes, I said.

"So you could be pregnant now," she said.

I had never had a failure of birth control before. I said no.

"I'm not giving it to you."

"What?" I asked.

She said that if I was pregnant, the morning-after pill could hurt the fetus. I blinked. I felt as though I had been banged across the head.

"But I'm sure I'm not," I said, my voice sounding faraway.

"I'm not giving it to you," she said.

We were in Iowa, a few hundred miles from where my father had been born, where a conversation that shared certain similarities had taken place sixty years before. This was not so far from Eureka, where my grand-mother had been convinced to have my father, where somehow she had been reassured. Now here I was, unmarried, unready in the most basic ways to be pregnant, frankly before I even was, and this stranger, a woman doctor, saw only this: she did not approve of my behavior. I was struck by the nature of coincidence in life in which you encounter others who can influence you, for their own purposes or for what they believe to be yours. I don't know exactly what happened between my grandmother and her doctor; I knew that at that moment, by this doctor, I was not being seen.

I was breathless. I had thought I was being conscientious by coming here, obsessive maybe, making sure that I would not get pregnant at a time and place in my life where it would be impossible. She did not look me in the eye. By her reluctance, I believed she was saying—pay the price. Don't have sex. This seemed like an intrusion of another sort altogether—of herself.

Now, years later, I look at this woman and feel sad for her, the way she needed to simplify me, to see me as a cliché. How much easier it is to tell people what to do, how to behave, when you refuse to see them as complicated. How hard it is, to see each person's emotional life as individual and precise, to understand that you cannot understand the whole of another person's burdens. Is that kindness, the ability to actually listen to a person? Did my grandmother secretly want to have a fifth child, and simply want to hear that she was capable of handling this? How easy it is, especially for someone in a position of authority—a doctor, a teacher, a politician—to want to push other people's ideas aside and ignore the troubling, aggravating precision of individual life.

At the time I stood up, as though ready to grab what I wanted from her, but she turned, clutching her clipboard, with a strange, rehearsed calm, and walked to her next appointment. I wanted to do violence to her. I stood there, trembling. I began to cry. She had everything at that moment, the ability to give me the care I wanted, which was merely a high dose of the birth control pill; instead, she walked out of the room.

I walked out, shaken, and my friend drove me to the university hospital.

At the hospital, the medical resident, a sweet man in his early twenties, listened to my story.

He said, "Sure."

(Later, I found out that the morning-after pill works three ways: it can inhibit or prevent ovulation; change the uterine lining, making it hard for a pregnancy to implant; or inhibit sperm/egg transport through the uterus. All three could work at once. If a pregnancy had already been established, it would not work.)

I loved that second doctor, how he trusted my story, how he understood what I needed and did the simple act—give the morning-after pill to me.

I went home and took the pill. I remember little from the effects of it; it seemed strange that my period had come because I had summoned it. Then it was done. I had not a single regret; when I saw the blood from the summoned menstrual period, I felt an enormous lightness, a coldness lifting—I felt I had been anchored again. My body had been returned to me.

I look at that moment and what is most memorable to me is how that woman doctor and I were strangers to one another. We sat on two metal chairs in the dim hallway of the women's clinic and she did not know me, and did not want to trust me. What did she see when she looked at me?

I believe she saw someone she wanted to punish. She did not see me as a young woman trying to negotiate her life in her own particular way. She saw me as someone whose behavior should be changed. But why did she see me as such when I was coming to her, suddenly, with my own definite medical need, my own desires? What would have helped her see me as a person?

For years, I did not want to have children. Slowly, I met Robert, the man whom I chose, and who, to my great fortune, chose me. We married and then, when I was 33, we had a visit. A friend of my husband's visited us with his 2-year-old, and I watched them, as though observing a secret new species: parents. I watched the way our friend talked to the girl, how he handed her a box of juice, how he could (or appeared to) listen to seemingly endless nattering about princesses and fairies as though she were discoursing on Proust. The father and child seemed to inhabit a planet of intimacy different from the rest of us. I was suddenly horribly jealous. It seemed almost an accident of feeling as sudden as my desire not to have them. My arms felt bare, empty. I was frightened by this sudden need; when they left, I wept.

Now, many years later, Robert and I have our two choices: one is eight years old and one is four. I remember the night when each child was made, the mundane quality of the following morning, the way the traffic flowed on the avenues outside our window, the same shocking way it would after a death. There was the peculiar sense that we were allowed to become this new breed, parents, and without a license. When the pink line appeared, two weeks later, on the pregnancy test, I showed it to Robert. We were so stunned at the finality of this, the surreal knowledge that we would be joined by another, that we both turned around and quickly went back to work. It was as though we didn't want anything to be different, though we knew it was. We did not love the new being yet— the child's entrance still felt like a bombardment—though we wanted the person who would be born in nine months. It was a startling, new feeling, this wanting, utterly different from anything I'd felt before—it was quieter, a readiness. The wanting was there because we were different—because, in some mysterious part of ourselves, Robert and I were ready. Before truly understanding it, we wanted to share our lives, share the love we had discovered for each other, with a child; along with our son, growing within me, there was a new, mysterious love growing, embryonic within both of us, a strange and new protectiveness.

Robert and I set up a corner in our one-bedroom apartment that would be Jonah's corner. We began to make room for him, this person we did not yet know. His belongings began to arrive before he did—packages floated in containing toys, clothes, a bassinet. We watched it accumulate with a kind of bewildered excitement and dread.

Our love for our child truly began later, with a startling and immense violence, when Robert and I first held Jonah. After his birth, I held my arms out tentatively, trying to appear to be a mother, and the doctor placed him in my arms. Jonah was newborn, damp, wiry, animal. We looked at each other. He seemed to recognize me, in some mysterious primal way; he was guessing that I was his mother, as I was guessing that he was my son. The tenderness of this shared yearning, the beauty of the presence of his tiny feet and hands and arms made me suddenly, desperately, grip him. My husband and I were breathless at the magnificence of our son, this person who belonged to us. He was here; he was ours; we were his. We were, at that moment, forever changed.

We were parents.

I did not want to ever let him go.

I remember my astonishment at my children's relentless belief in their right to be in the world, at the furious way they run across playgrounds, at their belief that history has started with them. They find it amusing, the photos of their parents when we were younger, when their mother and father were, hilariously, children; it is a secret among parents, that we remember the world before them.

I stand at the park, watching the children streak across the grass, each one an accident of some sort, even if they were planned. I am an accident, but so are you. We are accidents of timing, of love, of yearning. We are accidents of parents who did not know if they wanted us, of parents who did. We are here, in the year 2007, on this planet, our feet clinging to the surface of the earth. We are temporary. We are mysterious. We are, at the first dark flickering of our lives, so unknown that it is impossible to legislate about us. We may become a person, or we may not. I watch the children in the park and I think of my grandmother Mary jumping off the stairs. I think of the way my grandmother Ardie worried about my aunt for every moment of her life, how she never escaped the burden of her fear for Joan, how my aunt sat, drugged, alone, in her room, waiting. I think of how my aunt liked to give me presents—Tic Tacs, a pack of gum. I think of the doctor at the women's clinic, her tight, grim expression, the way she gripped her prescription pad and said firmly, "I'm not giving it to you." I think of the precise mystery of each person on this planet, how every person is brave in some ways and not others.

I think of the impossibility of legislating bravery.

The sun burns down on the park.

The children run.

THE RAW EDGES OF HUMAN EXISTENCE:
The Language of Roe v. Wade
by Francine Prose

Jul 2012

"WE FORTHWITH acknowledge our awareness of the sensitive and emotional nature of the abortion controversy, of the vigorous opposing views, even among physicians, and of the deep and seemingly absolute convictions that the subject inspires. One's philosophy, one's experiences, one's exposure to the raw edges of human existence, one's religious training, one's attitudes toward life and family and their values, and the moral standards one establishes and seeks to observe, are all likely to influence and to color one's thinking and conclusions about abortion. In addition, population growth, poverty, and racial overtones tend to complicate and not to simplify the problem."

These beautiful, cadenced sentences occur early in the majority decision, written by Supreme Court Justice Harry Blackmun, in the landmark case, *Roe v. Wade*, or, as it is more properly known, *Jane Roe, et. al. v. Henry Wade, District Attorney of Dallas County*. The case was decided by the United States Supreme Court on January 22, 1973, and since then has, perhaps needless to say, served as a lightning rod for immoderate and often extreme expressions of what Justice Blackmun rather mildly terms "vigorous opposing views." Its essential correctness, which is obvious, and its equally obvious failure to take the measures that in subsequent years would have prevented states from so restricting abortion that it is technically legal yet all but practically unavailable for large numbers of girls and women—all that has been argued for decades by passionate opponents and advocates. And some of this debate has involved people who—like myself, I will admit—have a sense of what *Roe v. Wade* means without having much bothered to read what it actually *says*.

In fact, it's reading that I heartily recommend, not only because of what it *does* say, but for the intelligence and grace with which it says it. You can download the text of the ruling from the internet and easily skim or skip the parts you don't understand, the necessary detours into legalese.

And you can read the rest for pleasure and for the chance to observe the workings of a mind (or group of minds) expressed in measured language that is blessedly simple and logical as it endeavors to take on a subject that, as Blackmun suggests in the paragraph above, is the very opposite of logical and simple. It contains a mini-history of abortion and of the popular and legal views of abortion from antiquity to the present, and it struggles to puzzle out how the Constitution should be interpreted in cases of this sort. Reading *Roe. v. Wade* strengthens and restores your faith in the human ability to reason and to put the result of that reasoning into comprehensible language.

Like so many of the political events that have most profoundly affected our lives, the *Roe. v Wade* decision has lodged in our minds but, over time, shed its details and its specificity so that it has gradually been transformed from a particular case into a symbol of a woman's (perpetually, it would seem) endangered right to choose whether or not to continue a pregnancy. It is a controversy so fraught with high emotion that— since we are speaking of language—every word choice is loaded with meaning and association, so much so that I found myself rewriting the previous sentence several times, rejecting other, more inflammatory ways of describing that choice: whether or not a woman will carry a child to term, whether she will abort a fetus, and so forth. Among the striking things about *Roe v. Wade* is that, while it considers questions of prenatal life, of viability and of "quickening," the pregnant woman is always— essentially and rightly—at the heart of the debate.

In 1970, a pregnant woman named Norma L. McCorvey (or "Jane Roe") sued the state of Texas, where abortion was currently illegal. A district court sidestepped the issue by ruling in favor of Jane Roe but refusing to pass an injunction that would prohibit the enforcement of the law. The case was first argued before the Supreme Court in 1971, and then reargued beginning in October, 1972, when, as the opening of the ruling tells us, "A pregnant single woman (Roe) brought a class action challenging the constitutionality of the Texas criminal abortion laws, which proscribe the procuring or attempting an abortion except on medical advice for the purpose of saving the mother's life."

The early sections of the document establish Roe's legal right to sue and efficiently deal with issues central to this case and future cases—for example, the fact that "the natural termination of Roe's pregnancy did not moot her suit" and excepting pregnancy "from the usual federal rule that an actual controversy…must exist at review stages and not simply when an action is initiated." Later in the ruling, the judges rather charmingly expand upon the reasoning behind this exception: "The normal 266-day human gestation period is so short that the pregnancy will come to term before the usual appellate process is complete. If that termination makes the case moot, pregnancy litigation seldom will survive much beyond the trial stage, and appellate review will be effectively denied. Our law should not be that rigid. Pregnancy often comes more than once to the same woman, and in the general population, if man is to survive, it will always be with us."

A few pages into the ruling, we find the sentences quoted at the beginning of this essay: a wise and marvelously dispassionate summation of the particular difficulties and complexities surrounding the question of abortion, a controversy that necessarily involves "one's philosophy, one's experiences, one's exposure to the raw edges of human existence, one's religious training, one's attitudes toward life and family and their values, and the moral standards one establishes and seeks to observe." The phrase that stands out and stays with you is, of course, the reference to "the raw edges of human existence." Even as it's hard to say what precisely the phrase means, we immediately intuit the depth and sympathy with which it embraces the range of circumstances that might cause a woman on those raw edges to admit that she is unable to raise a child, as well as the pain and grief and regret that any of these situations and decisions might occasion.

After citing the grounds on which Jane Roe took on the Texas statute—that it interfered with the concept of personal liberty guaranteed by the Fourteenth Amendment and the right to privacy protected by the Bill of Rights—the ruling offers a compressed history of abortion law, beginning in classical antiquity, when abortion was "resorted to without scruple, except, interestingly," when it was considered "a violation of the father's right to his offspring." It ascribes the "rigidity" of the Hippocratic oath on its origin in Pythagorean dogma, which represented "only a small sample of Greek opinion," then moves quickly into a consideration of common law, which used "quickening"—the first perceptible movement of the fetus in utero—as the marker dividing a legal procedure from an illegal one. In general, quickening was believed to occur between the sixteenth and eighteenth week of pregnancy, though, tellingly, "Christian theology and the canon law came to fix the point of animation at 40 days for a male and 80 days for a female, a view that persisted until the 19th century." In England, in 1803, the abortion of a quickened fetus was made a capital crime, but abortion law was slower in coming to the United States. "It was not until after the War Between the States that legislation began generally to replace the common law. Most of these initial statutes dealt severely with abortion after quickening but were lenient with it before quickening." Gradually, the laws became stricter, until by the end of the 1950s, "a large majority of the jurisdictions banned abortion," unless "performed to save or preserve the life of the mother."

"At the time of the adoption of our Constitution, and throughout the major portion of the 19th century, abortion was viewed with less disfavor than under most American statutes currently in effect. Phrasing it another way, a woman enjoyed a substantially broader right to terminate a pregnancy than she does in most States today." The justices go on to imply that some of the responsibility for this change lies with the American Medical Association, which has officially opposed abortion since 1857.

In section VII of the document, the justices explain the basis for their decision: "This right of privacy, whether it be founded in the Fourteenth Amendment's concept of personal liberty, as we feel it is, or, as the District Court determined, in the Ninth Amendment's reservation of rights to the people, is broad enough to encompass a woman's decision whether or not to terminate her pregnancy. The detriment that the State would impose upon the pregnant woman by denying this choice altogether is apparent. Specific and direct harm medically diagnosable even in early pregnancy may be involved. Maternity, or additional offspring, may force upon the woman a distressful life and future. Psychological harm may be imminent.

Mental and physical health may be taxed by childcare. There is also the distress, for all concerned, associated with the unwanted child, and there is the problem of bringing a child into a family already unable, psychologically and otherwise, to care for it. In other cases, as in this one, the additional difficulties and continuing stigma of unwed motherhood may be involved. All these are factors the woman and her responsible physician necessarily will consider in consultation."

[margin note: giving up fl adoption? not easy, though.]

How lucid and transparent the language is, how economically and thoroughly the passage takes into account the harsh realities, the unfortunate experiences on the "raw edges of existence" that might compel a woman and her responsible physician to consider an undesirable but unavoidable alternative. And how compassionately it wishes to spare women—and just as importantly, the children they are forced to bear— the prospect of "a distressful life and future."

[margin note: sigh. Laws v. convenience/ experience? I agree wl pro-choice, but ruling premise+ lang. left so much open to attack...]

Subsequently, the ruling shifts from a consideration of the rights of the pregnant woman to that of the rights of the unborn. There is another brief historical survey—this one of the idea that life does not begin until birth. The mini-history spans the view of the Stoics to the opinion, interestingly enough, of the majority of Catholic thinkers until the nineteenth century, when it became Church dogma that life begins at the moment of conception.

The justices do not agree. "The word 'person,' as used in the Fourteenth Amendment, does not include the unborn...In short, the unborn have never been recognized in the law as persons in the whole sense."

[margin note: voting age?]

So when the ruling goes on to affirm the state's right to regulate abortion after the first trimester, it is not because of the personhood of the unborn but rather in consideration of the health of the mother. "Because of the now-established medical fact...that until the end of the first trimester mortality in abortion may be less than mortality in normal childbirth. It follows that, from and after this point, a State may regulate the abortion procedure to the extent that the regulation reasonably relates to the preservation and protection of maternal health."

Reasonably. Reasonably. That one word is the great strength and the great beauty—and also perhaps the great weakness—of *Roe v. Wade*. The

presumption of, and the faith in, reason could neither foresee nor take
into account the irrational opposition to abortion that would, in the years
following the justices' decision, result in laws requiring parental notifica-
tion and waiting periods, that would prohibit the use of federal funding
for abortions and forbid military hospitals from performing the procedure,
all measures that would make abortion impractical and unavailable for
many girls and women, especially those living in rural areas, the young
and the poor—in short, the ones living closest to those raw edges and
most often in desperate need of medical intervention.

Because for all the wisdom and beauty and logic of *Roe v. Wade*, the
document does betray a certain failure of the imagination. You can see it
most clearly in the section in which the judges consider traditional arguments against abortion—the desire to protect prenatal life and the wish to
safeguard women from a medically dangerous procedure, dangers that,
the court notes, have been obviated by the adoption of "modern medical
techniques," and (though this is not explicitly stated) the widespread use
of antibiotics and other means of preventing infection. But the objection
that the court dismisses most lightly and offhandedly is the one to which
it should, perhaps, have paid closer attention.

"It has been argued occasionally that these laws were the product of a
Victorian social concern to discourage illicit sexual conduct. Texas, however, does not advance this justification in the present case, and it appears
that no court or commentator has taken the argument seriously. The
appellants and amici contend, moreover, that it is not a proper state purpose at all and suggest that, if it were, the Texas statutes are overbroad in
protecting it since the law fails to distinguish between married and unwed
mothers."

What Justice Blackmun and his assenting colleagues are too reasonable to understand is how much the rulings against abortion have, in fact,
had this intention in mind—that is, the desire to control women and their
sexuality, and beyond that, a distrust for sexuality in general and female
sexuality in particular. That is something that has been taken very seriously indeed, though few will admit it. It is a view in direct opposition to
the essentially life-affirming and respectful sensibility that suffuses every

[handwritten margin note:] I have no idea how I feel about this. It's kinda the welfare argument.

[handwritten margin note:] I really don't know how true this is.

clear and well-written sentence of *Roe v. Wade*, the language whose moderation and beauty is thrown into sharp relief by the very different and highly inflammatory language of the dissenting opinion, authored by Justice Byron R. White:

"The Court apparently values the <u>convenience</u> of the pregnant mother more than the continued existence and development of the life or potential life that she carries…I cannot accept the Court's exercise of its clear power of choice by interposing a constitutional barrier to state efforts to protect human life and by investing mothers and doctors with the constitutionally protected right to exterminate it."

So "women" (the term used most frequently in the majority opinion) have become "mothers," "maternal health" has become "convenience," "protection" has become "extermination." How far we have come from the language of reason and of sympathy for our fellow humans, for women who must make these difficult and painful choices that occur on—and in fact define and demarcate—the raw edges of human existence.

I agree with this author's sentiment. However, she extols the virtues of the court case based on its language and Constitutional premise, both of which I find rather weak. The first half of White's quote (dissenting) is true, based on how the case was decided/worded, but I personally don't agree w/ the 2nd half.

Roe v. Wade is a sad, sad case for the pro-choice community to base its debate on. I agree with the decision, but not the decision making. It's frustrating.

TODO: read it!

BIOGRAPHIES

STEPHANIE ANDERSEN lives with her dog Daisy in Pennsylvania where she teaches English and writes. She is presently working on a memoir about giving her daughter up for adoption.

K.A.C. is a pseudonym.

JANET MASON ELLERBY is a Professor of English at the University of North Carolina Wilmington. She is the author of *Intimate Reading: The Contemporary Women's Memoir*, and the forthcoming *Following The Tambourine Man: A Birthmother's Memoir*.

A founding editor of the literary journal, *Ecotone*, KIMI FAXON HEMINGWAY received her MFA from the University of North Carolina Wilmington, where she currently teaches memoir writing and English Composition.

CAROLYN FERRELL is the author of the short story collection *Don't Erase Me* which won the Art Seidenbaum Award of *The Los Angeles Times* Book Prize, the John C. Zacharis Award given by *Ploughshares*, and the Quality Paperback Book Prize for First Fiction. Her stories have been anthologized in *The Best American Short Stories of the Century*, edited by John Updike, and *Giant Steps: The New Generation of African American Writers*, edited by Kevin Young. She lives with her husband and children in the Bronx.

DENISE GESS is the author of the novels *Good Deeds* and *Red Whiskey Blues*, and the coauthor of the nonfiction book, *Firestorm At Peshtigo: A Town, Its People and the Deadliest Fire in American History*. Her personal essays have been published in the anthologies *Remarkable Reads: 34 Writers and Their Adventures in Reading* and *The Horizon Reader*, in *Philadelphia Stories*, *Wild River Review*, and *The Sun*. She's currently working on a collection of essays, *Bad For Boys*. She is an assistant professor of creative writing at Rowan University in Glassboro, New Jersey.

KATIE ALLISON GRANJU is the author of *Attachment Parenting* and a contributor to several anthologies. Her essays and articles have appeared in *The New York Times*, *Salon.com*, *Brain, Child*, *Hip Mama*, *Parenting*, and many other publications. She lives in Tennessee with her husband and three children, and is expecting baby #4. She has a blog at www.katieallisongranju.com

SANDY HINGSTON, a senior editor at *Philadelphia Magazine*, lives outside Philadelphia with her husband and teenaged son and daughter. Her work has appeared in *More*, *Self*, *Prevention*, and *Women's Health*.

ANN HOOD is the author of, most recently, *The Knitting Circle*. Her other books include *Somewhere Off the Coast of Maine* and *An Ornithologist's Guide to Life*. Her essays and short stories have appeared in many publications, including *The New York Times*, *The Paris Review*, *O*, *Food and Wine*, and *Traveler*. She lives in Providence, RI.

PAM HOUSTON is the author of two collections of linked short stories, *Cowboys Are My Weakness*, which was the winner of the 1993 Western States Book Award and *Waltzing the Cat* which won the Willa Award for Contemporary Fiction. Her stories have been selected for volumes of *Best American Short Stories*, *O. Henry Awards*, *The Pushcart Prize*, and *Best American Short Stories of the Century*. Her first novel, *Sight Hound*, was a finalist for the Colorado Book Award. She is the Director of Creative Writing at UC Davis, and divides her time between Colorado and California.

VELINA HASU HOUSTON, Ph.D., is a playwright whose works are produced internationally. She founded and directs the Master of Fine Arts program in Dramatic Writing at the University of Southern California School of Theatre, where she is a professor of theatre.

SUSAN ITO lives in Oakland with her multigenerational family. She is the coeditor of *A Ghost at Heart's Edge: Stories & Poems of Adoption*. Her essays and fiction have appeared in *Growing Up Asian American*, *Hip Mama*,

Making More Waves, The Bellevue Literary Review, and elsewhere. She is the fiction coeditor at *Literary Mama,* an online literary journal, where she also writes a monthly column about life in the Sandwich Generation.

ELIZABETH LARSEN was a member of the team that created *Sassy* magazine and was also an editor at *Utne Reader.* Today she's a freelance writer whose work has appeared in numerous publications, including *Child, Travel & Leisure,* and *Ms.*

KATE MALOY is the author of the novel, *Every Last Cuckoo,* and the memoir *A Stone Bridge North.* She is coauthor of *Birth or Abortion? Private Struggles in a Political World.* Recent essays can be seen in *The Kenyon Review* and the Seal Press anthology *For Keeps,* edited by Victoria Zackheim.

DEBORAH MCDOWELL has written widely for both academic and general audiences. Her publications include *"The Changing Same": Studies in Fiction by African American Women, Leaving Pipe Shop: Memories of Kin,* as well as numerous articles, book chapters, and scholarly editions, most recently *Narrative of the Life of Frederick Douglass.* Extensively involved in editorial projects pertaining to the subject of African American literature, she founded the African American Women Writers Series for Beacon Press and served as its editor from 1985-1993, overseeing the republication of fourteen novels from the late-nineteenth and early-twentieth centuries. She also served as a period editor for the *Norton Anthology of African American Literature,* contributing editor to the D.C. *Heath Anthology of American Literature,* and coeditor with Arnold Rampersad of *Slavery and the Literary Imagination.* She is the Alice Griffin Professor of Literary Studies at the University of Virginia.

Author of *Red House: Being a Mostly Accurate Account of New England's Oldest Continuously Lived-In House* and the poetry collection *Bandit Letters,* SARAH MESSER has received fellowships and grants from organizations including the Provincetown Fine Arts Work Center, the Wisconsin Institute for Creative Writing, and the National Endowment for the Arts. Her work has appeared in *The Paris Review*, *The Kenyon Review*, and *Quarterly West*, as well as several anthologies, including *Legitimate Dangers: Poets of the New Century*. She lives in North Carolina, where she is an associate professor of creative writing at The University of North Carolina Wilmington.

JACQUELYN MITCHARD is the author of the No. 1 New York Times best-selling novel, *The Deep End of the Ocean*—chosen as the first book for Oprah Winfrey's Book Club. She subsequently wrote five other best-selling novels, *The Most Wanted*, *A Theory of Relativity*, *Twelve Times Blessed*, *Christmas, Present*, *The Breakdown Lane*, *Cage of Stars* as well as an essay collection, *The Rest of Us: Dispatches From the Mothership*. Mitchard has published three children's books—two young children's novels, *Starring Prima!* and *Rosalie, My Rosalie*, as well as a children's picture book, *Baby Bat's Lullaby*. Her next novel, *Still Summer*, is forthcoming. Her first Young Adult novel *Now You See Her,* came out early this year. She lives in Wisconsin with her husband Christopher Brent, and their seven children.

CATHERINE NEWMAN is the author of the parenting memoir *Waiting for Birdy*, and the weekly columns "Dalai Mama" on wondertime.com and "Bringing Up Ben and Birdy" on babycenter.com. She has written essays for *O: the Oprah Magazine* and the best-selling anthology, *The Bitch in the House*. She lives in Massachusetts with her family.

FRANCINE PROSE is a novelist and critic whose works include the novels *A Changed Man* and *Blue Angel*, which was a finalist for the National Book Award. Her works of nonfiction include *Reading Like A Writer: A Guide For People Who Love Books and For Those Who Want to Write Them*, *The Lives of the Muses: Nine Women and the Artists They Inspired* and *Caravaggio: Painter of Miracles*. She is the recipient of numerous grants and awards, among them the Dayton Literary Peace Prize, Guggenheim and Fulbright fellowships.

ASHLEY TALLEY is a writer and teacher from southern Virginia. She has a BA from Brown and an MFA from UNCW. She lives in coastal North Carolina where she is completing a novel.

KATHERINE TOWLER is the author of the novels *Snow Island* and *Evening Ferry*. She has been awarded fellowships from the New Hampshire State Council on the Arts and Phillips Exeter Academy, where she served as the Bennett Fellow. She teaches in the MFA Program in Writing at Southern New Hampshire University and lives with her husband and two doted-on cats in Portsmouth, New Hampshire. For more about her work, visit her website at www.katherinetowler.com.

HARRIETTE E. WIMMS lives in Baltimore, where she is the proud and busy mother of a 3-year-old boy. She is completing her Ph.D. in child clinical psychology and community psychology at the University of Maryland, Baltimore County. Her dissertation explores the experiences and perceptions of doctoral students of color in psychology. She has an M.S. in developmental psychology from Johns Hopkins University and a B.S. in English from Towson State University. Her poetry has appeared in the anthology *From the Listening Place: Languages of Intuition*.

ACKNOWLEDGMENTS

First, thank you to to Nina de Gramont, a fantastic co-editor, who made this vision we had one New Year's Eve into an amazing reality. Thank you to Eric Simonoff, Peter Steinberg and Rebecca Gradinger for great advice and help in getting this book into the world. Thank you to the brave team at MacAdam Cage—David Poindexter, Scott Allen, Julie Burton, Melissa Little, Melanie Mitchell, and especially, to our editor Kate Nitze, for such deep and wonderful enthusiasm for this project and for sharing our vision for this book. Thank you to our contributors for sharing their stories with such generosity and honesty. Thank you to my parents, David and Meri Bender, for showing me how a complex view of the world is the one of most tolerance; to Suzanne and Aimee Bender, for endless and precious support. Thank you to friends and family whose ideas and enthusiasm about this project helped along the way: Margaret Mittelbach, Jennie Litt, Dana Sachs, Rebecca Lee, Wendy Brenner, Sarah Messer, Virginia Holman, Jessie Costa, Karen and Josh Vogel, Bill McGarvey, Katherine Wessling, Frances Siegel, Perrin Siegel, Norma Varsos and Natalie Plachte-White. Thanks to Talia Bilodeau at the National Women's Law Center for believing in this project and giving us so much help. And thank you, especially, to my husband Robert, for your precious love and for your wisdom about everything, and to Jonah and Maia, our two blessings who astound us every day. —*Karen E. Bender*

Tiffany Salter

KAREN E. BENDER is the author of a novel, *Like Normal People*. Her fiction has appeared in magazines including *The New Yorker, Granta, Zoetrope, Ploughshares, The Harvard Review,* and *Story,* and has been anthologized in *Best American Short Stories, Best American Mystery Stories,* and the *Pushcart Prize* series. She has received grants from the Rona Jaffe Foundation and the National Endowment of the Arts.

ACKNOWLEDGMENTS

First of all, thanks to Karen Bender for bringing this project into my life, and for being such a generous and inspiring co-editor. Thank you Peter Steinberg and Shannon Firth at Regal Literary for hard work and unwavering support. Everyone at MacAdam Cage has been so brave and enthusiastic: David Poindexter, Scott Allen, Melanie Mitchell, Melissa Little, Julie Burton, and especially our wonderful and talented editor Kate Nitze. Thanks always to my parents, Carol and George de Gramont. Thanks to the many friends who tolerated me and cheered me on, especially Danae Woodward, Mel Boyajian, and Alicia Erian. Thanks to Shawna Kenney, Dan Lee, Amy Cherry, and Sarah Messer for leading us to contributors we might not have found on our own. Thanks to Pamela English for all her help and hard work. Many thanks to Charles Siebert, for valuable input on my essay. Many, many, many thanks to David Gessner, who loved, supported, and advised me every step of the way. And most of all, thanks to our contributors, who had the courage and honesty to tell their stories. —*Nina de Gramont*

David Gessner

NINA de GRAMONT is the author of a collection of short stories, *Of Cats and Men*. Her first novel, *Gossip of the Starlings*, is forthcoming. Her work has appeared in a variety of publications including *The Harvard Review*, *Isotope*, *Post Road*, *Nerve*, *Exquisite Corpse*, and *Seventeen*.